NATURAL HISTORIES

25 EXTRAORDINARY SPECIES
THAT HAVE CHANGED OUR WORLD

BRETT WESTWOOD AND STEPHEN MOSS

JOHN MURRAY

First published in Great Britain in 2015 by John Murray (Publishers)
An Hachette UK company

First published in paperback in 2016

1

A CIP catalogue record for this title is available from the British Library

ISBN 978-1-47361-703-2
Ebook ISBN 978-1-47361-702-5

Typeset in Garamond by Palimpsest Book Production Limited, Falkirk,
Stirlingshire

Printed and bound by Clays Ltd, St Ives plc

John Murray policy is to use papers that are natural, renewable and recy-
clable products and made from wood grown in sustainable forests. The
logging and manufacturing processes are expected to conform to the environmental regulations of the country of origin.

John Murray (Publishers)
Carmelite House
50 Victoria Embankment
London EC4Y 0DZ

www.johnmurray.co.uk

To all at BBC Natural History Unit Radio:
long may they inspire armchair naturalists everywhere

CONTENTS

INTRODUCTION

When we no longer look at an organic being as a savage looks at a ship, as at something wholly beyond his comprehension; when we regard every production of nature as one which has had a history; when we contemplate every complex structure and instinct as the summing up of many contrivances, each useful to the possessor, nearly in the same way as when we look at any great mechanical invention as the summing up of the labour, the experience, the reason, and even the blunders of numerous workmen; when we thus view each organic being, how far more interesting, I speak from experience, will the study of natural history become!

Charles Darwin, *On the Origin of Species*

Natural Histories is the result of a close collaboration between two of Britain's greatest institutions, the BBC Natural History Unit and the Natural History Museum. They have formed a partnership to celebrate the wonder and variety of the natural world, through some of its most extraordinary and fascinating creatures. They have done so by bringing together two sometimes disparate but closely linked strands: nature and culture, exploring the profound impact that nature has had on human society over the course of history.

The series and this book tell the often surprising stories of twenty-five astonishing species that have managed to get under the skin of our society and change the way we see the world. From snakes to squid, brambles to butterflies, corals to crocodiles and dinosaurs to daffodils, *Natural Histories* – in each episode or chapter – takes a single species, or group of plants or animals, and explores its complex connections with our own, human world.

So we learn about the Thames whale, which inspired an outpouring of compassion when it found itself stranded in the centre of London; and the much smaller but equally fascinating flea, immortalised in poetry by John Donne and celebrated in the last century by Mexican nuns, who made a few extra dollars by selling fleas dressed in exquisitely made miniature costumes.

Some of these creatures, like the dinosaurs and mammoths, are extinct; and yet their stories remain as modern and compelling as those of the parrot and the polar bear. Why is the lion called the 'king of beasts'? It's fascinating to examine how this particular (sometimes rather lazy) animal became such a potent symbol of power. How did the shark become shorthand for everything that we were afraid of? And the cockroach for disgust and revulsion, to such an extent that a Rwandan radio station's comparison of the Tutsi people to cockroaches was considered an incitement to the genocide of 800,000 people? There are some unexpected creatures here that you may never even have heard of: such as burbot – but this very different fish has an amazing story to tell involving a Finnish heavy metal band and the Russian playwright Anton Chekhov. More familiar cultural references include Monty Python (dinosaurs rather than parrots), *Moby-Dick*, *Crocodile Dundee* and of course *Jaws*, with its unforgettable (albeit mostly unseen) shark.

The biology of each plant or animal is explored along with its cultural history, featuring people whose stories are inextricably intertwined with the star species of each episode or chapter. David

Attenborough on gorillas to Wordsworth on daffodils, Harry Potter to Alfred Russel Wallace, and the poet John Clare to the polar explorer Apsley Cherry-Garrard. Each story tells us both about the indefatigable strength of the human spirit, the unexpected ways in which we have interacted with the species featured and, most of all, the profound connection we have with the natural world, as Sir Michael Dixon, Director of the Natural History Museum, points out: 'We're always looking for new ways to challenge the way people think about the natural world – its past, present and future.'

A (Very) Short History of Natural History

For most of the 100,000 or so years that modern human beings have existed, our relationship with nature has been a utilitarian one: plants and animals were there to be gathered or killed and then eaten. Our ancestors wore animal skins to keep them warm, and burned the oil found in some plants and animals to provide fuel. Plants were also used as primitive medicines, to provide building materials, and later to feed domestic animals or, in the case of grasses such as wheat, to make food.

As humanity became more civilised, things began to change. Nature wasn't simply there to be taken advantage of any more. The oldest cave paintings, from the Palaeolithic era, date from around 35,000 years ago. These are the first natural history artworks. Over 340 caves have been discovered across France and Spain alone. Using charcoal and yellow and red ochre, large wild animals, such as bison, horses, aurochs (an extinct wild ox) and deer run across the cave walls in every continent, while drawings of humans are relatively rare. Henri Breuil argued that the paintings were a hunting magic meant to increase the number of animals. From a modern perspective, it is hard to comprehend why these early hunters chose to portray these creatures in this way: was it for some kind of religious or superstitious reason; or did they have a more practical use, to teach youngsters how to hunt?

Throughout early civilisations gods were often pictured in animal form – most notably in the ancient Egyptian pantheon where Sobek the crocodile god rubs shoulders with hawk-headed Horus and cat-headed Bastet. The Greeks were fascinated by the colourful beliefs of the Egyptians (see Chapter 18: Crocodiles) but they were determined to make sense of the world too. The turning point came with Aristotle (384–322 BC) who first turned natural observation into a science. In his hugely influential nine-volume *History of Animals*, he described how a chick developed inside the egg, the social organisation of bees and observed that some sharks gave birth to live young.

Until relatively recently, our ancestors lived and worked mainly on the land, cheek by jowl with plants and animals. Nature was mainly regarded as something to be exploited for human benefit, an attitude that found support in the Book of Genesis: 'And God said unto them, "Be fruitful, and multiply, and replenish the earth, and subdue it: and have dominion over the fish of the sea, and over the fowl of the air, and over every living thing that moveth over the earth".' It could not be clearer: mankind was very firmly in charge, and the natural world was a seemingly unlimited resource to be used – and abused – for our benefit.

But some time around the middle of the second millennium changes came about. In western Europe at least, the notion of dominion over living creatures became increasingly tinged with responsibility as a duty to a divine creator. Slowly and almost imperceptibly at first, but then much more rapidly, our attitudes to the wildlife around us altered.

Five hundred years later, we continue to exploit the natural world (even though we now know to our cost that it is indeed both finite and rapidly disappearing); yet we also celebrate, love and appreciate it as never before in human history.

This modern way of looking at nature began here in Britain.

There were pioneers such as Gilbert White, the rector of the Hampshire parish of Selborne, whose celebrated natural history of his village and its surroundings continues to be read today, more than 200 years after it was first published; and the seventeenth-century butterfly enthusiast Eleanor Glanville, who was considered insane because she spent her time 'in pursuit of butterflies'.

The scientific and cultural revolution of the Enlightenment in the eighteenth century was swiftly followed by the Industrial Revolution of the eighteenth and early nineteenth centuries, when society changed rapidly and fundamentally. Philosophers began to question what had gone before, including the idea that we as human beings held a special place above nature; science went from superstition to practical and measurable experiments; and people began to appreciate that the natural world might indeed not be as boundless as we had once supposed.

At the same time, wider society changed too. People moved in their millions from the countryside to towns and cities: and in doing so discovered a deep nostalgia for their rural heritage. This, along with a rise in living standards and an increase in what would come to be called 'leisure time', led to a rapid rise in 'hobby nature': interests such as botanising, birdwatching and butterfly collecting soon became fashionable pastimes amongst the newly emerged middle classes.

Thus, paradoxically, it took a move away from nature to allow people to appreciate it properly; an appreciation that gave birth to the deep and complex relationship many Britons enjoy with the natural world today. This is evinced by the popularity of TV programmes such as *Springwatch*, and of another BBC Radio 4 series and accompanying book, *Tweet of the Day*, which held the nation (or at least those prepared to get up at the crack of dawn) enthralled by the therapeutic properties of birdsong.

Not that we should be surprised at this. In 1964 the psychologist Erich Fromm coined the term 'biophilia' – literally 'the love of life' – to describe our innate human need to make connections with living things. Later, US biologist Edward O. Wilson refined the term to refer specifically to what he regarded as our innate need to make links with the natural world, or as he put it, 'the connections that human beings subconsciously seek with the rest of life'.

As *Natural Histories* will reveal, our links with nature have, over the past few centuries, influenced every aspect of human society: from high to popular culture, including classical and pop music, visual art, plays, poetry and novels, films and TV, and the very language that we speak. This is a global phenomenon: all around the world wildlife and nature are embedded in religious belief, cultures and societies.

We have had a lifelong fascination with the natural world – we are both unable to remember a time when we were not captivated by the wild creatures around us. We have been fortunate to have turned our enduring passion into our work: as broadcasters, writers and public speakers, and if we can enthuse others with the joys of connecting – or reconnecting – with the natural world, then we'll feel amply rewarded.

Most of us engage with nature because we enjoy it for its own sake, but it's reassuring to know that there are enormous benefits to be gained too. It is now widely accepted that contact with the natural world brings measurable improvements to our physical, emotional and mental health; for many it can also provide an extra spiritual dimension to our lives.

Natural Histories aims to help us better understand and appreciate this deep and crucial connection. By telling the stories of each plant or animal, and tracing the many different and surprising ways in which human beings have connected with them, we hope to unravel the complexities of our relationship with nature, which continues to delight, enthral and enlighten us, and always will.

The Making of the Series

Radio 4 has a long history of bringing natural history
to life for listeners, but this is the first time we have
embarked on a project of this scale and variety.

Gwyneth Williams, Controller, BBC Radio 4

Natural Histories is based on the eponymous Radio 4 series produced
by the Natural History Radio department of the BBC Natural
History Unit. The department has made many renowned series
from *Shared Planet* and *Saving Species* to the award-winning *Tweet
of the Day*, but *Natural Histories* has proved their biggest and most
exciting challenge so far.

The natural world has always governed our lives. At the most
basic level we need animals and plants to survive, but this radio
series has set out to explore the more unusual and dramatic ways
in which we have been influenced by wildlife, and how it has got
'under our skin'.

Natural themes in human lives have been repeated and reinforced
down the ages in art, music, religion, commerce and cuisine, in
countless different ways. Although, in the twenty-first century,
humanity has often been described as disconnected from the natural
world, the aim behind our series was to prove that this could
hardly be further from the truth. Our lives are still being enriched
by wildlife in new and continually inventive ways. Who, for example,
would have thought that mammoths, once an essential stalwart of
human existence in the Ice Ages, would resurface from the permafrost as unlikely heroes of an animated film? Or that daffodils, a
source of memory and reflection for William Wordsworth, would
yield a drug to alleviate the early effects of dementia? This element
of surprise was a key ingredient in all the programmes: we wanted
listeners to say 'I never knew that.'

There was no shortage of fascinating potential subjects. The
daunting task of assembling the often complex stories around them

was made easier by the partnership forged with London's renowned Natural History Museum, whose vast collections and scientific expertise provided a core for each programme. The skin of Happy Jerry, a mandrill brought to London from West Africa on a slave ship where he was taught to smoke and swill gin, immediately sparked the theme of how we view our closest relatives, the primates. The skull of a lion unearthed at the Tower of London provided a fresh insight into the role that the 'king of beasts' has played in human monarchy.

Mary Colwell, the series producer and major scriptwriter, was also very keen to shine a light into the more obscure or forgotten corners of the natural world. Though her suggestions of coral, sea anemones and burbot were initially met with raised eyebrows, these proved alluring and entrancing subjects and led to all kinds of memorable moments. (Brett, for one, certainly never expected to be eating a medieval burbot torte, decorated with gold-leaf, on air.)

Once the list of candidates had been whittled down to twenty-five, it was time to explore the riches of the Natural History Museum. Mary Colwell recalled the first time she saw the skeleton of the northern bottlenose whale that tragically died in the Thames in 2006 dwarfed by the Natural History Museum's vast collection of cetacean remains: 'Seeing the Thames Whale in the off-site storage area of the Natural History Museum was an extraordinary and humbling experience. It was so small compared to the rows of jaws of blue and sperm whales, their backbones tailing far into the distance. I felt completely in awe of these huge creatures.'

Tom Bonnett, who recorded many of the interviews for the series, was fascinated by another huge creature:

Recording in the bowels of the Natural History Museum was at times an eerie experience. When we visited the giant squid's lair, I taped the echoing sound of our footsteps as we descended the stairs, senses heightened by the muffling headphones. The rest of the team had brought back tales of countless wide-eyed creatures staring from pickling jars, so I was full of anticipation. When I stepped inside the tank room, there, dominating the centre of the room, was the 10-metre tank housing the museum's giant squid, Archie. I was a pane of glass away from something that struck fear in sailors for centuries. I found myself keeping half an eye on it, allowing myself to imagine that if I turned away, even for an instant, it might begin to stir.

Finding contributors to discuss general natural history and the exhibits was straightforward, thanks to collaboration with the specialists based at the museum. But the interaction between wild-life and humans often called for imaginative leaps from the series' team. Ellie Sans, who researched much of *Natural Histories*, remembers one particular breakthrough (also on giant squid):

Researching this series was a challenge and a delight. I was used to talking to scientists about familiar topics but now, although I was still talking to academics, they were specialists in art, literature, media, sociology, music, philosophy, history and more . . . We wanted someone to explain our fascination with sea monsters, and finding someone who has studied the reasons we seem to like scaring ourselves was a challenge. When I eventually tracked down Mathias Clasen at Aarhus University in Denmark and his work on why people so enjoy horror in films, books and games, it was a bit of a eureka moment.

For Mary Colwell, the mammoth programme yielded some surprising contributors including the writer of one of her favourite animated films: 'Michael J. Wilson, the writer of *Ice Age*, was an excellent and important contributor. His research into mammoths for the film script was a revelation.'

Andrew Dawes, assistant producer of the series, was particularly impressed by the zeal of the scientists and other enthusiasts, both at the Natural History Museum and all over the world, to discover everything about some of the less obviously appealing subjects in the series: 'I especially loved George Beccaloni describing finding cockroaches in Australia near a town which had tried to promote cockroach tourism, or Theresa Howard talking about fleas with such passion before taking us to the immaculate Miriam Rothschild cabinets packed with 90,000 microscope slides of specimens.'

———•———

The aim of *Natural Histories* has been to illuminate the often surprising connections that still bind us to the natural world. In this book, we've had the opportunity to chase up even more of the stories and research some of the fascinating links that the radio programmes simply weren't long enough to include. This is not a handbook or an encyclopaedia: there are plenty of those already. In these twenty-five chapters, poetry and folklore jostle with science and history: we want to inspire armchair naturalists everywhere to find out more. From mandrills to mandrakes, these creatures and phenomena are a fundamental part of our past and our present, and will continue to be so in our future. We guarantee that you will never see the natural world in the same way again.

Brett Westwood and Stephen Moss
August 2015

Radio 4 Natural Histories: www.bbc.co.uk/programmes/b05w99gb
Natural History Museum: www.nhm.ac.uk

There are 193 species of monkeys and apes, 192 of them are covered with hair. The exception is a naked ape self-named Homo sapiens.

Desmond Morris, *The Naked Ape*

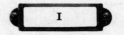

Monkeys and Apes

Cousins – A Mirror to Ourselves

The scene was much the same as the end of many royal dinners in the early nineteenth century: a curious blend of decorum and informality. Much wine had been drunk. The men lit their pipes and began a more relaxed conversation. But one guest was not happy. It was his first royal dinner and he'd been on his best behaviour until now. Although he too smoked a pipe and enjoyed a glass of gin, he was unable to join in the discussions around him. He was getting increasingly agitated, because he was jealous of the king's marked attentions towards one of the lady guests. After all, George IV had long been notorious for his womanising, even though the beautifully made clothes, fashionable haircut, and even the corsets he was squeezed into could do little to improve the physical appearance of the ageing and corpulent king. Nevertheless, it was common knowledge that noble families were still careful not to leave their unmarried daughters alone in his company.

Finally the guest had had enough. The exact details of what happened next are unclear. What we do know is that the offending diner was summarily ejected from the royal presence before he could wreak any more havoc. Which, being a male mandrill – the world's largest species of monkey, and about the size and weight of a ten-year-old child – he probably would have done.

*

Mandrills are the largest of more than 150 different species of Old World monkeys (the family *Cercopithecidae*). They are only found in a small corner of West Central Africa: in the dense tropical rainforests of Cameroon, Equatorial Guinea, Gabon and the Republic of the Congo. They can be very hard to see in the wild because unlike other monkeys they often hunt on the forest floor; but if you do catch a glimpse of one, it is not easily forgotten. The males are one of the most striking, and certainly the most colourful, of all the world's primates, as conservationist and primatologist Ian Redmond describes:

> Male mandrills are the most spectacular monkeys – like a bigger, stockier baboon with a brightly coloured face and rear end. The face is most peculiar, with ridged skin and a nose like an enormous red phallus, where the nostrils become testicles and the nose is shaped like a penis. It's as if they are wearing a badge that says, 'I've got big genitalia on my face!'

The bizarre colours and shapes at both ends of the mandrill are, like many similar features in nature, the result of sexual selection; over many generations, females have preferred males with larger and more brightly coloured features, which has created an evolutionary pressure towards more prominent ones. Mandrills have long fascinated scientists: Charles Darwin wrote in *The Descent of Man* that 'no other member in the whole class of mammals is coloured in so extraordinary a manner'.

Even today we know little about the mandrill. They are nervous of people, with good reason, as Ian Redmond explains:

> Sadly I've only ever seen mandrills dead on a bushmeat trader's slab – literally piles of them. They often move around in large hordes, consisting of several family groups that have come together, maybe hundreds of them. And because they move around the forest talking to each other, grunting and crowing, hunters with dogs are able to round them up and shoot them.

Human slavery was not finally abolished until 1833, and so at this time vast numbers of people were still being transported on slave ships from Africa. Among them were stowaways. Happy Jerry – the mandrill that would go on to so offend the king – arrived in Bristol from the Gold Coast of West Africa in 1815, the same year as the Duke of Wellington's victory over Napoleon at Waterloo. Born in the rainforest, he had been captured by hunters as a very young animal, so young that he adopted the captain and crew of the slave ship that had bought him as his new family, and mimicked their behaviour, picking up their habits in the same way that any young primates – including human children – learn. Later he gained a taste for strong gin and pipe tobacco, both of which he would happily consume while sitting in his favourite armchair.

Jerry was put on display outside the Exeter Exchange, a Georgian shopping mall on London's Strand which also housed a menagerie. Jerry shared his new home with lions and tigers, whose loud roars would often startle passers-by and crowds in the street below. His fame soon spread, with throngs of people – sometimes including Wordsworth and Byron, who were regular visitors – coming to see this genial and very human-like primate. Finally word reached the ear of the king who, always on the lookout for new and unusual experiences, issued the fateful invitation to dinner.

Happy Jerry cut a rakish figure in Regency England. There was great sadness all round when the mandrill died in 1831. He'd provided entertainment and enlightenment and a window into a very different world for fashionable Georgians, whom he amused and appalled in equal measure. So much so that he was stuffed and mounted, then at some later date unstuffed so that today his folded skin rests in the Life Sciences Mammal Collection of the Natural History Museum. Principal Curator Richard Sabin accounts for his appeal: 'It was a fascination with his human-ness – the elements of humanity that he displayed – but every so often he would remind people that he was a wild animal, and show it. Fortunately people like to be shocked as well as entertained.'

Monkeys and apes are the creatures most like us on earth: our closest relatives. And together, we have been on quite a journey.

We are especially captivated by the group of higher primates known as the 'great apes', in the family *Hominidae* (the name itself is an indication of the closeness between these animals and human beings). These six species – the western and eastern (also known as lowland and mountain) gorillas, Bornean and Sumatran orang-utans, the chimpanzee, and its smaller relative the bonobo – are our closest living relatives, so it's hardly surprising that we find them fascinating.

Apes – which also include the nineteen species of gibbon – differ from the world's 300 or so monkeys in several important ways. The most obvious difference is that apes do not have tails, while most monkeys (though not quite all) do. Apes are also generally larger, have better sight, and in the case of the chimpanzee and gorillas, can use tools and have developed a rudimentary form of language. And whereas monkeys can be found in both the Old and New Worlds – baboons, macaques, colobus monkeys and others in Asia and Africa; and tamarins, marmosets, capuchins and their relatives in South and Central America – apes are only found in the Old World continents of Africa (chimps, bonobos and gorillas) and Asia (gibbons and orang-utans).

Our relationship with the great apes has been a long and complex one. Our prehistoric ancestors hunted them for food, a custom that remained sustainable for centuries until the invention of reliable and accurate firearms gave one side an unfair advantage over the other. Since then, the population of all the great apes has declined, partly through over-hunting, but also because of habitat loss, especially in South East Asia, where the two species of orang-utan are now highly endangered. Another problem is the spread of human-borne infectious diseases: not only serious ones such as Ebola, but even apparently harmless viruses including the common cold, which can prove lethal to chimpanzees and gorillas.

Scientists have long studied the higher primates; indeed chimpanzees and gorillas have been the subject of more in-depth studies than almost any other species of wild mammal. Gorilla scientist Ian Redmond argues that spending long periods of time with these animals, our closest relatives on earth today, has given him a unique insight into their lives:

> It's about having that inter-species friendship with a wild animal who's not dependent on you – you're not feeding them, you're not doing anything to them other than watching them to observe their natural behaviour – but their natural behaviour includes interacting with friendly beings who happen to be around them – and that's us.

The physical similarity between humans and the great apes is striking and when we look into their eyes we cannot help but see ourselves reflected back. Yet these intriguing animals can seem so near to us and yet also so distant. Ian Redmond is fascinated by the similarities but also the differences:

> We used to describe the other apes as 'sub-human primates' – now we use the term 'non-human primates'. But we are apes – genetically we are very close to chimps and bonobos – so it is fascinating to observe them and see things they do that are very like us, and also the things they do very differently.

Of all the human encounters with the great apes through history, one stands out: a famous film sequence first broadcast on the landmark BBC TV series *Life on Earth* in 1979. Consistently voted one of the most memorable TV moments of all time, it involves presenter David Attenborough going to meet a troop of gorillas in the volcanic forests on the border between Rwanda and Zaire. Attenborough sets aside his script and simply turns to camera, letting his emotions speak for him:

There is more meaning and mutual understanding in exchanging a glance with a gorilla than any other animal I know. Their sight, their hearing, their sense of smell are so similar to ours that we see the world in the same way as they do. They live in the same sort of social groups with largely permanent family relationships. They walk around on the ground as we do, though they are immensely more powerful than we are. And so if there were ever a possibility of escaping the human condition and living imaginatively in another creature's world, it must be with the gorilla.

That sequence was a turning point for these gentle giants. For the very first time, millions of people watching at home saw them as peaceable animals, living as a family and allowing another species to come close to their young and even play with them. It showed a bond of trust that was both humbling and challenging, especially so because for much of our history we have treated gorillas as dangerous monsters. It is this continual tension between regarding apes as either our cousins or our enemies that has given rise to such misunderstanding between us, and has ultimately defined our relationship.

Humans lived alongside these animals in the African rainforests for millennia, but everything changed when, during the eighteenth and nineteenth centuries, the age of exploration coincided with the development of more lethal and accurate weapons. The invention of the gun changed not only the way human beings relate to each other but also human–animal relationships too. Suddenly, these large and powerful animals could be brought down at a distance, with little or no risk to the human hunter. In the age of exploration and acquisition that dominated the Victorian period, the gun was a valuable tool.

Expeditions were mounted to bring back specimens for museums and private collectors, and intrepid hunters became the celebrities of their day, recounting their adventures in bestselling books. In *Adventures and Explorations in Equatorial Africa*, published in 1861,

French-American explorer Paul Du Chaillu recounted the day his party tracked a huge male gorilla – the first time the existence of these mighty beasts had been reliably confirmed:

Suddenly an immense gorilla advanced out of the wood straight toward us, and gave vent, as he came up, to a terrible howl of rage, as much as to say, 'I am tired of being pursued, and will face you.'

It was a lone male, the kind which are always most ferocious. This fellow made the woods resound with his roar, which is really an awful sound, resembling very much the rolling and muttering of distant thunder . . .

We at once gathered together; and I was about to take aim and bring him down where he stood, when Malaouen stopped me, saying in a whisper, 'Not time yet.'

We stood, therefore, in silence, gun in hand. The gorilla looked at us for a minute or so out of his evil gray eyes, then beat his breast with his gigantic arms – and what arms he had! Then he gave another howl of defiance, and advanced upon us. How horrible he looked! I shall never forget it.

Once again, Du Chaillu lifts his gun to fire, and once again his guide stays his hand. By now he is fearful that they have let the beast get too close, and that it will kill them:

Again the gorilla made an advance upon us. Now he was not twelve yards off. I could see plainly his ferocious face. It was distorted with rage; his huge teeth were ground against each other, so that we could hear the sound; the skin of the forehead was drawn forward and back rapidly, which made his hair move up and down, and gave a truly devilish expression to the hideous face. Once more he gave out a roar, which seemed to shake the woods like thunder; I could really feel the earth trembling under my feet. The gorilla, looking us in the eyes, and beating his breast, advanced again.

'Don't fire too soon,' said Malaouen; 'if you do not kill him, he will kill you.'

This time he came within eight yards of us before he stopped. I was breathing fast with excitement as I watched the huge beast.

Malaouen said only 'Steady' as the gorilla came up. When he stopped, Malaouen said 'Now!'

And before he could utter the roar for which he was opening his mouth, three musket-balls were in his body. He fell dead almost without a struggle.

The gorilla was a huge male, about the height of a small man, tall with enormous, muscled arms and powerful hands and feet, far stronger than any human, but still, as Du Chaillu observed, strangely humanoid in appearance: 'While the animal approached us in its fierce way, walking on its hind legs and facing us as few animals dare face man, it really seemed to me to be a horrid likeness of man.'

Encounters like this – an angry male gorilla charging at a hunter – became all too common. The prowess of the hunter was celebrated in set pieces of shocking taxidermy in museums around the world, as Ian Redmond explains: 'When the specimens came back they were mounted in a way that depicted that moment. It's like a nineteenth-century version of a YouTube hit – in the hunter's mind there's that moment when he pulled the trigger and the animal died, and that vivid image was captured for ever . . .'

It wasn't long before another new invention – the cinema – realised the box-office potential of monster apes attacking defenceless humans – or, as in one 1933 thriller – falling in love with them. It may be more than eighty years old, but the original *King Kong* (there have been numerous sequels, remakes and spin-offs, as well as computer games, theme-park rides and countless parodies) remains as popular as ever.

The simple plot is deceptively powerful. Kong is a giant gorilla who, having been brought to the very human world of New York as 'the eighth wonder of the world', goes on the rampage. While wreaking havoc on the terrified city, he falls in love with a beautiful young girl, memorably played by Fay Wray, whose terrified screaming when Kong takes her in his giant hands is one of cinema's most iconic moments. *King Kong* had all the elements of a great movie, and was based on a very real perception of apes at the time. They were still the aggressors who took any chance to attack us.

This view began to change during the second half of the twentieth century. An important turning point was another film, *Gorillas in the Mist*, which brought to our attention the pioneering work of Dian Fossey, the American gorilla scientist who showed us the intimate lives of these gentle giants – and the threats to them from poaching.

Dian Fossey was determined to discover more about the lives of wild gorillas, not simply by the traditional 'sit and observe' method favoured by most zoologists, but by getting to know them as individuals and families. So for almost two decades she studied a group of gorillas in the mountainous forests of Rwanda, making major advances in our knowledge and understanding, especially of how they communicate, what they eat and their social relationships.

In late 1985 Fossey was murdered as she slept in her cabin – possibly by poachers or an employee with a grudge, but maybe also because she opposed gorilla tourism, which brought major benefits to the local economy. The last entry in her diary presciently read: 'When you realise the value of all life, you dwell less on what is past and concentrate more on the preservation of the future.'

However, Fossey's legacy might still have been forgotten, were it not for the huge worldwide success of *Gorillas in the Mist*. Although the film is a drama, not a documentary, it is hard to overestimate its influence on people's attitudes, as Ian Redmond describes:

> *Gorillas in the Mist* reached audiences that you can only dream of getting to; because of the publicity and the numbers of people who were inspired by Dian Fossey, we've turned things around. The

film engaged the world in that issue and as a result of that the countries with mountain gorillas have managed to protect them, and the movie is an important part of that.

Gradually, through the influence of this film, David Attenborough's encounter with mountain gorillas and many more books, documentary films and stories, a more realistic view of apes began to emerge, one that we are familiar with today. Children were also encouraged to think about a two-way relationship with animals in cartoons and in the film *Dr Dolittle*, based on Hugh Lofting's books. Talking to the animals is exactly what Dian Fossey did: she learned gorilla-speak to show the gorillas she was not a threat, which allowed us to get those wonderful, close encounters we see on film. As a newly qualified biologist, Ian Redmond had the good fortune to work with Fossey, and remembers how she did it: 'She learned to use their little quiet vocalisations they make to each other – contact calls to keep in touch with the rest of the group. By using a reassuring sound, a friendly sound, Dian learned that eventually they will accept you, almost as an honorary member of the family.'

Dian Fossey wasn't the first person to be curious about the behaviour of primates, and the way their lives intersect with ours. In the late seventeenth century, more than a hundred years before Happy Jerry came to London, Edward Tyson – one of the foremost anatomists of his day – managed to obtain the body of a young chimpanzee. Like Jerry, this animal had been taken on board a ship in West Africa and treated as if it were a child. When the ship docked in London, Tyson spoke to a sailor who had looked after the animal, to find out how it had behaved during the long voyage from Angola to London:

> After our pygmy [*sic*] was taken and a little used to wear clothes,
> it was fond enough of them, and what it could not put on himself
> it would bring in his hands to some of the company on the ship

to help him put on. It would lie in a bed, place his head on the pillow, and pull the clothes over him as a man would do, but was so careless as to do all nature's occasions there [too].

The chimpanzee also learned to eat and drink – mostly in moderation:

After it was taken and made tame, it would readily eat anything that was brought to the table, and very orderly bring his plate thither to receive what they would give him. Once it was made drunk with punch, and they are fond enough of strong liquors, but it was observed that after that time it would never drink above one cup, and refused the offer of more than what he found agreed with him.

As a committed member of the temperance movement, Tyson's report of the chimp's moderate drinking habits may well have been recast to carry a moral message for his readers. Professor Erica Fudge, expert in animals and culture, explains: 'You get the sense that even back then these sailors were unable to view this anthropoid animal as anything other than anthropoid, and they wanted this to be a little human, and they obviously enjoyed its company . . .'

For Edward Tyson, the chimpanzee provided him with an opportunity to test out one of his theories about human intelligence. This was long before Darwin developed his theory of evolution by natural selection, and scientists viewed the world in a far more ordered way, taking their inspiration from classical thinkers such as Aristotle. As Erica Fudge, Professor of English Studies at the University of Strathclyde and Director of the Animal Studies Network, points out: 'What Tyson discovered was that chimpanzees are closer to humans on more factors than they are to monkeys. He argued that what this tells us is that this little creature is what he calls the nexus of the human and the animal.'

But that wasn't the only thing Tyson found out. As he dissected the animal, he discovered that its vocal cords were remarkably similar to that of a human being; and yet if that were the case, why couldn't the chimp speak? This offered further proof for Tyson that the chimp was an intermediary between the higher humans and the lower monkeys:

> He can't discover the difference between the human and the animal in terms of speech in the body, and that then allows him to go back to the older story, which is that humans are different from animals because we have a thing called 'reason', which of course you can never find in the body – it's just a kind of spiritual essence that makes us different. And so the fact that the chimpanzee has vocal cords, yet doesn't speak, reinforces the status of humans as the speaking creature.

But although one view saw apes and humans as separated by the power of language, not everyone agreed with this. One contemporary theory was that the apes had actually worked out that if they did speak in front of us then we would enslave them; as we had already done with the unfortunate human residents of West Africa.

It's an amusing story but we shouldn't be too smug that we no longer treat chimps like this. They may not be drinking gin any more, but children were being taken to see chimpanzees' 'teaparties' at London Zoo until 1972. And even more recently PG Tips featured chimpanzees dressed up as the Tipps family, voiced by famous comedians from Bob Monkhouse to Peter Sellers, enjoying 'a lovely cuppa' in their TV adverts. There was outcry when the campaign finally stopped in 2002. Chimpanzees look so much like us that it's almost impossible not to turn them into mini-humans.

Even so, there's no doubt that we've come a long way since we first became amused by a pygmy chimp and a pipe-smoking mandrill. Our relationship with our closest wild relatives has taken many twists and turns over the centuries, and is currently undergoing yet another transformation. The scientific focus is now on the interconnectedness of life on earth, but that can be hard to accept when we are so removed from the forests and mountains where many primates live. The media has a big role to play in helping twenty-first-century humanity to accept that we are part of a web of life, not simply a dominant species that can do with the world what it wants, as Richard Sabin explains:

> In recent years we have extracted a huge amount of very useful information from people in the field studying primates; we understand more about the way they interact with each other, that their language is quite complex, they have learned behaviours they pass on to their young and then to other groups – how they learn the way we do, and so on.

Yet even as we finally begin to properly understand the lives of our closest relatives, we have paradoxically put them in greater danger than ever before. All six of the great apes are now classified by the International Union for Conservation of Nature (IUCN) as either endangered or (in the case of the Sumatran orang-utan and western gorilla) critically endangered, with habitat loss, hunting for bushmeat and the spread of disease the greatest threats to their future. After all, if they do disappear, it won't simply be their loss, but ours too, in Ian Redmond's view:

> The frightening thing is that just as we are beginning to understand and respect non-human primates more we are in danger of losing them, because not everyone has that understanding. The sad fact is that if we succeed in exterminating our closest relatives we will lose, because they are essential to the health of the forest; their salvation is our salvation.

We'll leave the last word to chimpanzee specialist Charlotte Uhlenbroek, who reveals the wonder she feels as a human, looking straight into the eyes of a great ape when they and their families begin to trust you:

I was always fascinated by what makes us human, and when you're in the forest with chimpanzees day after day, it gives you a real sense of belonging – of being at home in the world, having your family around you. But more than anything else I feel a wonderful sense of interconnectedness with the natural world.

I knew that *Jaws* couldn't possibly be successful.
It was a first novel, and nobody reads first novels.
It was a first novel about a fish, so who cares?

Peter Benchley, author of *Jaws*

2

Sharks

Fear and Loathing

Imagine a hunter that is lithe and sleek, the embodiment of elegance and poise. An animal so supremely in harmony with its environment, so masterful and impressive, that it has inspired poems, novels and music – and works of art that have profoundly challenged our deepest assumptions. A predator whose sheer physicality holds us in thrall, whose image alone can suspend us between terror and admiration.

Recognise it? Maybe a piece of music will help; a piece so famous, so instantly recognisable that you only need to hear the first two notes to know exactly what you are listening to. Those are enough to strike fear into your heart and send a shiver up your spine. And they are enough – for some people at least – to stop them ever swimming in the sea again . . .

When composer John Williams first played his theme for *Jaws* to Steven Spielberg, the director assumed that it was some kind of joke. How could such a basic melody possibly be strong enough to underscore the action of a blockbuster movie? Yet it worked. As Williams himself said, the theme grinds away at you, 'just as a shark would do, instinctual, relentless, unstoppable'. The trailer – voiced by Orson Welles – only added to the sense of menace: 'There is a creature alive today that has survived millions of years of evolution without change, without passion, and without logic. It lives to kill: a mindless, eating machine. It will attack and

devour anything. It is as if God created the devil and gave him
. . . jaws.'

It was the summer of 1975, and suddenly even feeding the
goldfish seemed dangerous. *Jaws* sparked mass hysteria, as though
this one film had stirred a collective terror buried deep in our
primordial psyche. Its villain was not human, but a huge, apparently vengeful, great white shark that, especially in the sequels to
the film, appears to be engaged in a vendetta against the holiday-
makers at a fictional US east coast resort, Amity Island.

But this is no ordinary shark. After the first, apparently random,
attacks, as the film goes on it appears to target individuals, including
the crew sent to try to kill it. Eventually the shark is blown to
kingdom come. But not before it has taken its toll in both human
lives and the collective psyche of the people and community left
behind. By the end, the shark's malevolence has become almost
human.

Jaws broke every box-office record going, soon overtaking *The
Godfather* as the highest grossing movie in US history, a record it
held until the release of *Star Wars*. It won three Academy Awards
(including Best Original Score), regularly appears in lists of the
best movies of all time, and spawned three not very good sequels,
two theme-park rides, two musicals and several bestselling computer
games.

But in the process, *Jaws* unwittingly created a negative image
of sharks that we can never fully erase. Its lethal, emotionless
assassin, a ruthless killing machine apparently dedicated to hunting
down defenceless swimmers, has turned the shark into the most
feared – and ultimately one of the most hated – animals on the
planet.

Jaws was based on a novel written by US author Peter Benchley.
It very nearly didn't appear at all: having had several ideas rejected,
Benchley was on the verge of giving up writing for a living. Even
when the idea – loosely based on a true-life story of a fisherman
catching a great white shark off the coast of Long Island – was
finally accepted, the book almost never saw the light of day, as

the publisher was unhappy with the tone and demanded rewrites. But eventually, in 1974, it was published, and a year later Steven Spielberg made it into his celebrated film.

Benchley and Spielberg understood the power of anthropomorphism, and both realised that the shark was the perfect villain, a new and original 'baddie' just waiting to be exploited. Before *Jaws*, sharks had occasionally appeared as cinematic villains, such as in the James Bond films *Thunderball* (1965) and *Live and Let Die* (1973). But with the portrayal of the great white in *Jaws*, something changed fundamentally, as John Ó Maoilearca, Professor of Film and Television at Kingston University, explains: 'Suddenly the idea that you could have a 20- to 30-foot predator that still exists to this day, that will kill you and can eat you whole, seemed to be a strange discovery for the public imagination.'

For many cinemagoers, the most terrifying aspect of the shark in *Jaws* is not its appearance, but the fact that you don't actually see it at all until towards the end of the film. It was almost as if the idea of the shark was more powerful – and infinitely more terrifying – than the reality of the creature itself. As Richard Kerridge, nature writer and Lecturer in Creative Writing at Bath Spa University, points out, it played magnificently on our primal fear of the unknown; of an attacker lurking out of sight, somewhere in the depths of the oceans, but which has its cold black eyes fixed firmly on us:

> The fear of the shark is so intense partly, I think, simply because of the sea. For most of us, the ocean is still an alien place: it's uncanny, vast and comparatively empty. So when we're swimming there is always a lurking sense of vulnerability, particularly a fear of what might come up from beneath. That fear of the great mouth coming up from the dark depths below is a very primal one. The deep sea also represents the vastness of the universe in which we are tiny, vulnerable and insignificant.

Ironically, the reason we don't see the shark for so long in *Jaws* was not an artistic decision, but a practical and financial one. The model sharks Spielberg had commissioned simply did not look frightening enough, and nor were they easy to manipulate in the open ocean where the film was being shot. With time and money rapidly running out, Spielberg followed the great master of suspense, Alfred Hitchcock, and decided not to show the shark for the first two-thirds of the film. As he remarked, it's what you *don't* see that is truly terrifying. Turning the shark from a real animal into an unseen menace changed the whole course of the narrative, and added immeasurably to the suspense, as John Ó Maoilearca notes: '*Jaws* is a very effective horror film about a monster you cannot see, and it has been used as a formula ever since – the Ridley Scott film *Alien* was pitched as "*Jaws* in Space".'

But the more we regard sharks as a uniquely terrifying killer, the less we really understand about them. So what exactly are sharks, and why are they so good at what they do?

Sharks have been around for perhaps 400 million years. They long predated dinosaurs, which first appeared about 230 million years ago, let alone mammals (which have been around for some 200 million years), birds (roughly 150 million years) and *Homo sapiens* (a mere 200,000 years). Their longevity has enabled them to hone their skills as the sea's top predators, as Hooper, the shark scientist played by Richard Dreyfuss in *Jaws*, wryly observes: 'Out there is a perfect engine, an eating machine that is a miracle of evolution – it swims and eats and makes little baby sharks – that's all.'

The dominance of sharks over such a long period of time also means that the many species of fish that are preyed on by sharks have been shaped by them, as the Canadian environmentalist Paul Watson has indicated. The way they look, behave, swim, camouflage and defend themselves have all been moulded – through natural selection – by being hunted by sharks.

However, by no means are all sharks huge, fearsome predators. Sharks range in size from the massive whale shark – the largest fish in the world, at roughly 10–12 metres long and weighing up to 21.5 tonnes – to the tiny dwarf lanternshark, a kind of dogfish whose maximum length is just over 21 centimetres. And despite their huge size, the whale shark and its cousin the basking shark – the second largest fish on the planet – are filter feeders, eating nothing larger than krill.

All sharks, from the smallest to the largest, share a number of distinctive features. Their teeth are not fixed into their jawbone, as with mammals, but instead are embedded into their gums. This enables them to be constantly replaced during the fish's life, so that it always has the strongest, sharpest possible set available. Sharks have several rows of replacement teeth ready and waiting, each moving gradually forward on the animal's jaw until it is needed.

Like skates and rays, but unlike bony fish, sharks' skeletons are made from cartilage, a flexible material only about half the density of bone, which means that the shark can save energy as it swims. To compensate for any potential weakness, they also have a network of toothlike fibres known as 'dermal denticles' on the outside of their skin, which adds strength and helps to reduce water turbulence. Sharks swim using their powerful tails, which produce rapid thrust, enabling them to accelerate swiftly when pursuing their prey. And most famously, they must keep moving: some species – though by no means all – have to swim forward constantly in order to breathe, a behaviour that has embedded itself in popular culture as a metaphor for human progress.

There are almost 500 different species of sharks in the world. Yet only about a dozen of these have ever attacked human beings, and just three – great white, tiger and bull sharks – are responsible for the vast majority of fatal attacks. Of these, the great white – the star of *Jaws* – is by far the most feared. Great white sharks can reach almost 6.5 metres in length and may weigh as much as 2,000 kilos. They can live up to seventy years – longer than any other fish of their type – and swim at more than 56 kilometres per hour.

Found in many of the world's warmer oceans, great whites are most frequently seen off the coasts of Australia, the United States, Mexico, Japan and South Africa. Surprisingly, perhaps, they are also regularly spotted in the enclosed and shallow waters of the Mediterranean, and have even been reported off the coasts of Britain – though most, if not all, of these 'sightings' are thought to be of smaller species such as the porbeagle shark. And as biologist and patron of the Shark Trust Ian Fergusson points out, when you do come face to face with a great white, you know it:

> It's a quite incredible experience. There is this moment of pure adrenaline, when you look into the depths of the Pacific Ocean, and you see for the first time just that glimpse of white and black, the traditional colour scheme of the great white shark, beneath the boat, and coming up slowly to look at you. And in that moment, you recognise just how tiny and puny *Homo sapiens* is compared with this incredibly powerful animal – an animal every bit as intelligent as any of the terrestrial apex predators.

The word 'shark' first enters general usage in the middle of the sixteenth century, at the beginning of the age of discovery, when a specimen was apparently brought back to London by Captain John Hawkins from an expedition to West Africa. Before that, sharks were known as 'sea dogs' – hence the name 'dogfish', which is still used for some smaller species today.

Some linguists believe that the word 'shark' derives from the Mayan word *xok*, which would have been pronounced 'shok'. However the word 'sharke' (meaning a large sea fish) appeared in a letter written by Thomas Beckington, a civil servant (and later Bishop of Bath and Wells) as early as 1442. A more plausible alternative is that 'shark' derives from the German *schorck*, meaning 'villain' or 'scoundrel'.

In the 400 years or so since the word came into common usage, it has spawned a wide range of meanings – mostly negative ones. Thus we have 'loan sharks', 'card sharks' (a variant, possibly through mishearing, of the phrase 'card sharp') or simply 'shark' – applied to lawyers, criminals and politicians to denote a particular kind of behaviour, as linguist Alice Deignan explains: '"Shark" is used to denote unscrupulous and greedy behaviour in business or occasionally legal dealings, particularly when this involves exploiting vulnerable people.'

The link between sharks and lawyers is a strong one. A US television series about a rapacious lawyer, starring James Woods, was simply named *Shark*. During the making of *Jaws*, Spielberg named the ill-fated mechanical shark 'Bruce' after his lawyer, Bruce Ramer. Cultural historian Dean Crawford wonders what sharks have done to earn such vilification:

> Did they chomp down on our prehistoric ancestors often enough to create an evolutionary memory, a kind of monster profile in the lower cortices of our brains? Or are we exercising that special combination of loathing and fascination that humans reserve for a predator at least as well designed and widely feared in its watery realm as we are on land?

Others, including Richard Kerridge, suggest that our view of these creatures as ruthless killers is largely based on their physical characteristics:

> Why they are so hard to like is partly because their faces are so immobile, so still, so lacking in the kind of features that give us meaning, and reassure us. The whole repertoire of the landscape of the face is missing – there is just this smooth, torpedo-like shape, that great mouth with those teeth, and those black, empty eyes. The phrase that comes up all the time in writings about sharks is 'blank and expressionless'. It's as if they represent what life might be like if it were ruthless and merciless, and not moral or kind at all. It's the creature against which most others can be seen as relatively kind.

Adrian Peace, Honorary Associate Professor of Anthropology at the University of Queensland, also highlights their lack of any behaviour with which we can empathise: 'Their appearance turns us off – they look mean and menacing, with beady eyes, but most important of all they appear to do nothing else but hunt. At least bears and lions play with their offspring, but you never see sharks do anything but hunt. That explains why we so readily demonise this particular animal.'

This demonisation goes back further than we might assume; at least three-quarters of a century before the release of *Jaws*. In his 1897 poem 'The Shark', Lord Alfred Douglas (friend and lover of Oscar Wilde) cleverly melds the whimsical and menacing to create a vivid portrait of a ruthless, pitiless hunter:

> A treacherous monster is the Shark
> He never makes the least remark.
>
> And when he sees you on the sand,
> He doesn't seem to want to land.
>
> He watches you take off your clothes,
> And not the least excitement shows.
>
> His eyes do not grow bright or roll,
> He has astonishing self-control.
>
> He waits till you are quite undressed,
> And seems to take no interest.
>
> And when towards the sea you leap,
> He looks as if he were asleep.
>
> But when you once get in his range,
> His whole demeanour seems to change.
>
> He throws his body right about,
> And his true character comes out.

It's no use crying or appealing,
He seems to lose all decent feeling.

After this warning you will wish
To keep clear of this treacherous fish.

His back is black, his stomach white,
He has a very dangerous bite.

When it comes to our fascination with sharks, poetry, metaphors and the continued fame of *Jaws* are only the tip of the iceberg. Sharks also feature in both classic and contemporary art, most famously perhaps in two very different works more than two centuries apart.

The first of these, dating from 1778, is an oil painting by the American portraitist John Singleton Copley, *Watson and the Shark*. The original, now in Washington's National Gallery of Art, depicts a dramatic scene that took place in the harbour at Havana in 1749, when a young cabin boy named Brook Watson was savaged by a shark, losing his leg before being rescued. Watson later rose to become Lord Mayor of London, and commissioned the painting himself, perhaps to showcase his youthful heroism. Although undeniably vivid and powerful, the painting is badly let down by the artist's portrayal of the fish itself, which looks more like a crazed mutant dolphin than a shark.

No such accusations of inaccuracy can be levelled at the maker of the second piece of art, the bad boy of modern British art, Damien Hirst. That's because instead of a painting, drawing or sculpture of a shark, his 1991 artwork – entitled *The Physical Impossibility of Death in the Mind of Someone Living* – features the entire body of a 4-metre-long tiger shark preserved in formaldehyde inside a huge, steel-framed glass case, its mouth open as if ready to attack.

If *Jaws* played with the fears generated by *not* seeing a shark,

Hirst's work did exactly the opposite, creating an image from which we are unable to hide. As he explained, using a phrase from the original *Jaws* novel, he chose this particular creature to 'represent a fear'. In doing so, he shook the foundations of the art world to the core, as art expert Giovanni Aloi from the Chicago School of Art observes:

> It was a landmark piece for Damien Hirst. Some claim that it is the most important art piece in the twentieth century, and in many respects it changed the audience's relationship with contemporary art. Standing in front of the cabinets, the point that Hirst wanted to make was that we experience death a fraction of a second before becoming dead . . .

Just as, presumably, seeing a shark coming towards you would be your last experience of life. The artwork certainly created headlines, with the *Sun* newspaper commenting on the cost: '£50,000 for a fish without chips!' More seriously, Hirst was criticised for using a real animal in his work, especially because the shark had been killed to order, which many people found morally reprehensible. But as Aloi argues, he was only following the long tradition going back to the classical art of the Middle Ages and Renaissance of using animals – or parts of animals – to create artworks:

> Many insects and molluscs were used to produce hues and pigments that could not be produced in any other way. Sometimes it would take 12,000 creatures to make only 1.4 grams of pure dye, so the animal sacrifice involved was absolutely disproportionate. There are many animals disappearing into the beautiful classical paintings by people like Titian and Leonardo that we all love, whereas Damien Hirst has only killed a shark. This is a paradox we need to consider before demonising a work of contemporary art.

Most critics were positive about the artwork, with one noting that: 'The shark is simultaneously life and death incarnate in a way you don't quite grasp until you see it, suspended and silent, in its tank.'

But not everyone was quite so impressed. Veteran Australian art expert Robert Hughes suggested that, with such grossly inflated prices being paid for increasingly bizarre works, the international contemporary art market had become 'a cultural obscenity':

> The term 'avant-garde' has lost every last vestige of its meaning in a culture where anything and everything goes . . . A string of brush marks on a lace collar in a Velásquez can be as radical as the shark that an Australian caught for a couple of Englishmen some years ago and is now murkily disintegrating in its tank on the other side of the Thames. More radical, actually.

The 'dead shark', as it became known, had originally been commissioned by multimillionaire art collector Charles Saatchi, who later sold it to a US hedge fund manager for a sum variously reported to be between $8 and $12 million. Unfortunately for the new owner, the shark had not been preserved properly, and soon began to deteriorate. When it was replaced by a completely new specimen in 2006, it raised interesting questions about what constitutes an original artwork.

There is no getting away from the fact that both Hirst's shark in formaldehyde and the shark in the film *Jaws* represent sharks as killing machines to the general public. But this is not a universal attitude. In parts of the world where people live their daily lives with sharks, their understanding of these fascinating and complex animals is far more nuanced. Traditional cultures in the Pacific didn't just see all sharks as killers, as Dennis Kawaharada, Professor of English at the University of Hawaii, explains: 'Sharks were a source of food, while man-eating sharks were ritually hunted as a rite of passage. But there were also sharks that were worshipped as ancestral gods, who were protectors, so a deceased family member could be transformed into a "guardian shark", which could then be sent to attack or kill enemies.'

Around the world there are many shape-shifter myths featuring animals that can assume human form. Sharks are no exception. One story tells of a young 'shark-man' born to a young woman following her love affair with a 'shark-god'. Appearing to be a normal human being, he accompanies his fellow villagers into the sea, transforms himself into a shark and seizes his victims. Eventually he is discovered and killed: 'The story is a lesson about obeying the warnings of the gods, but it also serves as a reminder to those who enter the ocean to be aware of their surroundings.'

There are tales of benevolent sharks too, those that assist people to navigate at sea, or which drive away man-eaters to protect coastal communities. These stories show how other cultures represent sharks in different forms, some dangerous, others altruistic. It is a varied and complicated view that reflects the need of seafaring people to share watery space with the creatures that also live there. Such myths are a product of a deeply spiritual approach to nature, as Dennis Kawaharada suggests: 'Most ancient people viewed all beings in nature as spiritual entities, which could both harm and help you. I think the concept behind the worship was to harness the benevolent spirits to do good for you, or to control the malevolent ones through worship and rituals and prayers.'

In recent times the coming of modern customs and lifestyles to Hawaii means that many of these traditional beliefs are inevitably fading; yet they still persist among fishing families, a sign of their potency and longevity.

With all the many ways in which we view sharks – both positive and negative – it is hard to get to the truth of the risk they pose to humans. Well-publicised reports of 'shark attacks' have led to a behavioural phenomenon that US lawyer, author and social psychologist Cass R. Sunstein calls 'probability neglect'. This is a form of cognitive bias, fuelled by the modern media, which means that we are unable to judge risks properly. As a result, we tend to grossly overestimate our chances of dying in rare but headline-hitting events such as a plane crash or shark attack, when the odds of such an event occurring are actually vanishingly small.

Statistics on shark attacks going back to the year 1580 produce a total of close to 3,000 shark attacks in 434 years (an average of fewer than seven a year), of which 548 (an average of just over one a year) proved fatal. In recent years, the number of fatalities has risen, with an average of four each year. This is partly because more are being reported, but also perhaps due to changes in shark behaviour caused by a lack of available food and global climate change, both of which are encouraging sharks to venture closer to shore and investigate potential new sources of food, including human swimmers.

Yet other top predators such as lions, leopards and tigers are responsible for far more human deaths, as indeed are domestic dogs, cows and horses. You are more likely to die driving to the beach, being stung by a jellyfish, or from a coconut falling on your head, or as actor-turned-marine-environmentalist Ted Danson put it, 'You're more likely to be killed by your toaster than a shark.' And even when you do venture into the water, in the US you are more than 3,000 times more likely to drown than to die from a shark bite.

Moreover, the majority of shark attacks are not fatal, suggesting that the shark is simply taking an experimental bite to check whether its victim is good to eat. This may not be much comfort if you are the person being experimented on, but it does suggest that our image of sharks as malicious, ruthless man-eaters might perhaps be mistaken. In fact sharks do not really want to eat human beings, because we are not fatty enough for them to digest easily, and don't have as much energy-giving blubber as seals – which may explain why most great whites only bite humans once. Unfortunately that single bite may still prove fatal, due to blood loss, trauma and shock.

The remote chance of actually being killed by a shark hasn't stopped some coastal communities from adopting the policy of the mayor of the fictional town, Amity, in *Jaws*, and killing any big sharks that venture near their beaches. The most recent example of this occurred in Western Australia in 2014, when the state premier Colin Barnett had baited hooks installed to try to catch the sharks. Despite widespread criticism from environmentalists, and suggestions that blood from the hooked fish may attract even more sharks, at the time of writing the policy continues.

The words we employ to talk about sharks are also important to the way we treat them. Adrian Peace has been looking at the language used in shark reports from Australian newspapers:

> What strikes me is the uniformity of the terms that are used to describe sharks when they come into contact with people. When the summer comes round here in Australia – 'shark season', as it's called – the terms used by the media are ones like lurking, lingering, prowling and loitering, and they're always doing these things near 'innocent' or 'unsuspecting' bathers. The most evocative words of all are menacing, terrorising and stalking – the Mafia menace, and assassins stalk, so this is really a very extreme suggestion of criminal behaviour on the part of sharks.

A 2014 report from the University of Sydney linked the demonising language used against sharks directly to government policy to cull them when an attack occurs. But things may be changing. Adrian Peace believes that a recent change of heart towards sharks may be due to a greater understanding of their behaviour, and a deeper empathy with what it means to be a shark: 'When sharks attack they are after all doing this in their natural territory. Not only that but they're also behaving naturally in the sense that they are driven by instinct to attack whatever happens to be in their space. They cannot really be held responsible for their actions.'

This more understanding attitude towards sharks is coming from surprising places, often being promulgated by the survivors of shark attacks, or their relatives, who plead with the authorities not to take revenge in their loved one's name. Following her lucky escape from being bitten by a shark in 2014, Australian teenager Kirra-Belle Olsson was at pains to point out that this was not the shark's fault: 'It's their home, they're only doing what they do every day. It's not like they say, "there's a person, I'm going to eat it".'

Elsewhere, notably in South Africa, whole communities tend to have a fairly benevolent attitude towards sharks, not least because the sharks generate a huge amount of revenue in eco-tourism opportunities, either from boat trips or the more controversial pastime of 'cage diving'. Controversial, because many boat operators are 'chumming' – putting fish offal into the water as bait – in order to attract more sharks, a practice that is likely to mean that sharks begin to associate humans with food and which could have dire consequences.

Of course the real problem is not that sharks might eat us, but that a significant number of human beings wish to eat sharks, rapidly hastening their global decline. We kill between 26 and 73 million sharks every year. As a result, with perhaps as few as 3,500 individuals in existence, the great white shark – the infamous 'star' of *Jaws*, and the most feared animal on earth – is now possibly rarer than the tiger. And large sharks are much more difficult than tigers to keep in captivity, making this top marine predator far more vulnerable to extinction.

Millions of sharks fall victim every year to a culinary trend sweeping the Far East. Shark fin soup is a favourite dish across much of Asia, including China, now the world's biggest economy. It is pretty tasteless but, like tiger parts and rhino horn, it is supposed to increase sexual potency. Unscrupulous and unregulated fishing fleets simply catch huge numbers of sharks, cut off the fins, and then throw the mutilated animals back into the ocean to die a slow and painful death. The figures are staggering: China alone is estimated to harvest 10,000 tonnes of shark fin every year, resulting in the deaths of tens of millions of sharks; and this does not take into account the largely unreported illegal trade.

Ironically, one of the leading voices supporting a revision of our attitude towards sharks was the author Peter Benchley. Following the huge success of *Jaws*, Benchley's novel went on to sell an estimated 20 million copies, making him a very rich man indeed. But with wealth and success came guilt: that he, perhaps more than anyone, had been unwittingly responsible for our negative attitudes towards sharks, resulting indirectly in the deaths of millions of sharks worldwide.

He resolved to make up for this by supporting shark conservation through articles in newspapers and magazines, in his 2001 book *Shark Trouble*, and by acting as a spokesman for environmental organisations. He even suggested that he would not have written the novel had he known then what sharks were really like: 'The shark in an updated *Jaws* could not be the villain; it would have to be written as the victim; for, worldwide, sharks are much more the oppressed than the oppressors.'

Perhaps he was too hard on himself. After all, we have always viewed sharks with suspicion and fear and they are never going to be as popular in conservation terms as giant pandas, polar bears, tigers or elephants. But the fear seems to be something we like, if we can feel it at a safe distance. It is a thrill. That is what the appeal of *Jaws* was all about. As Oliver Crimmen, Senior Curator of Fish at the Natural History Museum recalls, the '*Jaws* effect' was far from being entirely negative: 'After the book and the film came out there was a big leap not only in public interest in sharks but also in scientific research. When Peter Benchley visited the museum in the last years of his life I was able to tell him this, and I think it did console him.'

After Benchley's death in 2006, his widow declared that the global hysteria fostered by *Jaws* was not his fault, and that 'he took no more responsibility for the fear of sharks than Mario Puzo [author of *The Godfather*] took for the Mafia'. Ultimately, Benchley had grown to understand what any naturalist knows: that sharks behave in the way they do because that is the way evolution has programmed them; they are predators – they eat other animals: 'We provoke a shark every time we enter the water where sharks happen to be, for we forget: the ocean is not our territory – it's theirs.'

It is possible to see the face of a great white shark as possessing a doglike eagerness rather than malevolent cruelty. Our relationship with sharks is changing, and our desire to conserve them is growing. Whether it will spread sufficiently quickly to save them is another matter, but Ian Fergusson is cautiously optimistic:

> We are certainly on the right course. Despite all of the still-ongoing media hyperbole that surrounds sharks, there is a growing swell in public opinion that is becoming more positive towards them. We are slowly getting new generations to start to embrace the idea that this is an animal worth protecting. You will hear innumerable scientific debates as to why they should be saved, but let me simplify it for you: sharks are cool fish to have in the ocean, and wouldn't it be a boring place without them?

A fallen blossom
Returning to the bough, I thought –
But no, a butterfly

Arakida Moritake

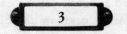

Butterflies

The Dark Side of Beauty

It had been a long, hard and uncomfortable day, just one of many long and uncomfortable days in the depths of the steaming rainforest of the Molucca (now Maluku) Islands of northern Indonesia.

Alfred Russel Wallace was hot, tired and sweaty; a state of affairs he had grown to accept, if not exactly enjoy, during his travels around this remote and hostile archipelago. He had put up with these discomforts for five years and would endure them for a further three, during which time he was to collect a phenomenal 126,000 specimens of birds, butterflies and beetles. He was a collector extraordinaire. Unlike most of the scientific establishment, with neither family wealth to draw on nor friends in high scientific places, Wallace was funding his travels by finding and selling specimens to enthusiasts back in England. And despite being a self-taught naturalist who had left school at fourteen, he had managed to come up with a theory that was to revolutionise science.

The previous year, 1858, he and Charles Darwin, the most famous scientist of his day, had had papers jointly presented to a distinguished audience at the Linnaean Society in London, in which each outlined a theory of evolution by means of a process that would come to be known as 'natural selection'; a theory each had worked out independently of the other.

Of the thousands of creatures Wallace was to collect during his long life, one particular butterfly stood out as the most special. At first, all he glimpsed was a brief flash of gold in the darkness of the foliage; then he had a slightly better view and noticed that the wings were patterned in bold yellow and black. Finally, it settled on a flower just a few yards in front of him. Moving slowly forward, Wallace's heart was beating so loudly he thought it might frighten the insect away, but it stayed put, greedily drinking the flower's nectar. Inch by inch, Wallace moved near enough to pounce. Then, with a rapid swish of his net, the butterfly was captured.

Despite his long experience as a collector, Wallace was flabbergasted by its sheer beauty, as he recalled in his bestseller of 1869, *The Malay Archipelago*:

> The beauty and brilliancy of this insect are indescribable, and none but a naturalist can understand the intense excitement I experienced when I at length captured it. On taking it out of my net and opening the glorious wings, my heart began to beat violently, the blood rushed to my head, and I felt much more like fainting than I have done when in apprehension of immediate death. I had a headache the rest of the day, so great was the excitement produced by what will appear to most people a very inadequate cause.

Wallace's passion soars off the page, his pure, unadulterated obsession with nature. This insect was indeed new to science, and is sometimes known by the name of its discoverer: Wallace's golden birdwing. Its scientific name *Ornithoptera croesus* also emphasises its bright colour: Croesus, the King of Lydia (now western Turkey) from the sixth century BC, was legendary for his overflowing coffers of gold.

Wallace was amassing his butterflies, along with many other creatures, at the height of the Victorian collecting frenzy. The specimens he assembled, along with his detailed notes, have proved invaluable to modern naturalists. We owe the collections in most of our museums to the labours of these nineteenth- and early twentieth-century naturalists who travelled the world, often in extreme and dangerous conditions, to collect animals and plants.

The American poet Robert Frost called butterflies 'flowers that fly and all but sing'. It's a powerful image. The butterfly is the essence of a warm spring or summer day and we use it as a symbol of fragility and frivolity: people with butterfly minds skip from one subject to another.

But surely the attraction of butterflies is that they are only with us for a short time, their seasonal flights having a poignancy that tugs us back to sunny days. Even now, whenever he sees small tortoiseshell butterflies, Brett is seven years old again, a young hunter lurking by the buddleia bush at his grandparents' back door, armed with a net taller than himself. The lasting memories of such fleeting encounters and the chance to collect butterflies make them so irresistible.

Colourful and highly mobile, it's no surprise they have captured our imagination in art, music, literature, religion and science and, of course, hobbies. More than almost any other creature, butterflies have come to embody a rich and varied panoply of symbolic and cultural meaning. Their colours and patterns, short and ephemeral lives, delicacy and spirituality, and, above all, their apparently miraculous transformation from earthbound larvae to creatures of the air, have contributed to our perennial fascination with these beautiful creatures.

There is even mythology surrounding the word 'butterfly'. For example, it is sometimes asserted that the word was originally 'flutterby', describing the flight of the insect. (Sadly this is no more than a charming thought.) Another suggestion is that the word – a contraction of 'butter-coloured fly' – comes from a single familiar species, the brimstone, which is often the first butterfly to appear in spring; the males are indeed strikingly yellow.

There is a stronger clue in the German word for butterfly: *Schmetterling*. According to author and entomologist Peter Marren, *Schmetter* derives from a dialect word meaning 'cream' or 'sour milk', while another folk name is *Milchdieb*, meaning 'milk thief'. This may refer to the ancient Teutonic belief that witches stole milk from cows, which links with a strange phenomenon where butterflies were known to gather in large numbers when milk was being churned into butter outdoors. Perhaps, Marren suggests, butterflies are somehow drawn to a chemical pheromone in the milk or butter itself. However, *schmettern* is also the German verb meaning to beat, smash or crash, which might lead us to suggest an equally plausible derivation of the word: that it comes from the Old English verb *beatan* (also meaning 'to beat'), and simply refers to the action of the insects' wings as they fly through the air.

The words for butterfly are clearer in most other languages than in English. Thus the French have *papillon*, itself derived from the Latin word *papilio* meaning 'tent' (hence our modern English word 'pavilion') and referring to the shape of the wings. The Italian word *farfalla* is more familiar in its plural form, as *farfalle*, the name for the pasta shaped like a bow tie (or butterfly!), while the Spanish *mariposa* has a religious origin which derives from the phrase '*la Santa Maria posa*, meaning 'the Virgin Mary alights' – presumably a reference to a butterfly landing delicately on a flower. The Norwegian *sommerfugl* translates as the evocative 'bird of summer', but of all the different words for butterfly, surely the most fascinating is the ancient Greek *psyche*. The root of many modern terms including psychology, psychiatrist and psychic, to the Greeks it meant 'spirit' or 'soul', as Peter Marren explains:

> The Greeks were the first people to adopt butterflies into their philosophy and world view. They noticed that the caterpillar turns into a pupa which seems to be dead, almost as if the caterpillar has made its own coffin, and then suddenly the pupa splits open and out comes this angelic butterfly, a spiritual insect that flies off into the sky and is no longer bound by the earth.

This is, however, only one of many different ways – albeit perhaps the most powerful – in which we have incorporated butterflies (and their complex life cycle) into our view of the human world.

Butterflies have come to symbolise life and death, heaven and hell, freedom and imprisonment, joy and despair. In doing so they have entered our lives – our psyche, one could even say – in a way few other creatures have managed to do apart, perhaps, from birds. As the Chinese philosopher Zhuangzi wrote in the fourth century BC: 'I do not know whether I was then a man dreaming I was a butterfly, or whether I am now a butterfly dreaming I am a man.'

Butterflies are bittersweet. Their transient beauty inspired the tragic figure of Puccini's Madame Butterfly. Religious paintings use butterflies to symbolise resurrection, or as portents of doom. There's more on both of these later. Muhammad Ali famously said he could dance like a butterfly, but sting like a bee. It's probably safe to say that he wasn't speaking as a dedicated lepidopterist, but rather his comment reflects the fact that as a society we have always watched butterflies closely, fascinated by their lives from egg to caterpillar to adult.

Only birds – in all their variety and conspicuousness – rival butterflies as exemplars of human qualities, emotions and passions. Thus butterflies are perceived as beautiful, fragile and ephemeral, as indeed they are: most are strikingly patterned; they can be easily damaged or killed; and few live more than two or three weeks.

Beauty and fragility are an irresistible combination, that ephemeral and fleeting psyche that we strive to capture and pin down. It's an image that inspired John Fowles's dark novel *The Collector*, the tale of a lepidopterist who 'collects' a young woman and keeps her in a basement. This idea is central to Puccini's opera *Madame Butterfly* with its tragic heroine, a young Japanese woman, so beautiful her devious suitor, Pinkerton, compares her to a fluttering butterfly, so captivating he must capture her, even though it will damage her wings. In one of the most moving scenes, Madame Butterfly sings about how it feels to be pinned down like this:

> They say that overseas
> if it should fall into the hands of man
> a butterfly is stuck through
> with a pin
> and fixed to a board!

Her words prove prophetic: later, rejected by Pinkerton, Madame Butterfly stabs herself with her father's hara-kiri knife. Pinkerton's response is equally telling about why we still see butterfly collections as pieces of art:

> There's some truth in that;
> and do you know why?
> So that it shouldn't fly away again.
> I've caught you . . .
> You're mine.

———•———

The most wide-ranging and powerful images of butterflies refer not to the adult insect we see on spring and summer days, but to the process by which this creature comes about; one of the most extraordinary examples of metamorphosis in the whole of the animal kingdom.

If a visitor from outer space were to be shown the life cycle of a bird or a mammal, it would presumably make some kind of sense: the fertilised egg (or embryo) gradually develops – either inside or outside the mother's body – until it produces a small version of the adult creature. But butterflies and moths undergo the most extraordinary change, in which the three stages following the hatching of the egg appear so different it is hard to believe they belong to the same species, let alone represent three stages in the life cycle of a single individual. As the US architect and inventor Buckminster Fuller pointed out: 'There is nothing in a caterpillar that tells you it's going to be a butterfly.'

Thus the egg hatches into a caterpillar, a typical insect larva that is basically an eating machine with legs. Having hatched, most caterpillars feed voraciously, often on a single species of food plant. As they grow, they pass through several stages known as 'instars', in which they moult their outer skin to reveal a new layer beneath. During the last of these stages, the caterpillar develops proto-wings, hidden beneath its outer casing.

Once the caterpillar is fully grown – a process that may take several weeks or even months – it is ready to enter the next stage of its life cycle: pupation. This is perhaps the most incredible transformation of all, from a mobile, active caterpillar into a static, apparently inactive, pupa. During this stage the insect undergoes the various processes that alter it from the caterpillar into the adult butterfly – changing its body shape and growing the wings it will need to fly.

When it finally emerges, the adult butterfly cannot immediately fly, so is very vulnerable to being eaten by predators. Its wings gradually unfold, inflate and dry (a process that usually takes between one and three hours) before the adult butterfly finally takes to the air. Yet although its lifespan may be brief – certainly compared with its time spent as an egg, caterpillar or pupa – it is this stage of the insect's life that we most often celebrate. As the comedian George Carlin wryly observed: 'The caterpillar does all the work, but the butterfly gets all the publicity.'

Most representations in art – indeed almost all the best-known examples – at first appear to be overwhelmingly positive, yet this is perhaps because we are seeing them from our own, modern perspective, as Peter Marren explains:

Artists did not always paint a butterfly for its own sake, but as a symbol, an embodiment of some abstraction, whether moral or religious. Because they were the nearest thing in the natural world to our idea of a spirit, butterflies tended to symbolise the world beyond, a prefiguration of the afterlife that awaits us . . . Butterflies were part of the creation of our world and, like all life, we could learn from them. They were at once real and metaphors. They were a promise of a world beyond, and in this life they put us in our place.

Nowhere is this more apparent than in the work of the Dutch Renaissance artist Hieronymus Bosch. As you look closely at his masterpiece *The Garden of Earthly Delights*, created in the opening decade of the sixteenth century, it takes time to find the butterflies among the plethora of human and animal characters. But searching reveals several examples of butterflies depicted in ways we find quite hard to understand nowadays.

There is a fearsome-looking 'butterfly-monster' with the body of a man and the head of a butterfly (it is not clear which species, though it does show the peacock's false 'eyes'), thrusting his sword into the stomach of an unfortunate captive. Nearby, what is clearly a meadow brown, augmented with the head and claws of a bird, attacks another victim, while what may be a painted lady feeds greedily on a blue thistle, which in turn emerges from the body of a homunculus.

We still struggle to understand the extremity of Bosch's butterfly imagery: the drab meadow brown was once seen as a spy from hell, the small eye-spots on its wings being the equivalent of satanic closed-circuit TV, noting misdemeanours for future reference. The association between the meadow brown and the powers of darkness is still commemorated in the scientific name for the species' genus *Maniola*, which roughly translates as 'little spirit from the underworld'.

Even butterflies we find beautiful today held a sinister meaning in the past. Take the red admiral, a common visitor to our gardens, with its velvet black wings slashed with red. That colour combination gave rise to all manner of dark thoughts. Although the English name was previously 'admirable', perhaps reflecting its popularity, it once had a far more sinister significance, as Peter Marren points out: 'Red is a very rare colour in butterflies, and although to us it is beautiful, in the past it was seen as sinister, as an echo of darkness and flames, and of hell – hence this became the butterfly from hell.'

Thus red admirals appear as representations of evil and hellfire in many late medieval and Renaissance artworks, often juxtaposed with white butterflies representing innocence, purity and hope. The red admirals are often to one side, in the shade, perched on a faded bloom or decaying fruit, or with grotesque birdlike heads, making them 'look like little devils' or, perhaps, damned souls. Peter Marren also points out the French word for the red admiral is *Vulcain* – after Vulcan, the blacksmith of the gods.

In *Floral Wreath with Madonna and Child*, a religious still-life painting by the seventeenth-century Flemish artist Daniel Seghers, two butterflies are shown: a large white and a red admiral. While the Virgin Mary is looking at the white butterfly, the eyes of the young Christ are gazing at the red one, a symbol both of sin and death but also, perhaps, a reminder of the crucifixion.

Ironically enough, today these two butterflies are regarded in an almost diametrically opposite way. Whereas the red admiral, a migrant from southern Europe or North Africa, is now seen as a welcome sign of spring, the appearance of any of the familiar 'cabbage white' butterflies is a signal for gardeners, allotment owners and vegetable growers to reach for their pesticide spray. But not, hopefully, before they have stopped to take a closer look at these fascinating insects.

When we see a butterfly – especially once it has perched so we can take a closer look – we are often captivated by its colour and markings. And just as we often take an anthropocentric view of birdsong as nature's gift to us, rather than as an essential tool in the biological process of courtship and breeding, so it is easy to view butterflies' wings as pleasing and attractive, without ever stopping to wonder at the purpose of their complex patterns.

As with many bright colours in nature, the reds and oranges serve as a warning: that the insect may be toxic or at least distasteful to predators. The 'eyes' on the upper wings of many butterflies

– notably the familiar peacock – are also a defence mechanism: they fool a hungry bird into pecking at the wing tip rather than the insect's body so that it can escape alive, albeit often with a damaged wing.

A new theory, proposed by Philip Howse in his 2014 *Seeing Butterflies* (subtitled *New Perspectives on Colour, Patterns and Mimicry*), suggests that these patterns are even more complex than one might assume. Howse argues that butterfly wing-patterns don't just send generic messages to a predator; instead, by mimicking specific creatures, including caterpillars, spiders, bumblebees and even birds of prey, they send targeted warnings.

Their patterns hold other messages for us, including mathematical formulae, which it takes an art historian to unmask. Giovanni Aloi, from the School of the Art Institute of Chicago, who specialises in the representation of animals in art, outlines another reason we find butterflies so appealing:

> It's not just the bright colours – there's something more to the structure and pattern of the wings that we humans find particularly fascinating. It's been argued that the golden section, which is the ratio of proportional perfection in classical art, is contained in the wings of butterflies – they have a kind of primordial appeal.

The 'golden section' (also known as the 'golden ratio', and represented by the Greek letter *phi*) was discovered by the ancient Greeks. They used it in their art and sculpture as it has a special appeal to the human eye. It is also found widely in nature, for example in the whorls of a snail's shell, the pattern of seeds on the head of sunflowers, the shape of spiral galaxies and the whirling cloud patterns of hurricanes – even the shape of a human face demonstrates the golden section. When something is pleasing to us, it probably follows this particular mathematical structure.

But the golden ratio isn't just pleasing to the eye; it actually has a stabilising, calming, comforting effect, as Giovanni Aloi explains: 'When we look at butterflies, especially in the traditional specimen cabinet configuration found in museums where the wings are spread out in a symmetrical fashion, we are instantly – almost subliminally – captivated by the golden ratio that is captured in the shapes and patterns on the wings.'

Such detail was not lost on one group of men who became obsessed by butterflies: the Victorian collectors, who were so numerous they were even commemorated – and indeed satirised – in the popular fiction of the period. Among the varied cast of minor characters in Anthony Trollope's *Barchester Towers*, Dr Vesey Stanhope stands out as the epitome of clerical absenteeism, as Trollope makes clear: 'Years had now passed since he had done a day's duty, and yet there was no reason against his doing duty except a want of inclination on his own part.'

Nominally the rector of two parishes in this fictional diocese, he has lived for a dozen years in Italy, where he appears to have spent most of his time collecting butterflies – much to the disgust of the redoubtable Mrs Proudie, wife of the new bishop.

We can smile at Trollope's barbed portrait, as is the author's intent. But Dr Stanhope was by no means untypical of the clerical profession at this time. In his detailed study *The English Parson-Naturalist*, Patrick Armstrong traces a passion for butterflies among churchmen back to the seventeenth-century theologian and naturalist John Ray, with whom 'the adventure of modern science begins'.

Ray combined his love of God and fascination with nature in a way we can still relate to today:

> You ask what is the use of butterflies? I reply to adorn the world and delight the eyes of men; to brighten the countryside like so many golden jewels. To contemplate their exquisite beauty and variety is to experience the truest pleasure. To gaze enquiringly at such elegance of colour and form designed by the ingenuity of nature and painted by her artist's pencil, is to acknowledge and adore the imprint of the art of God.

Later parson-naturalists with a particular interest in butterflies included the nineteenth-century evangelist F.O. Morris, who produced some of the most sentimental, inaccurate (yet hugely popular) writings on nature ever published; the Revd Leonard Jenyns, who kept accurate diaries on the butterflies of Cambridgeshire; and the best known of all, Gilbert White, author of *The Natural History of Selborne*.

What these men had in common was a good education, plenty of what we would now call leisure time, and the ability – indeed a duty – to wander the highways and byways of their parish without being considered suspicious, at a time when anyone doing so without due cause would have been regarded as either mad, bad or both.

By the late nineteenth and early twentieth centuries, however, a passion for natural history was no longer considered a niche interest; indeed it was becoming rather fashionable, especially among the landed gentry, in what butterfly enthusiast Matthew Oates describes as a 'Victorian and Edwardian obsession'.

Of all these gentlemen-collectors, perhaps the most colourful was Sir Vauncey Harpur Crewe, 10th Baronet, of Calke Abbey, a former Augustinian priory in Derbyshire. Harpur Crewe was a genuine English eccentric: generous with servants and employees but tight-fisted with his own family; a committed anti-smoker who banished his daughter from her home for the rest of his lifetime for smoking a single cigarette; and violently opposed to any form of modern transport – not just motor cars but even bicycles.

His obsession was the amassing of an enormous collection of natural objects, including birds and their eggs, moths and particularly butterflies. On his death in 1924, the vast majority of his collection was sold in order to pay death duties, but a large number of specimens still remain at Calke Abbey, which is now in the hands of the National Trust.

Matthew Oates showed us through dusty rooms full of specimens geological, entomological, ornithological. He described the 'glorious clutter' of a shabby room with rows and rows of shelves stacked with cardboard boxes which, on closer examination, reveal Harpur Crewe's obsessive nature – even by the standards of his day.

One case contains twenty-five silver-washed fritillaries, neatly pinned and mounted, as bright as when they were first caught on a single day in the New Forest. Although a few of the specimens display the classic orange and black upper wings of this large butterfly, the majority are an iridescent silvery-green in shade. These are of the very rare form *valezina*, an odd colour variant only found in females, and only then in large colonies. To have obtained so many of these specimens in a single day reveals how common this now rare butterfly must once have been.

This kind of obsession is reminiscent of another popular pastime of this period, stamp collecting. Like an album full of identical stamps, some showing a single imperfection that paradoxically makes them more valuable, these rows and rows of butterflies are testament to a single-minded obsession. But Oates sees a fundamental difference in the collecting of natural rather than man-made objects: 'These are better than Penny Blacks, as they were living things, the result of a complex metamorphosis that produced an atypical butterfly, unique in time and place.'

The reason men such as Sir Vauncey Harpur Crewe were so enthusiastic about collecting, while their successors – including Matthew Oates himself – are still so passionate about finding and documenting living butterflies, Oates believes, is connected to love, memories and a quite understandable obsession with beauty: 'People collect memories – deliberately or inadvertently. Vauncey Harpur Crewe was collecting memories of great adventures with wildlife. Admittedly he killed it, he shot it, he caught it, he pinned it, and he kept it as specimens – but don't think for a moment that he didn't love these things.'

As butterflies have declined in number and the fashion for collecting them has become both illegal and widely considered immoral, we have perhaps lost something of our connection with these beautiful and fascinating creatures. But all that changed during the Whitsun bank holiday weekend in late May 2009, when Britain was invaded – by painted ladies.

The painted lady is one of Britain's most attractive and enigmatic butterflies. Pale orange, with black wingtips spotted with white, it looks rather like a washed-out version of a red admiral and, like that species, it migrates here each spring from Spain or North Africa. But while red admirals are a regular annual arrival – like swallows or cuckoos – painted lady numbers vary dramatically from year to year; some summers they are few and far between, while in other years they can be fairly common. Yet nothing could have prepared us for the arrival of millions – perhaps tens of millions – of painted lady butterflies during that memorable spring and summer.

The invasion was the result of an incredibly successful breeding season earlier in the year due to heavy winter rains which produced a profusion of the food plants on which the caterpillars feed. Favourable weather conditions, with light southerly winds, then allowed the newly emerged adult butterflies to fly through Spain and France, and then across the Channel to Britain. The first sightings were on the coasts: staff at one Norfolk nature reserve counted fifty flying past every minute, with 18,000 in total in just a few hours.

For the rest of the summer, the butterflies just kept on coming, and the sight of them whizzing past with a flash of orange became commonplace throughout the British Isles. They then bred and laid eggs that hatched into caterpillars, which pupated to produce a new generation of adults in early autumn. These were then observed for the very first time heading off from south coast headlands on their long journey to their original homeland in the Atlas Mountains of Morocco.

The effect of perhaps as many as 1 billion painted ladies adorning the British summer was extraordinary: even people who never normally notice wild creatures were fascinated by these little insects and their epic journey to arrive here, and the invasion was a regular feature in newspapers and on TV news bulletins.

Yet by the following year the normal pattern had resumed: painted ladies were decidedly few and far between and we had returned to a world in which, as Alan Bennett put it in his play *Forty Years On*, 'a butterfly is an event'. What a different world from the one just a century or so ago when Sir Vauncey Harpur Crewe could collect dozens of now incredibly rare butterflies in a single day.

H.G. Wells wrote in his 1895 novel *The Wonderful Visit*:

> If it were not for collectors England would be full, so to speak, of rare birds and wonderful butterflies, strange flowers and a thousand interesting things. But happily the collector prevents all that, either killing with his own hands or, by buying extravagantly, procuring people of the lower classes to kill such eccentricities as appear . . . So one may go through England from end to end in the summer time and see only eight or ten commonplace wild flowers, and the commoner butterflies, and a dozen or so common birds, and never be offended by any breach of the monotony.

But even though collectors did take many specimens, there were millions more, and these depredations made little or no difference to population levels, apart perhaps in the cases of a few very rare species.

What has devastated Britain's butterflies – and much of the rest of the country's lowland wildlife – is the way we have chosen to farm the countryside since the end of the Second World War, using chemical pesticides and herbicides to raise yields, and destroying wildlife-rich but unproductive habitats such as hedgerows and field margins to increase productivity. Butterflies – especially grassland specialists – have been particularly badly hit by these changes and, as a result, the majority of Britain's fifty-plus species are in serious decline.

Conservationists have fought back, and are still doing so. Bold and colourful species such as the swallowtail have now come to stand for conservation of habitats: in this case the fenland of East Anglia. The large blue, which disappeared from Britain in 1979, has been successfully reintroduced, while the Duke of Burgundy and high brown fritillary are being actively conserved to prevent further declines.

Now Britain's butterflies face a new challenge, one that presents both a threat and an opportunity: global climate change. If, as predicted, temperatures do rise, we are likely to lose species such as the mountain ringlet which, as its name suggests, lives only at high altitudes in the Lake District and the Scottish Highlands. Down at the other end of the country, new species from continental Europe are already arriving: large tortoiseshell (which used to breed here), scarce tortoiseshell, long-tailed blue and the wonderfully named Queen of Spain fritillary may all permanently colonise southern England during the coming decades.

Yet unless we change the way we manage the countryside to make room for wildlife, most will continue to be confined to the edges, the margins, the little parcels of land we set aside as nature reserves, whereas rightfully they should be something we see so often we take them for granted – part and parcel of our daily lives. Today they may be symbols of our harmonious relationship with nature, a utopia where people and wild creatures are at one, but the reality is very different. And if we allow them to disappear, we run the risk of losing far more than just a few species of insects.

Whether colourful, dowdy or pure white, butterflies continue to take hold of us, guiding our philosophy, art, music and literature. The power of the butterfly remains undiminished. Its transformation from egg to caterpillar to chrysalis to flying 'winged blossom' still transfixes us with wonder. The last word goes to William Wordsworth and his poem, 'To a Butterfly':

> I've watched you now a full half-hour;
> Self-poised upon that yellow flower
> And, little Butterfly! indeed
> I know not if you sleep or feed.

How motionless! – not frozen seas
More motionless! and then
What joy awaits you, when the breeze
Hath found you out among the trees,
And calls you forth again!

This plot of orchard-ground is ours;
My trees they are, my Sister's flowers;
Here rest your wings when they are weary;
Here lodge as in a sanctuary!
Come often to us, fear no wrong;
Sit near us on the bough!
We'll talk of sunshine and of song,
And summer days, when we were young;
Sweet childish days, that were as long
As twenty days are now.

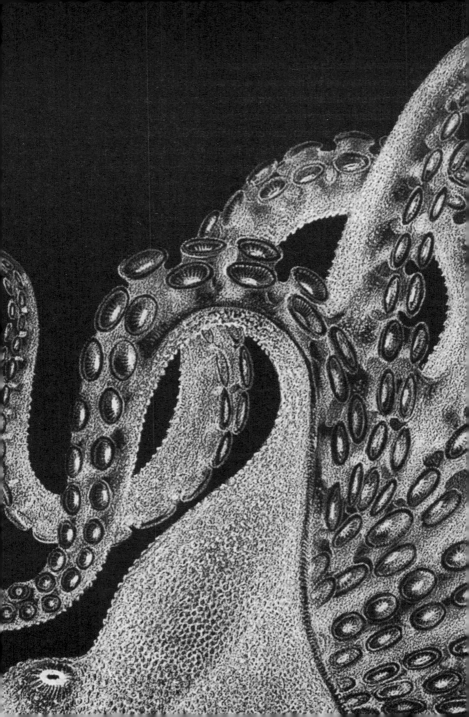

By this time three of the crew, Bill included, had found axes, and one a rusty cutlass, and all were looking over the ship's side at the advancing monster. We could now see a huge oblong mass moving by jerks just under the surface of the water, and an enormous train following; the wake or train might have been 100 feet long. In the time I have taken to write this, the brute struck us and the ship quivered under the thud; in another movement, monstrous arms like trees seized the vessel and she keeled over; in another second the monster was aboard, squeezed in between the two masts, Bill screaming 'slash for your lives'. But all our slashing was to no avail, for the brute, holding on by his arms, slipped his vast body overboard, and pulled the vessel down with him; we were thrown into the water at once, and just as I went over, I caught sight of one of the crew, either Bill or Tom Fielding, squashed up between the masts and one of those awful arms.

Captain Floyd's account of the sinking of the *Pearl*,
The Times, 4 July 1874

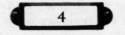

4

Giant Squid

Fear of the Unknown

The scientists in the submersible couldn't believe their eyes. Seven hundred metres below the surface of the Atlantic Ocean, near Chichi Island off the Japanese coast, they had finally come face to face with the kraken of legend. Suspended head-first and spotlit by the beams of the submarine, there it was in full view and perfect focus; arms clamped to a lump of bait, calmly watching them with eyes the size of dinner plates. Almost all the reported encounters over the centuries had involved this sea monster viciously attacking any potential predators. That day back in 2012 was the first time anyone had managed to get close enough to film the giant squid in its natural habitat, so their hearts were beating madly, not just through fear, but with the sheer thrill of discovery.

Monsters are meant to be scary, and we have a rich tradition of stories about these particular entities. In his atmospheric poem 'The Kraken', Alfred Tennyson tried to capture the mystery surrounding it:

> Below the thunders of the upper deep;
> Far far beneath in the abysmal sea,
> His ancient, dreamless, uninvaded sleep
> The Kraken sleepeth: faintest sunlights flee
> About his shadowy sides; above him swell
> Huge sponges of millennial growth and height;

And far away into the sickly light,
From many a wondrous grot and secret cell
Unnumber'd and enormous polypi
Winnow with giant arms the slumbering green.

The poem concludes with a warning that one day the kraken
will come up from its deep-sea world and reveal itself to us:

There hath he lain for ages, and will lie
Battening upon huge sea worms in his sleep,
Until the latter fire shall heat the deep;
Then once by man and angels to be seen,
In roaring he shall rise and on the surface die.

Tennyson recognised the power of these monsters to thrill us, but
how accurate are our perceptions of them, and how have they
changed as, over time, we have learned more about the real creatures on which these myths and legends are based?

We may not have seen a sea monster but most of us have met one
in our nightmares and imaginations. Monsters and the sea – they
go together like vampires and castles or zombies and graveyards.
In our minds certain places seem to hold fear and that fear is
distilled into a monstrous form. We've always done it. Our fear
of sea monsters has a long and distinguished pedigree in myth,
legend and literature. It goes all the way back to ancient Greece,
to the tale of Odysseus and his rather troublesome journey back
from Troy to Ithaca. Among the many trials he and his crew had
to face was the sea monster Scylla.

The various descriptions of Scylla give her a tentacled body
including six heads on long necks, each armed with rows of
murderous teeth. In *Metamorphoses*, Ovid described her transformation from beautiful nymph to monster. When she rejected the
advances of the sea god Glaucus, he went to the sorceress Circe
for a love potion. When Circe decided she wanted Glaucus for

herself, she vowed to eliminate her rival, poisoning the pool in which Scylla bathed, and turning her into a hideous monster, who was always on the offensive.

The most famous description of the monster in action comes from Homer's *Odyssey*. Dressed in his armour, sword in hand, Odysseus stood ready to fight her off at the prow, but when she pounced, her thrashing arms proved too fast for him:

> Then we entered the Straits in great fear of mind . . . We could see the bottom of the whirlpool all black with sand and mud, and the men were at their wit's ends for fear. While we were taken up with this, and were expecting each moment to be our last, Scylla pounced down suddenly upon us and snatched up my six best men. I was looking at once after both ship and men, and in a moment I saw their hands and feet ever so high above me, strug-gling in the air as Scylla was carrying them off, and I heard them call out my name in one last despairing cry. As a fisherman, seated, spear in hand, upon some jutting rock throws bait into the water to deceive the poor little fishes, and spears them with the ox's horn with which his spear is shod, throwing them gasping on to the land as he catches them one by one – even so did Scylla land these panting creatures on her rock and munch them up at the mouth of her den, while they screamed and stretched out their hands to me in their mortal agony. This was the most sickening sight that I saw throughout all my voyages.

Scylla wasn't real of course, but she wasn't totally fanciful either. The descriptions of those long heads and tentacles must have emerged from genuine encounters with octopuses or squid, either at sea or as beach-bound wrecks. Giant squid are not solely referred to in classical poetry. Both Aristotle and Pliny described creatures of huge dimensions in their works of natural history. The head of Pliny's giant squid caught off the coast of Spain was 'equivalent in size to a cask of fifteen amphorae' (more than 600 litres) and could hardly be encircled by a man with both arms. The tentacles were upwards of nine metres long and covered in knots 'like those on a club'. Its body weighed over 300 kilos.

Fuelled by tales from sailors returning home from the edge of the world, with stories of their ships being wrapped in multiple slimy arms, the legend of the kraken was born. The story of the kraken has been around since at least the late thirteenth century, when an old Icelandic saga describes a journey across the Greenland Sea where the sailors meet a couple of enormous sea monsters. One was called Hafgufa, which literally translates as 'sea mist', a creature of such gigantic proportions that it could swallow whales whole, seeing ships and sailors as rather more of an hors-d'œuvre. This marine behemoth apparently remained submerged for long periods before lunging above the surface with its huge jaws, engulfing everything in its orbit.

This monster was not only in our imagination: serious naturalists believed in its existence too. In his 1735 work *Systema Naturae*, the book that laid the foundations of modern scientific classification, Carl Linnaeus officially recognised a giant sea monster living in the seas off Scandinavia as a member of the squid or octopus family, and (rather strangely, given its huge size) named it *Microcosmus marinus*, meaning 'small sea world creature'. However, he did admit to having no first-hand experience of the species, adding, 'It is said to inhabit the seas of Norway, but I have not seen this animal . . .' Unsurprisingly the entry was quietly dropped from later editions.

In the mid-eighteenth century Erik Pontoppidan, the Bishop of Bergen, included the kraken in his *Natural History of Norway*, describing it as an island-sized creature with arms that could engulf and drag down the largest man-of-war. More dangerous than the beast itself was the whirlpool it created. Another Scandinavian author, the Swede Jacob Wallenberg, likened the kraken to the Leviathan of the Old Testament book of Job, Jonah's whale (see Chapter 25: Whale).

But as time went on, our idea of sea monsters began to change. As we explored the oceans over the following centuries, and gradually increased our knowledge of marine life, the Scylla-type monster and the kraken merged into a genuine, living creature: the giant squid.

In 1861 the French steamer *Alecton* was just off the Canary Islands when the crew sighted what was described at the time as a 'sea-monster'. They chased after the creature and eventually managed to harpoon it; then they attempted to haul it up on to the deck using ropes. Unfortunately the ropes cut through the animal's body and the head end slid back beneath the waves, leaving only the spear-shaped tail behind.

The *Alecton*'s captain later submitted his account of the incident to the French Academy of Sciences, only to have his claim to have caught a sea monster firmly rebuffed by a member of the academy, Arthur Mangin. Mangin pronounced that no 'wise' person – 'especially a man of science' – would 'admit into the catalogue those stories which mention extraordinary creatures like the sea serpent or the giant squid, the existence of which would be . . . a contradiction of the great laws of harmony and equilibrium which have sovereign rule over living nature as well as senseless and inert matter'.

The giant squid takes pride of place as the personification of the terror of the deep sea. No wonder, with its huge conical body, enormous eyes, long tentacles with tooth-fringed suckers and – instead of a mouth with teeth – a huge, pointed beak. To us it is unearthly, grotesque and mysterious; the perfect alien living almost invisibly among us. Its habitat is the inky blackness of the deep ocean, far beyond the reach of sunlight, and we are only afforded tantalising glimpses of this beast when a gobbet of suckered arm washes ashore, or an injured specimen is found roiling in a deep-sea trawler net. As we'll discover, that can be exciting enough, and challenging for the specialists at London's Natural History Museum, but there's more to sea monsters and our need for them than you might think.

Mathias Clasen, Assistant Professor in Literature and Media at

Aarhus University in Denmark, identifies our fascination with monsters – both real and imaginary – as a basic human need:

> I would argue that a monster is an unnatural, dangerous creature; but there are borderline cases where naturally occurring creatures are so strikingly weird that they look unnatural to us. One example would be the giant squid, which is, almost literally, a monster. It's very big, it looks weird, it has a very strange morphology, so just looking at a giant squid with its strange beak and long tentacles with suction cups containing teeth, it is almost in itself monstrous.

The giant squid may indeed be a real creature, but it is a very alien-looking one. Most encounters with this strange animal are on the surface, when the squid is sick or dying and so lashes out with those long tentacles when a boat approaches. Over time, its strange behaviour and appearance inevitably led to associations with sea monsters, as Edith ('Edie') Widder, CEO and senior scientist at the Ocean Research and Conservation Association in Florida, points out:

> You've got this creature that has eight lashing arms and two slashing tentacles growing straight out of its head; it's got serrated suckers and a parrot beak that can rip flesh. It's got an eye the size of your head, a jet-propulsion system and three hearts that pump blue blood – I think that's about the most alien thing you could ever imagine.

Humans are often fearful of creatures that don't conform to the way we expect animals to look – like us. Spiders, snakes and scorpions are classic examples of this irrational fear of 'otherness' as are squid, as Emily Alder, Lecturer in Literature and Culture at Edinburgh Napier University, indicates:

> Unlike say, mammals, with whom it's easy for humans to identify, the kraken is monstrous – it defies the familiar body organisation

of other animals, and raises questions about how the natural world is organised; but at the same time it appears to have recognisable features – parallels of hands and a face; like humans but not like humans.

Paradoxically, as Emily Alder explains, the more we got to know about the real giant squid, the more the creature took centre stage in fictional depictions of sea monsters: 'I think it's really after the Enlightenment, and all its expansion of knowledge about the natural world, that the kraken becomes a kind of real, biological entity, as well as a mythological one; and that seems to stimulate fictional stories to a much greater extent.'

Two famous works of nineteenth-century fiction – both set on the high seas – feature sea monsters: Herman Melville's 1851 novel *Moby-Dick* and Jules Verne's 1870 work *Twenty Thousand Leagues Under the Sea*. In the former, Captain Ahab's ship the *Pequod* comes across a huge creature, which the chief mate describes as:

> the great live squid, which, they say, few whale-ships ever beheld, and returned to their ports to tell of it . . . A vast pulpy mass, furlongs in length and breadth, of a glancing cream-colour, floating on the water, innumerable long arms radiating from its centre, and curling and twisting like a nest of anacondas, as if blindly to catch at any hapless object within its reach. No perceptible face or front did it have, no conceivable token of either sensation or instinct, but undulating there on the billows, an unearthly, formless, chance-like apparition of life.

In *Twenty Thousand Leagues Under the Sea*, a thrilling tale of man against squid, Verne's Captain Nemo comes across a pack of 'poulpes' (which strictly translated from the French means 'octopuses', but is usually rendered into English as 'giant squid'), which attack the *Nautilus* and kill a sailor. It is 'poulpe' fiction at its best:

What a scene! The unhappy man, seized by the tentacle and fixed to the suckers, was balanced in the air at the caprice of this enormous trunk. He rattled in his throat, he was stifled, he cried, 'Help! help!' These words, spoken in French, startled me! I had a fellow-countryman on board, perhaps several! That heart-rending cry! I shall hear it all my life. The unfortunate man was lost. Who could rescue him from that powerful pressure? However, Captain Nemo had rushed to the poulpe, and with one blow of the axe had cut through one arm. His lieutenant struggled furiously against other monsters that crept on the flanks of the *Nautilus*. The crew fought with their axes. The Canadian, Conseil, and I buried our weapons in the fleshy masses; a strong smell of musk penetrated the atmosphere. It was horrible!

For one instant, I thought the unhappy man, entangled with the poulpe, would be torn from its powerful suction. Seven of the eight arms had been cut off. One only wriggled in the air, brandishing the victim like a feather. But just as Captain Nemo and his lieutenant threw themselves on it, the animal ejected a stream of black liquid. We were blinded with it. When the cloud dispersed, the cuttlefish had disappeared, and my unfortunate countryman with it. Ten or twelve poulpes now invaded the platform and sides of the *Nautilus*. We rolled pell-mell into the midst of this nest of serpents, that wriggled on the platform in the waves of blood and ink. It seemed as though these slimy tentacles sprang up like the hydra's heads. Ned Land's harpoon, at each stroke, was plunged into the staring eyes of the cuttle fish. But my bold companion was suddenly overturned by the tentacles of a monster he had not been able to avoid.

Even well over a century after it was written, this still makes for terrifying reading.

Another classic account came from H.G. Wells. In 1896 Wells published *The Sea Raiders*, a book that piqued the public's imagination with a particularly ferocious version of the giant squid that Wells termed *Haploteuthis ferox*. These huge creatures terrorise the coast of England, horribly devouring any humans who have the misfortune to encounter them:

> The rounded bodies were new and ghastly-looking creatures; in shape somewhat resembling an octopus, with huge and very long and flexible tentacles, coiled copiously on the ground. The skin had a glistening texture, unpleasant to see, like shiny leather. The downward bend of the tentacle-surrounded mouth, the curious excrescence at the bend, the tentacles, and the large intelligent eyes, gave the creatures a grotesque suggestion of a face. They were the size of a fair-sized swine about the body, and the tentacles seemed to him to be many feet in length.

The hero of the book, Mr Fison, was 'horrified, of course, and intensely excited and indignant, at such revolting creatures preying upon human flesh'. After shouting at them, he tries to drive them off by throwing rocks at them, but they move towards him, 'making a soft, purring sound to each other'. It is Wells's refusal to have the creatures defeated by the humans that appeals to Emily Alder: 'I like *The Sea Raiders* partly because the creatures get away with it. Often in late Victorian gothic literature the monster is subdued, destroyed and punished in the end. But these monsters appear, terrorise the sea for a few months and then they vanish, and nobody knows where they have gone.'

Verne and Wells based their accounts on what was then known about the real-life kraken but neither was a writer with any tendency to underplay the dramatic. This raises an interesting question: how important is accuracy and how real do our monsters need to be? Is it that we need monsters, we have to have something to frighten us and battle against? And that no matter what the facts really are, we will distort them?

Our continued obsession with these monsters in literature, over such a long period of time, raises a question. Do we need them for reasons that may not always be obvious, least of all to ourselves? The way they are portrayed – in myths, novels and films – suggests that we actually enjoy being scared witless. Mathias Clasen has made a special study of monsters in films, games and books:

> The striking thing about these kinds of monsters is that they don't really exist, but they play a huge role in our mindscapes: in our dreams, our nightmares, our stories, myths, and so on. So monsters say things about human psychology, and I would argue that we can't help but project fearful monsters into our surroundings.

He believes that to really understand why this should be, we need to look at human evolution and biology:

> Humans are the most successful large animal on the planet, but we are also fragile, and unspecialised, and weak; and possibly the most fearful organism on earth. We're afraid of things that exist in the world, but we're also afraid of things that only exist in our own imaginations. Given our inability to defend ourselves against predators, what we do is to anticipate and imagine danger, and in doing so we tend to embellish and exaggerate naturally occurring dangerous creatures, and make them monstrous – even more terrifying.

Watching monster films, reading scary books or playing frightening fantasy computer games could be seen as the mental equivalent of going to a gym. Just as having a fit body allows you to run away from danger fast, or to turn and fight off an attacker, so a mind exercised by role-play helps prepare us mentally for the decisions we would make in any terrifying situation. They also, as Mathias Clasen explains, give us a paradoxical form of comfort:

> All the objects and the situations in the world that scare us and frighten us become fascinating. So we love watching TV shows about zombies, as it allows us to get an insight into our own reactions to fearful situations – but in a safe context. After all, almost nobody dies from watching a horror film.

So reading about, or even playing the part of, a monstrous giant squid terrifying little humans in the middle of a vast, hostile sea is really a rehearsal for a genuinely dangerous situation that we might one day encounter. But is any of it based on any reality? In the unlikely event of coming face to face with a giant squid, is it likely to start gnashing its enormous beak and grabbing us with its sucker-covered tentacles? Jon Ablett, Curator of Molluscs at the Natural History Museum, thinks not: 'When people think of the giant squid they think of them pulling down boats and attacking sailors, but the depths they live at means this really isn't possible. The only time they are seen at the surface is when they're dead or in distress.'

There are, though, some suggestions that during the Second World War submarines may have been attacked – or at least investigated – by giant squid. But not all such encounters have been so hostile. In 2012 Edie Widder was part of the ground-breaking project to film a 3-metre-long giant squid some 14 kilometres off the coast of Chichi Island in the North Pacific.

Previously the only footage of a giant squid was of a specimen that had been hooked by a fishing boat. There were photographs taken in 2004 by Japanese scientist Tsunemi Kubodera, who submerged a camera deep into the sea, but capturing the giant on moving film has proved remarkably difficult. This is not for want of trying, but squid are easily frightened away by the bright lights and the noise of the vessels and equipment. Edie's experience, though, was entirely different. The lure they used to attract the giant was a metre-long diamondback squid lit by a light that mimicked deep-sea bioluminescence. The sub itself used quiet electric thrusters that made a minimal amount of noise.

Edie remained on the surface in the research boat, but was in constant contact with her colleagues operating the sub beneath them. They thought they might get a glimpse, if they were really lucky, of this terrifying monster, but what appeared centre stage and in perfect focus in front of the submersible was a strikingly beautiful animal, filmed for the very first time in its deep-sea home. Breathtaking footage shows the squid suspended in the blackness, 700 metres below the surface, looking inquisitively at the submarine in front of it. For Edie Widder, the giant squid surpassed her wildest expectations:

> To see it so brilliantly bronze and silver, it really did look as if it were carved out of metal. The arms were undulating, the huge, blue eye was staring at us most of the time, I thought almost with an intelligence; and the detail was so astonishing after expecting to see just a fleeting glimpse, and instead you could study it, and that was magic.

But there were more surprises to come. When the sub returned to the surface, the scientists examined the diamondback squid they had been using as bait, expecting it to have been ripped to shreds by that fearsome beak. And yet as Edie recalls, the squid had fed very delicately, taking only small pieces of flesh. This is a result of a bizarre quirk of squid anatomy: because the animal's gullet passes through its brain, it must feed slowly and very carefully to avoid causing damage to itself. In turn, though, it is only vulnerable to a single predator: the giant sperm whale, which at up to 19 metres long and weighing as much as 70 tonnes, dwarfs even the monstrous giant squid.

The picture that is emerging of this mighty mollusc is of a gentle giant that is scared of loud noises and bright lights, an epicure that pecks delicately at its food and that seems to show both curiosity and intelligence. Hardly a Scylla or a kraken. We know that squid have titanic battles with sperm whales, because sometimes the whales' skins are scarred with sucker marks as the smaller creature tries to defend itself. But the giant squid is certainly not the aggressive man-eating predator the old stories have led us to believe.

And the more we find out about the squid, the more fascinating it becomes. So there was enormous excitement when a massive specimen was found in a fishing net off the Falkland Islands in 2004. Jon Ablett of the Natural History Museum was in charge of its preservation:

> It was sent over frozen on a commercial boat, which meant it was in really good condition. The first thing we did was defrost it, which took about four days, and made me pretty unpopular because deep-sea squid have ammonia in their tissues, and when it defrosted it released this into the atmosphere, making most of the building smell of urine for quite a few days. Once it was completely defrosted we began the fixation process, injecting the tissues with formalin dissolved in seawater, which stops the tissues from rotting.

Ablett and his colleagues named the giant squid Archie, after its scientific name *Architeuthis dux*; only later discovering, to their embarrassment, that the specimen was in fact a female. Archie now resides in a huge 10-metre-long tank, specially made for the museum by the company that previously made tanks for the artist Damien Hirst. Unfortunately the scientists are not entirely sure how heavy the specimen is because when they tried to weigh the animal, it was so heavy it broke the museum's scales: 'All we can say is that it is over 200 kilos, and it took thirteen of us to haul it into its tank.'

And there she sits today, in the Spirit Collection of the Natural History Museum, one of the largest and best-preserved giant squid specimens in the world. We can now stand and look at her eye to enormous eye, and when we do, somehow she doesn't seem like a monster any more. As we discover more and more about the biology and lifestyle of these mysterious creatures, is there a danger that their power to scare us will eventually fizzle out? Will we have to turn our highly charged imaginations to another unexplored realm – space perhaps – and come up with a new breed of scary monster? Mathias Clasen suggests that monsters of one kind or another will always be with us: 'There is no inclination that scientific progress has banished monsters from the shadows of our imaginations, so we will probably continue to be afraid of very strange things, including sea monsters.'

Emily Alder agrees, and believes that there is still a huge amount to learn about these mysterious creatures and the places where they live: 'Really we know very, very little about the deep sea: even now, there's only so far down we can get, and it's hard to collect specimens or conduct research; so it's still a very mysterious region of the globe from which it's not hard to imagine that all kinds of mysteries might lurk.'

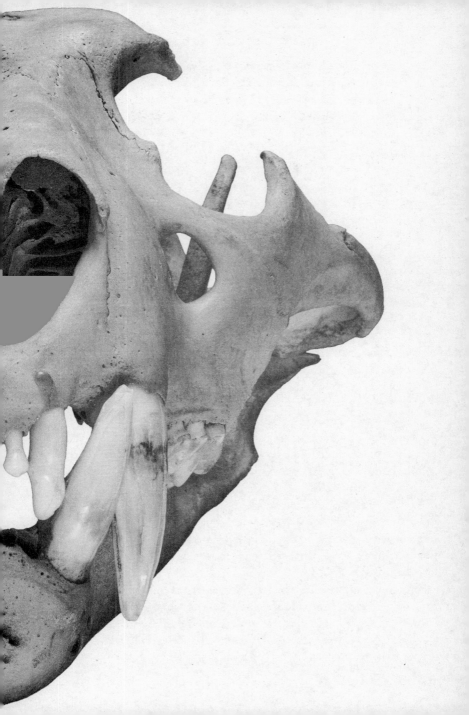

I am not afraid of an army of lions led by a sheep; I am afraid of an army of sheep led by a lion.

Alexander the Great

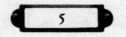

Lions

Power and Prestige

At first, as the workman heard the clang of metal against stone, he must have thought he'd struck his spade against a rock. But as he poked and prodded the surrounding earth, he realised that the object was in fact an animal's skull. And not just any old animal: the size, together with the huge, pointed teeth, meant that this had to be a big carnivore.

After the remains were taken to the Natural History Museum for experts to examine, it soon became clear from their size and shape – especially the huge canines – that the skulls were both lions. But it wasn't until 2005, seventy years after the original find, that they were subjected to modern carbon-dating techniques, and the truth was finally revealed: that they were hundreds of years old.

One animal had lived between 1420 and 1480, around the time of the bloody Wars of the Roses. The other was even older: dating back to the turbulent century between 1280 and 1385, from the time of the Crusades to the height of the Hundred Years War. Even more unexpected was the place where the skulls had been found: not some remote location on the African savannah, but far closer to home: the moat that surrounds the Tower of London. This was the oldest lion discovered in Britain since cave lions became extinct here towards the end of the last Ice Age, at least 12,000 years ago.

Today the Tower of London is one of the most popular tourist attractions in the whole of the United Kingdom, with over 3 million visitors a year. Some come to walk in the footsteps of Anne Boleyn, who was executed there in May 1536, and whose ghost reputedly stalks the corridors at night, carrying her severed head under her arm. Others want to see the Crown Jewels, the Beefeaters and the famous ravens, which, should they ever leave the Tower, will reputedly herald the downfall of both Crown and country.

Centuries ago, Londoners flocked there too, but they came to see a very different kind of spectacle: the Royal Menagerie. It is hard to imagine, in these days of books, wildlife television programmes and the Internet, just how exciting a visit to the menagerie must have been for people who would probably never have travelled more than a few miles from their home, let alone seen any animal fiercer than a fox.

The menagerie was first assembled by King John in 1210, just a few years before the hapless monarch was forced to seal the Magna Carta, changing the course of English history. John was following in the tradition of the greatest of all medieval monarchs, the Emperor Charlemagne, who had established no fewer than three menageries in present-day Germany and the Netherlands during his eighth-century reign.

William the Conqueror – King John's great-great-grandfather – also kept a menagerie at his manor near the Oxfordshire town of Woodstock, while many other European kings enthusiastically adopted the fashion for keeping wild animals. This was partly to entertain their courtiers, but also as a show of strength – especially important for a monarch as weak and helpless as John.

The Tower of London collection would become the biggest and longest lasting of the European royal menageries, and a major tourist attraction. Exotic creatures – including tigers, leopards, elephants and even a polar bear, which would regularly swim in the adjacent River Thames – were kept there for more than 600 years.

But the lions were the most popular exhibit: from the time that

Henry III was presented with three animals by the Holy Roman Emperor Frederick II in 1235, through the reign of King James I, who in 1622 had a stone platform built so that he and his royal guests could watch these mighty beasts fighting each other to the death.

Distinguished visitors who came to see them included Geoffrey Chaucer, Samuel Pepys and William Blake. From the reign of Queen Elizabeth I onwards the public were also allowed in, for an entrance fee of 1½d (equivalent to about £1 in today's money). Those who couldn't stretch to this simply brought along a dead cat or dog to be fed to the lions.

In 1275 King Edward I had the lions moved into a two-storey building that was renamed the Lion Tower, where they had separate cages for sleeping and daytime activities. Richard Sabin, Principal Curator of Vertebrates in the Department of Life Sciences at the Natural History Museum, reflects on what the presence of these mighty beasts would have meant to those coming to the Tower: 'People visiting the monarch would have had to pass through the Lion Gate. You can imagine how fearsome and terrifying it would have been to walk through an archway with lions above you and on either side. The whole idea was to reduce you to a quivering wreck before you reached the monarch.'

Certainly one distinguished prisoner was impressed: while imprisoned at the Tower in 1360, King John II of France paid a visit to the lions, living up to his nickname 'John the Good' by giving 20 shillings (equivalent to between £300 and £450 in today's money) to the fortunate keeper.

But the presence of these huge, fearsome beasts at the Tower was not without incident. On one visit in 1686, an unfortunate young woman named Mary Jenkinson was stroking one of the lion's paws when it suddenly grabbed her arm 'with his claws and mouth, and most miserably tore her flesh from the bone'. Doctors later amputated her arm but she did not recover, and died soon afterwards.

In the 1830s, after a lion had apparently bitten a soldier, the

Duke of Wellington – then Constable of the Tower – finally decided that this was no longer a suitable home for the menagerie. He had the remaining exhibits transferred to London Zoo, which had been opened a few years earlier, and also to Dublin Zoo in Ireland. The Lion Tower was demolished soon afterwards, though the Lion Gate remains standing to this day.

These real and symbolic versions of lions confirm the view that this is the indisputable 'king of beasts', with an air of power and authority that we both admire and envy. As a result we have taken the lion into the very heart of our society: into the corridors of power, into our art and literature, our painting and sculpture. Lions appear in myth and legend, and especially in religion. This central role is not confined to a single society or creed, for they are ubiquitous in societies throughout the world, even where they do not naturally occur. Of all our symbols, the lordly lion is one of the most potent, and one that goes back to the very beginnings of human civilisation.

In 1994, while exploring a cave system near the commune of Vallon-Pont-d'Arc in the Ardèche in southern France, three scientists stumbled across an extraordinary discovery. On the walls of the cave were hundreds of paintings: clear, confident markings depicting more than a dozen different kinds of animals, including panthers, bears and lions.

The paintings look as if they were painted only recently, and yet they are actually some of the oldest cave art so far discovered – dating back between 30,000 and 32,000 years. They have a dynamic, forceful – almost three-dimensional – quality, the result of techniques rarely found in other examples of prehistoric art: the background has been scraped clear for the artist to work on, and lines have been etched around the outline of each image to make them stand out. The lions are clearly engaged in a hunt, their bodies taut and low as if stalking their prey.

These paintings at the Chauvet Caves are just the earliest of countless examples of depictions of lions in art. We do not know what was in the minds of those prehistoric hunters as they created those vibrant images, but we do know that since the first humans began to write down their thoughts, they have regarded lions as embodying the very human concepts of power, prestige, strength and bravery.

One of the most famous surviving ancient monuments in the world, the Sphinx at Giza, dating back to at least 2500 BC, has the head of a man but the body of a lion. The Greeks named a settlement in the Nile Delta 'Leontopolis', meaning 'city of lions', while the Egyptians buried lions – which represented wealth as well as power – in their Pharaohs' tombs. Later, in roughly 1500 BC, accounts of Moses leading the Israelites out of Egypt noted that they carried banners decorated with images of lions. About the same time, the entrance to the Bronze Age citadel at Mycenae, in southern Greece, which has a sculpture of two lionesses above the arch, was known as the Lion Gate.

Other ancient North African and Middle Eastern cultures, including the Nubians, Mesopotamians and Persians, also featured lions widely in their iconography, as did the Greeks and Romans. Lions are prominent symbols in eastern cultures and religions too, including Hinduism and Buddhism. The legacy of these ancient peoples' obsession with lions lives on today. In cities throughout the world, carved lions can still be found on gates, bridges, tombs and temples, and there are also many lion statues, such as the famous bronzes beneath Nelson's Column in London's Trafalgar Square.

Lion symbolism has left its mark in less obvious ways. The mainly Sikh surname 'Singh' – now one of the commonest and most widespread family names in the world – comes from an ancient Vedic word meaning 'lion' (Asiatic lions of the race *persica* would have been common and widespread); while the nation of Singapore gets its name from the Malay words meaning 'lion city', even though lions have never been native to South East Asia.

Lions also feature widely in ancient writings: they appear in Aesop's *Fables*, the Talmud of Judaism, Koran of Islam and of course the Christian Bible, most famously in the tale of Daniel in the lions' den. Old Testament passages, including this verse from Proverbs, frequently extol the lion's bravery: 'The lion, which is strongest among beasts and turneth not away for any . . .'

Throughout history, rulers have frequently appropriated the lion's power and strength as a symbol of their own supremacy, as King John hoped to do when he created the Royal Menagerie. So it's hardly surprising that lions feature on the English royal coat of arms. But King John wasn't the first monarch to employ lions as a patriotic symbol: that honour goes to his older and more celebrated brother, King Richard I – also known, of course, as Richard the Lionheart, or as this French-speaking monarch would have referred to himself, 'Richard Cœur de Lion'.

Lions had been used in heraldry long before Richard came to the throne in 1189. They appeared in various forms, but always represented the traditional virtues of bravery, courage and strength. But it was a coat of arms featuring three lions given to Richard's paternal grandfather, Geoffrey of Anjou, when he was knighted in 1128, that changed the way we regard this animal for ever. Dr Paul Fox, a Fellow of the Society of Antiquaries, explains: 'What's fascinating about this shield is the way the lions were depicted, opening up a whole new chapter in the history of art. These are "lions rampant", in other words lions that are rearing up in a menacing, pugilistic pose.'

As Paul Fox points out, there are plenty of other examples of lions in art before that time, but they almost always featured the animals either on all fours or sitting down. And until Richard saw the lion's potential as a national symbol, coats of arms had usually been attached to individuals, not nations. At first, Richard chose a single lion rampant, but in 1198 this was altered to feature three lions passant (walking) to represent the king's rule over three of his most important realms: as King of England, Duke of Normandy and Duke of Aquitaine.

By adopting the lion as the symbol of English royal power, embodied in his nickname, Richard hoped to create an image of invulnerable strength that would enable him to defend his kingdom against internal treachery and foreign invaders. This was an essential strategy, because during his ten-year reign, until his death in 1199, Richard spent less than twelve months in England, spending the rest of the time away fighting in the Crusades.

Four centuries later, when the two crowns of Scotland and England were united under James VI and I in 1603, the three lions symbol was combined with the Scottish unicorn to create the royal coat of arms of the United Kingdom, a symbol still widely used today.

In 1996 the original symbol gained a new lease of life when it featured as the title of the most successful football song of all time (admittedly in a field not known for its excellence). The anthem 'Three Lions' (also known as 'Football's Coming Home') was written and performed by David Baddiel, Frank Skinner and the Lightning Seeds to coincide with England hosting the European Championships. Its title referred to the badge worn by every England footballer, and evoked the famous 1966 World Cup triumph over Germany. But even after 'thirty years of hurt', it didn't work – England lost in the semi-final to Germany (as usual, on penalties).

Yet the three lions symbol continues to inspire national pride, and of course will always be linked with Richard the Lionheart. It seems churlish to point out that although he is generally regarded by posterity as a strong king, most historians of the period now consider that Richard was just as poor a ruler as his younger brother John. Such, perhaps, is the power of the lion's image.

Nowadays, it's hard to spend more than an hour or so watching television, reading a newspaper or magazine, or walking down a high street, without seeing at least one example of a lion being used as a symbol. You cannot even eat a shop-bought egg without finding a red lion stamped on its shell (the stamp indicating that it has been laid by a hen vaccinated against salmonella). Lions can also be found on T-shirts, school badges, flags, chocolate bars and countless advertising hoardings. Companies using a lion as their logo include Peugeot cars, Löwenbräu beer (the name translates as 'lion's brew'), English football's Premier League, several football clubs including Chelsea and Aston Villa (and of course England), Cunard cruises, the rock band Queen, Sky Sports and, most famously of all, the Hollywood film giant Metro-Goldwyn-Mayer (MGM).

MGM can boast what is perhaps the longest continuous use of a lion as a commercial logo, since the roaring male lion first appeared at the beginning of its films back in 1924. Since then there have been seven different lions, the last of which, the aptly named Leo, has been in continuous use since 1957. But the MGM lions weren't just a symbol: several also appeared in a number of MGM films and TV commercials, including the Tarzan series. One widely circulated story suggests that an early MGM lion actually killed a man on set, but like so many good Hollywood stories, this appears to be an urban myth.

Other cinematic representations of lions include the Cowardly Lion in *The Wizard of Oz* (of which more later), Elsa the lioness in *Born Free*, and the most recent incarnation, Disney's *The Lion King*, a cinematic retelling of *Hamlet* – but with a suitably happy ending. Even happier for Disney, as the film has grossed almost $1 billion since it was first released in 1994 – making it the twentieth highest earning film of all time.

Lions aren't just used as symbols by companies, but also by individuals, perhaps in a quest to emulate the power and prestige achieved by Richard the Lionheart. Ethiopian emperor Haile Selassie, who reigned from 1930 to 1974, called himself the 'Lion of Judah', while Iraqi dictator Saddam Hussein named one of his army's tanks the 'Lion of Babylon'.

The social media site Instagram, on which users post photographs of themselves and their friends for all to share and see, has given rise to a new trend. Rich young Middle Eastern playboys pose with their latest expensive sports car, alongside a captive male lion. This is presumably designed to advertise their potency and prestige, ironically just as King Richard did more than eight centuries ago, when he wore a lion on his shield while fighting the infidels.

For all these people, lions represent a convenient, symbolic shorthand for the qualities they wish to display, ranging from simple prestige to a more overt (and sometimes sinister) display of power. We may scoff at such obvious symbolism; and yet when the British Lions rugby team take to the field, their sheer animal power is indicated by their very name.

Lions are not simply used to sell products or for personal self-aggrandisement. More subtle depictions of the power of lions feature prominently in literature, such as the character Aslan in C.S. Lewis's *The Chronicles of Narnia*. At first, Aslan (named from the Turkish word for lion) appears to be the classic representation of the symbolic animal: the all-powerful lord and guardian of Narnia. Yet as the story develops, we realise that Aslan has other qualities: as well as being powerful he can also be gentle. For Lewis himself, Aslan was the representation of the figure of Christ, combining the virtues of strength and mercy in a single, complex figure. The parallels are obvious: Aslan rules at a distance and sacrifices himself for his kingdom. But Ralph Pite, Professor of English at the University of Bristol, believes there is more to the character than this – Aslan represents both the authority and the wildness of lions, disappearing at the end of the story: 'I think there's the sense that the spirit that rules Creation – as C.S. Lewis would have seen it – is kingly, yet also inscrutable, unpredictable and untameable.'

For perhaps the most baffling image of a lion, we must turn to another symbolic representation, this time on a tin of Tate & Lyle's golden syrup. Look closely and you will notice a picture of a rotting lion carcass surrounded by a swarm of bees, together with the slogan: 'Out of the strong came forth sweetness'. This refers to the Old Testament story of Samson, who killed a lion and then noticed that a swarm of bees had taken over the carcass, making honey there. This in turn gave rise to the bizarre – and mistaken – ancient belief that bees can be spontaneously generated from the carcass of an animal (usually a cow), a process known as 'bugonia.'

The eponymous co-founder of Tate & Lyle, the nineteenth-century entrepreneur Abram Lyle, was known to be a religious man, but he may also have seen the chance to link his sugar-derived product with the more natural image of honey. But whatever the origin of the logo, it certainly worked: the design of the golden syrup tin has barely changed since it was first launched in 1885, and it recently entered the *Guinness Book of World Records* as Britain's oldest brand.

Amid all this symbolism, what of the animal at the centre – the lion itself? It is easy to forget that this is a real, living, breathing wild creature; and like all wild creatures it exists entirely independently of however we may choose to regard it.

One important aspect of the lives of lions is that, uniquely among the world's thirty-seven species of cats, they are social animals, living together in groups of up to half a dozen related females and their cubs. Male lions are often solitary, but may also live in pairs or small groups of up to six related individuals – either bands of brothers, cousins of a similar age, or simply cohorts that have ganged up together. Prides are usually headed by one or two dominant males.

Lions are not the largest of the big cats: that honour goes to the Amur (or Siberian) tiger. Tigers are both larger and heavier than lions, the biggest individuals being almost 4 metres from nose to tail, and weighing up to 325 kilos. In comparison, a male lion can reach a total length of about 3.5 metres and weighs up to 225 kilos. And yet a fully-grown male lion does appear to be very large indeed: perhaps because of its huge, bushy mane, or maybe simply because a male looks so huge compared with the females, which are typically about one-third smaller and lighter than their mates.

This may help to explain why we continue to regard the lion as uniquely magnificent, but does it match the reality of lions themselves? Powerful they may be, yet they can also appear – at least to the untrained human eye – lazy, sleepy and slow. But as lion expert Lizzie Bewick points out:

> In whose eyes are they lazy? They appear to be layabouts because we are diurnal, so we usually get to see lions in daylight, legs stretched out, comatose under a tree where they are shaded from the searing heat. They could have been active all night hunting, killing, fighting with hyenas, patrolling, or feasting – after which any sensible lion is going to be conked out come dawn!

Despite the impression often given by wildlife films, lions are not particularly efficient hunters. The vast majority of chases end with them pulling up short of their target, which escapes at speed. Only one in three hunts are successful – and that is when several animals hunt co-operatively; when a single lion is involved their success rate falls to less than one in five.

It is often assumed that most of the hunting is done by the lionesses rather than the males. In part this is true: it makes sense in a pride to have a division of labour, with the males defending their turf, meals, pride and offspring, while the lionesses bring home the bacon. But it may also be because almost all lion hunts ever filmed take place during the day, when a hunting male would stand out like a sore thumb because of his huge mane, which might show above even the longest grass. At night, when this is no longer an issue, males hunt more frequently; and they will also join forces with the females when they are pursuing a particularly large animal such as a buffalo, which may weigh more than a tonne.

Lions can and do hunt large grazing animals including wildebeest, giraffes and even, on occasion, baby elephants that have become separated from their herd. Yet they are also opportunists, taking prey as diverse as brown fur seals on the coast of Namibia, ostriches on the African plains, and a wide range of smaller items including mice, fish and even insects.

But lions do not always bother to kill to eat. Indeed in one of their main strongholds, the plains of the Serengeti in Tanzania, more than half their food items are obtained by scavenging. Lions are often joined at a kill by hyenas, which like them also both scavenge and kill for themselves, and may even use their superior numbers to snatch food away from their larger relative. But there are no prizes for knowing that hyenas are rarely, if ever, linked with the leonine virtues of strength and bravery.

Having eaten, lions spend much of their time asleep, sometimes for hours at a time, as carloads of frustrated tourists visiting Kenya's Masai Mara can bear witness. But even when resting, male lions must always be on the lookout for rivals. Intruding males may fight and drive away the incumbent ones, following which they will dispose of the deposed leader's offspring – killing the tiny cubs with a single bite while their mothers look on helplessly.

Life as a male lion is nasty, brutish and short. Most will not survive more than two or three years as one of the dominant males in a pride, especially if their buddy is killed, leaving them defenceless against a couple of younger, fitter rivals. So they cannot afford to waste any time and energy bringing up another male's cubs, but must impregnate the females and produce their own as soon as they can.

Not that lions are especially successful at mating. The male follows the female around for several days, mating quickly and often – roughly once every fifteen minutes or so, and up to seventy times in a single twenty-four-hour period. His persistence is essential: fewer than one in three matings result in the female becoming pregnant.

It is clear from looking at the lion's behaviour and lifestyle that the way we choose to represent the lion has very little to do with the animal itself. When a lion does stand up to a charging buffalo to protect its cubs, it is not being brave or virtuous, but simply reacting instinctively to defend its genetic heritage from attack. And yet, as wildlife filmmaker Adam Chapman observes, even as an experienced naturalist he cannot help associating what he sees when he watches lions hunting with the image of power and majesty:

> When you see a lioness moving through the tall grass, she just looks spectacularly lithe, athletic, and absolutely perfect for what she is about to do. Then when you see a big male following on behind, his mane blowing in the breeze, with that arrogant swagger, you really get a sense of why the male lion is such a symbol of power, of ruling over areas – because that is what they do when they hold their territories; they rule that area.

Not all symbolic uses of the lion go along with the widely held view that lions are brave, fierce and proud. Some turn the imagery on its head, as when in Cervantes's novel *Don Quixote* the eponymous hero declares that he will slay two lions to display his manliness, but when they are released they simply lie down in front of him and lick their paws. But the best known, and in many ways the most powerful, of these subversions is the portrayal of the Cowardly Lion in the movie *The Wizard of Oz*.

Based on an original 1900 novel by L. Frank Baum, which two years later was turned into a Broadway musical, the 1939 film is arguably the best-loved children's movie of all time, and indeed widely considered one of the greatest of all Hollywood films. Acres of print have been devoted to analysing the hidden meanings behind the characters and plot of *The Wizard of Oz*, but the consensus of most critics is that the Cowardly Lion is a classic satirical inversion of the cultural icon of the lion as the 'king of beasts'. Ralph Pite sums up this paradox:

> The Cowardly Lion is just a contradiction in terms, because the lion is the epitome of courage. But by acknowledging that he is afraid, the Cowardly Lion is actually braver than people who pretend to be brave. This is consistent with lots of people's thinking about courage: that it often consists of admitting your fearfulness. It's a

contradiction that reveals the underlying truth: that courage depends on an acknowledgement of fear.

So this lion knows he is meant to be brave, but struggles to find a way to be so. Ultimately, however, he does find his courage, by confronting his deepest fears, and is presented with a medal to mark his achievements. So like Dorothy's other companions, the Scarecrow (seeking a brain) and the Tin Man (searching for a heart), he does eventually find what he is looking for.

Although the Cowardly Lion remains a powerful antidote to the image of the lion as invulnerable, and although several other creatures – such as the eagle, tiger, leopard and elephant – are also used to represent strength and courage, the fact remains that when it comes to being a symbol of power and prestige, the lion still occupies the pole position. In the words of Dr Samuel Johnson, the lion remains 'the fiercest and most magnanimous of the four-footed beasts'.

Yet ironically, despite this admiration, this hasn't stopped us from persecuting lions relentlessly – in some cases to the edge of oblivion. And that leads us back to those lion skulls found in the moat at the Tower of London, and to the animal they came from. For these were not any ordinary lions, but animals from the distinctive race known as the Barbary lion. Also known as the Nubian, North African or Atlas lion, as these names suggest, the Barbary lion comes from the Mediterranean coast of North Africa.

Barbary lions were once found from Morocco in the west, through Algeria, Tunisia and Libya, to Egypt in the east. Isolated from other lion populations in Africa by the barrier of the Sahara Desert, and from those in Asia by the Sinai Peninsula and the Red Sea, by the Middle Ages these animals had grown bigger than their sub-Saharan and Asiatic cousins, and become one of the largest and heaviest of all lion races.

We can only imagine what they must have been like in their prime. That vast, flowing mane, surrounding the noble face with its staring eyes. The huge, muscular body, ready to spring into action at any time. And most of all, that ear-splitting roar, that even from a distance goes through your whole body like an earthquake.

The Tower of London wasn't the only place where Barbary lions were held in captivity. Many of the lions used to fight gladiators in the Colosseum of ancient Rome would have been Barbary lions – simply because they were easier to obtain than animals from sub-Saharan Africa. Tens of thousands of animals must have died during the carnage of that era, and were buried alongside their unfortunate human victims.

Special military units were sent abroad to capture these fierce and dangerous beasts, to provide a constant supply for the amphi-theatres, using a huge and complex infrastructure to transport them back to Rome. According to one Greek eyewitness writing in the second century AD, the captors had to risk their lives to snare the lions – being unable to use spears, as this might wound their precious quarry. One way of catching the beasts was to dig a pit and place a lamb inside, to lure the lion in. They also used nets, while some men even dressed up in sheepskins to attract lions, leading the impressed observer to write: 'O greatly daring men. What a feat they achieve, what a deed they do – they bear off that great monster like a tame sheep.'

But this was only the beginning of the Barbary lion's long, steady and irreversible decline over the next two millennia. As Richard Sabin notes, their very separation from other lions would have made them vulnerable:

The spread of human civilisations through the Nile Delta fragmented the lion populations in North Africa, and certainly would have led to the isolation of Barbary lions from other populations of lions in Africa. This would have reduced their ability to pass on their genes by breeding with other groups and made them much more vulnerable. They really didn't stand a chance.

Living in such a populated region also made the Barbary lion very exposed to hunting and caused a reduction in available prey animals.

By the early nineteenth century they had already vanished from coastal areas of North Africa. They clung on in the forested hills and mountains of Algeria until the 1880s, and survived in Tunisia for a decade or so longer.

In his 1914 work *The Book of the Lion*, explorer and politician Sir Alfred Edward Pease wrote of the Barbary lion's demise: 'During the nineties [1890s] I myself hunted almost the whole range of the Atlas [Mountains] . . . and never came across a single lion track.'

Pease also suggested one reason the lions might have become extinct here: 'The Algerian lions preyed on flocks and herds, and it was no uncommon thing for them to become man-eaters of the boldest and most accomplished kind; Gérard, who himself slew some thirty lions between 1848 and 1856, relates how one lion exterminated the population of a *douar* (a tribal assembly of tents), killing forty Arabs . . .'

During the first decades of the twentieth century a few solitary animals, pairs and small families were seen, with the last reliable sighting being of an animal shot by a French colonial hunter in 1922. However, there were several unconfirmed sightings during the period from the 1940s to the 1960s. Yet even if they did survive until then, we can now be certain that the Barbary lion is extinct in the wild. But does that mean it has gone for ever? That, of course, depends on whether there are any Barbary lions remaining alive in captivity; and if so, whether or not they are truly pure-bred individuals of this unique race.

Today, around thirty-five 'royal lions' are still kept in the zoo at Rabat in northern Morocco, which the authorities there have claimed are Barbary lions. So far DNA testing of some of these specimens, making comparisons with genetic material obtained from museum skins and bones, has not managed to confirm this claim: indeed, an initial test of five individuals concluded that they had *not* descended from Barbary lions, at least down the female, maternal line.

Nevertheless, even if these – and others held in various European zoos – are not pure-bred Barbary lions, this may not necessarily mean that the race is beyond recovery. If we can get an accurate genetic reading of captive lions, we may then be able to breed them with one another to select artificially for the Barbary genes.

That's the hope of Dr Simon Black from the Durrell Institute for Conservation Biology at the University of Kent, who has helped to create a studbook of captive animals in several European zoos that may have Barbary lion genes, a population he estimates to be about eighty animals. He believes that over several generations a captive breeding programme could, in theory at least, provide us with an animal that would look like – and to all intents and purposes be – a Barbary lion.

If this sounds like science fiction, consider the quagga. This distinctively dark-coated subspecies of the plains (or Burchell's) zebra could be found roaming the plains of southern Africa until the late nineteenth century, when it was finally driven to extinction by hunting.

In 1987 the South African biologist Reinhold Rau started the Quagga Project, attempting to recreate the extinct race by selectively breeding from plains zebras – those that already had the distinctive quagga-like striping on their rear body and hind legs. In early 2005 the first foal to resemble a quagga was born. Rau died the following year, secure in the knowledge that his dream to bring back the species had been at least partly accomplished. However it must be acknowledged that although the animals bear a remarkable resemblance to quaggas, genetically they remain different.

Until full-scale cloning can be developed, we will not be able to bring back any extinct race or species. And perhaps, even if at some time in the future we can, we should not be tempted to do so. The Natural History Museum's Richard Sabin is certainly not convinced of the benefits of bringing back recently extinct species or subspecies:

I think you have to examine the reasons why they went extinct in the first place – was it just over-exploitation or have we completely destroyed their natural environment? The technology may exist in the future, but if we bring them back, can we maintain a stable environment for the animals to live in, or will they just be sideshow oddities in a zoo that people pay to go and see? We just don't know.

But just because it may not be technically possible – or morally acceptable – to bring back the Barbary lion, those ancient skulls found in the moat at the Tower of London are still important, as Sabin explains:

> The fact that we hold the remains of these animals in our museum collections means that researchers have the opportunity to extract genetic data and compare it with that from closely related species which are facing extinction. This could help conservationists make decisions that might possibly slow or halt that process. So even though it has disappeared from the wild, the Barbary lion still has a very useful role to play.

In the meantime, what of the lion species as a whole? How is *Panthera leo* doing in the wild? The answer is, sadly, not very well at all. In 1950, when George and Joy Adamson were befriending Elsa the lion in what would become the book and film *Born Free*, there were an estimated 400,000 individual lions living in Africa. Even as recently as the early 1990s there may have been as many as 100,000 lions on the African continent.

Today there are thought to be fewer than 30,000, with numbers down by at least half in just thirty years. Few other large mammals have undergone such a rapid decline in such a short time. Several factors are to blame: habitat destruction, loss of prey to the growing trade in 'bushmeat', conflict with humans in an already crowded continent, and inbreeding caused by the genetic isolation of populations from one another.

The situation away from the main strongholds in eastern and

southern Africa is even more serious: the remnant population living in West Africa is now down to between 860 and 1,160 individuals.

In Asia, the situation is slightly more positive, in that there the population is at least growing rather than declining. But only about 400 Asiatic lions – a separate race, *Panthera leo persica*, also known as the Persian or Indian lion – still exist, all living in the Gir Forest in Gujarat, north-west India. This race was once found across much of temperate and tropical Asia, but like the Barbary lion it simply could not coexist with such a high human population.

Back in the lion's main stronghold, Africa, the situation has become so serious that the lion has now been officially listed as threatened – one level below endangered. The Director of the US Fish and Wildlife Service, which helped to achieve this increased status of protection, has publicly stated that if the declines continue, the African lion could be extinct in the wild by the year 2050.

So, ironically, as the number of lion symbols – and their uses – continues to increase at a dramatic rate, the number of actual living, breathing lions is falling almost as fast. Of course, even if the lion does become extinct it might still remain as a symbol of power and prestige: think of mythical creatures such as the unicorn and dragon, which are no less potent for never having existed.

Can we really imagine a world without lions; or at least a world where lions no longer exist in the wild, but are confined to cages in zoos, pacing up and down in front of crowds of visitors as bored as they are?

At the same time as revering the lion, we have chipped away at its existence until the whole edifice is in danger of imminent collapse. A metaphor, you might think, for the often paradoxical – and sometimes farcical – nature of our whole relationship with the natural world. Richard Sabin reflects on the long and complex relationship between lions and us:

> These specimens [the Barbary lion skulls] say an awful lot about
> the human attitude towards big, dangerous animals. We have spread

across the face of the planet, we've become the dominant species, but there are things that we envy in other animals – their power, their speed, their agility – and we try to control that. And I think that the fact that we've taken these big, dangerous animals into captivity speaks volumes about our own species.

Ugliest fish I've ever caught, slimiest too, but tastes just as good, if not better, than most fish!

Anonymous angler

Burbots

Unfamiliar Yet Fascinating

The lawyer lay on the wooden table in the back garden, glassy-eyed, mouth gaping and very, very dead. This was the first time Brett had been so close to one and he marvelled at the slimy skin, blotched with fungoid patches, the flattened, toadlike head and the long body.

The burbot – also known as the lawyer, because of its single goatee whisker (more on this later) – is a great rarity alive or dead in the British Isles, a fish ecologically out of water in a countryside that has forgotten its presence. Once this freshwater member of the cod family was abundant enough in some waters to be used as pig food, but now it is extinct here.

Some people would like to revive our relationship with this forgotten fish. Since it became extinct, Britain's anglers have always hoped it would return, even issuing 'Wanted' posters and, in the late 1970s, offering a £100 reward (about £650 at today's values) for any proven sightings. Yet on the other side of the pond in North America the burbot is so common it is often regarded as a pest; while in Russia it is hauled out of holes in the winter ice by hardy anglers, and the burbot hunt has been celebrated by none other than Anton Chekhov. Clearly this is a fish for connoisseurs, both culinary and conservation-minded, but in the British Isles it is now almost unknown.

So be honest – did you assume that the title of this chapter is a misprint for 'turbot', or perhaps a village in Wiltshire? And even if you have heard of the burbot, do you know anything about this skulking, frog-mouthed fish, apart from its rather unusual name? If you don't, you won't be the only one, for the burbot is, without question, by a long chalk the most obscure creature to appear in this book.

It must once have been far more familiar, at least judging by the variety of folk names for this large, ugly fish. As well as lawyer, these include Mariah, eelpout, freshwater ling, coney-fish, poor man's lobster, loach, lingcod, methyl, mud-blower, mother-eel and lush. Of these, freshwater ling is perhaps the most appropriate, for the burbot is indeed related to that species, and is the only freshwater representative of the *Gadiformes*, a large group of marine fish that includes many we enjoy eating, such as cod and hake.

The burbot is fairly large by freshwater standards, roughly 60–120 centimetres long and usually weighing between 3 and 8 kilos, though the world record, caught in Canada in 2010, tipped the scales at 11.4 kilos. It's a long, snaky fish, the mottled reptilian skin adding to the effect, though, unlike snakes, burbots are prodigiously slimy. Its fins are long but not strong and the fish are unable to withstand strong currents, hence their preferred territory in the mud of the river bed.

The earliest known reference to the burbot (under the alternative name 'eelpout') comes from the scholar Aelfric of Eynsham's *Anglo-Saxon Glossary*, published in the tenth century. It was clearly a common fish, as this account from Leonard Mascall's *Booke of Fishing with Hooke and Line* reveals: 'There is a kind of fish in Holland [Lincolnshire], which they call a poult . . . they come forth of the fennes brookes, into the rivers nigh there about . . . They have such a plentie in the fenne brookes, they feed their hogges with them.'

A millennium after it first appeared in our literature, the final British burbot probably breathed its last in 1969 when one (weighing just a pound) was caught in the River Great Ouse near Cambridge. East Anglia, Lincolnshire and around the Humber were its strongholds. It's an unusual distribution for a British freshwater fish, most of which are much more widespread. The burbot, though, remained true to its European origins and has a lot to tell us about our links with Europe. In England it only lived in rivers that flowed into the North Sea and which would have been connected to the Rhine in the post-glacial period, before we were separated from mainland Europe by the English Channel. It always preferred slow-flowing rivers, hiding under banks and on oozy bottoms, a lurker in the gloom rather than a swimmer in clear water.

Burbots become sexually mature at between four and seven years old, and the females spawn during the coldest months of the year, often laying their eggs – more than 1 million at a time – under a layer of ice. They feed mainly on other fish, such as stickleback, perch and trout, but they will also take insects and other aquatic invertebrates, and occasionally amphibians, birds and even snakes. This has led to their being, in turn, eaten by larger fish such as pike. To avoid being caught they tend to burrow into mud or silt during the day, only emerging at dusk to forage for food in these shallow northern waters.

A closer look at a burbot reveals a strange protrusion from its chin: a long, whiskery organ that gave the fish its main name, for burbot derives from the Latin *barba*, meaning 'beard'. This flexible antenna or barbel also enables it to find food in murky waters by touch. Its scientific name, *Lota lota*, comes from Old French for the fish, while in modern French the word *lotte* can refer either to the burbot or, more commonly on menus at least, the monkfish.

Today burbots can be found right round the northern hemisphere, across virtually the whole of Europe and Asia, and in North America from Alaska to the Atlantic, in cold-water rivers, streams and lakes, though they do enter brackish waters near the coasts when spawning.

The reason for its decline and disappearance is as shrouded in mystery as the murky waters where the burbot lives. It may have suffered from the loss of wetland habitat through drainage and development, or from a rise in pollution; or it could possibly have been an early victim of global climate change, having a marked preference for chilly waters.

Burbot fans have claimed that the burbot lives on in various English place names, such as Burbolt Lane (the old name for Downing Street) in Cambridge, and Barbot Hill Road and Barbot Hall in Rotherham. However, closer investigation has revealed that the fish remains uncelebrated: the de Barbots were an important South Yorkshire family, tenants of Barbot Hall during the four-teenth century; while 'burbolt' is almost certainly a corruption of 'bird-bolt', the name of a short, blunt arrow designed to kill small birds without piercing their skin.

But although the burbot wouldn't have won any prizes in a piscatorial beauty contest, with neither the majesty of the salmon nor the rainbow beauty of trout, it nevertheless has a fascinating story to tell.

The burbot was rescued from muddy obscurity by one thing: despite its bizarre appearance, it was extremely good to eat, as the eighteenth-century naturalist Thomas Pennant pointedly noted in his book *British Zoology*: 'It is a very delicate fish for the table, though of a disgusting appearance when alive.'

Its firm, white flesh appealed to poor and rich alike. And as the only freshwater species of the cod family, it was particularly sought after during Lent when fish replaced meat for forty days – and when wintry weather conditions meant that sea fish were only available in dried or salted form. As chef and cookery writer Xanthe Clay says: 'Anyone who could get their hands on burbot would have eaten it, as it was available in many of our cold, freshwater rivers. It was also very popular with royalty – especially its liver, which the Russians referred to as "the foie gras of the Tsars".'

Burbot torte was a favourite dish at medieval banquets. The flesh is dense and cod-like though less flaky with just a hint of river bed. First the whole fish was blanched, to remove its slimy coating and so its fine reptilian scales could be easily scraped off. Then a pastry case was built around the meat. This pastry (for special occasions sometimes overlaid with gold leaf) was not meant to be eaten but rather to protect the fish inside and keep it fresh.

Alexandre Dumas is best known today for his bestselling books *The Three Musketeers* and *The Count of Monte Cristo*, but he was also a keen gourmet and cook. In 1873, three years after his death, Dumas's *Le Grand Dictionnaire de Cuisine* was published, leading his contemporary Paul Lacroix to remark: 'Assuredly it is a great accomplishment to be a novelist, but it is no mediocre glory to be a cook.' In his book, Dumas wrote: 'The burbot is an excellent freshwater fish with some resemblance to the eel and the lamprey; some people confuse it with the loach, which is not nearly so good.'

Of all the various parts of a burbot, the most sought-after is definitely the liver – which can be up to six times the expected weight for a fish of this size. But it is not just the taste that is so appealing, but also the fact that it is very good for you, containing high levels of vitamins A and D, both essential for human health.

This was discovered quite by accident back in the 1920s, when a father and son from Minnesota, Joe and Ted Rowell, used burbot to feed the foxes on Joe's fur farm. They observed that the animals developed particularly soft coats, making them more valuable. Ted Rowell suspected that the foxes' fishy diet might be responsible, so he sent samples of oil extracted from the burbot's liver for analysis. Sure enough, burbot oil was found to have far higher levels of both the essential vitamins than cod-liver oil, and is also easier to digest, as it is less viscous than other fish oils.

This discovery changed Ted Rowell's life: he set up the Burbot Liver Products Company to produce and market the precious oil, a company that eventually became a multimillion-dollar enterprise. Today burbot liver is still highly prized by chefs, but most livers are processed to make into nutritional supplements.

But why are burbot livers so huge in the first place? It's all to do with the need to lay their eggs at the end of a long, hard winter, as Steve Simpson from the University of Exeter explains: 'During the summer they're munching away at anything that's available, building up large energy reserves in the liver. This grows to about

10 per cent of their body weight, which is like you or me having a liver the size of our leg.'

The burbot then lies dormant for most of the winter, a period as long as four or five months, without feeding. They then have to spawn – not, as Steve Simpson points out, because that's a good time for the adults, but because it is the best time for the baby fish, which will then have plenty of zooplankton to feed on during the spring and summer. But producing so many eggs takes its toll on the energy reserves of the female:

> The fact that burbot spawn at the end of the winter is remarkable. Most animals that overwinter without feeding, such as polar bears, are starving by the end of their hibernation. But at the end of the winter the burbot still have to dig deep into their energy reserves and spawn, which explains why they have such enormous livers.

The fish's greatest popularity as a food being at its time of reproduction at the end of winter, not to mention the sought-after twin delicacies of its liver (once swollen to ensure that its eggs are successfully spawned) and the sale of its eggs 'as a form of "caviar"', according to food historian Alan Davidson, must both have contributed further to the species' decline in Britain.

And it's not just being eaten that has put burbots under threat: it's the sheer breadth of their diet. They primarily eat other fish but, when these are in short supply, have been observed feeding on insects, frogs, snakes and even birds. Because everything is a potential meal, they are extremely liable to snap at lures, thus making them very easy to catch.

A burbot that proved somewhat harder to land features as the hero of 'The Fish', a short story by the late nineteenth-century Russian author Anton Chekhov. As a keen angler, Chekhov was well placed to tell the tale of the burbot – or as its Russian name directly translates, the 'eelpout' – which outwits both Russian peasants and their aristocratic rulers.

The story begins on a fine summer's morning, alongside a river: 'The air is still; there is no sound but the churring of a grasshopper on the riverbank, and somewhere the timid cooing of a turtle-dove. Feathery clouds stand motionless in the sky, looking like snow scattered about . . .'

This idyllic scene is somewhat spoiled by the presence of two peasants up to their necks in the water, thrashing about furiously as they try to get at something hidden in the roots of a willow tree. It is a fish: a burbot. And it won't budge. As the tale unfolds, so more and more people join in. Finally, after hours of effort, the burbot's head appears on the surface of the water; surely it can now be caught:

> A honeyed smile overspreads all the faces. A minute passes in silent contemplation.
>
> 'A famous eel-pout,' mutters Yefim, scratching under his shoulder blades. 'I'll be bound it weighs ten pounds.'
>
> 'Mm! Yes,' the master assents. 'The liver is fairly swollen! It seems to stand out! A-ach!'
>
> The fish makes a sudden, unexpected upward movement with its tail and the fishermen hear a loud splash . . . they all put out their hands, but it is too late; they have seen the last of the eel-pout.

The burbot has even been celebrated in the lyrics of a song, 'Burbot's Revenge', by the Finnish death metal band Kalmah. The chorus intones: 'Burbot's revenge . . . burbot's revenge . . . burbot's revenge . . .' It may not be appearing in the Eurovision Song Contest any time soon, but it does have a certain gruff charm, rather like the fish itself.

So, this obscure, slimy, rather reptilian fish turns out to have provided protein for peasants, haute cuisine for wealthy aristocrats, and inspired medicine, commerce, literature and song – well, Finnish death metal. What's not to love about the burbot, and why wouldn't we all want to see them back here in their native lakes, rivers and streams, in all their glutinous glory? Writer and campaigning environmentalist George Monbiot certainly does:

> It's this dark, mysterious, weird creature, which buries itself in the mud – and you're unlikely to see it, and that for me is part of its appeal. Somewhere down in those marshes and lakes the burbot lurks – and when you do see it, you'll be taken by surprise. For me it sums up the serendipity and wonder of these chance encounters with wildlife. Just knowing that it's there is something you can't put a price on.

But not everyone thinks reintroducing the burbot is such a good idea. In the US the fish is seen by many as a nuisance. So much so that the Utah division of Fishing and Game has imposed a 'catch and kill' regulation in the state's waterways. Alwyne Wheeler, a fish expert and former Curator of the Fish Collection at the Natural History Museum, admires the burbot but wouldn't necessarily want it back: 'The first question is why would you reintroduce them? If it's simply because they used to be there, that's not a very good argument. It would cost a lot of money and also wouldn't be very popular with anglers, as the burbot would eat the eggs and young of salmon and trout.'

This argument doesn't cut much ice with George Monbiot, who asserts that our conservation policy shouldn't be guided by people's hobbies. Others, though, take a more cautious approach, suggesting that before we try to bring it back, we need to pinpoint what made the burbot die out here in the first place. There is also the possibility that climate change may already have made the UK unsuitable for this cold-water fish.

But the burbot may be coming back all on its own. In the summer of 2010 two experienced anglers at different parts of the country separately claimed to have seen burbot swimming in our rivers: the first in the River Eden in Cumbria, and the second in the Great Ouse in Cambridgeshire – the self-same river where the last British-caught burbot was landed, more than forty years earlier.

Lifelong angler John Kitson spotted the River Eden fish, which rested for several minutes by his feet when he was wading in the river: 'It was unlike anything I'd seen in forty years of angling: blotchy, with a round head, a long dorsal fin and a stubby tail. When I got home I Googled a burbot image online and thought, Oh my God – that's it!'

The second sighting was made by French-born angler Emmanuel Hovette, close to the Pike and Eel pub in the village of Needingworth, and gains credibility from the fact that he not only has a Master's degree in fisheries, but has also fished for burbot in his native France:

> I was perch fishing when we spotted two marbled-brown, 2-foot-long fish which I'm certain were burbot, a species I've caught from the River Cher near Bourges on numerous occasions. I spotted them in clear water 1 metre deep and I immediately thought, Burbot. It was only when I returned home and went online that I realised they're meant to be extinct in the UK.

So if you fancy your chances of rediscovering this extinct fish, your best bet would appear to be a thorough search – during the evening or by night in summer – of rivers from Cumbria down through Yorkshire to East Anglia.

And even if there are not yet any firm plans to bring back the burbot, maybe one day it will once more glide serenely through (or rather lurk in the murkiest parts of) our rivers. Until then, we should stand back and admire a fish that was once a proud – if perhaps obscure – member of our British fauna, and which has been celebrated in so many different ways: through literature, medicine, nature watching, heavy metal music, or simply on our plates.

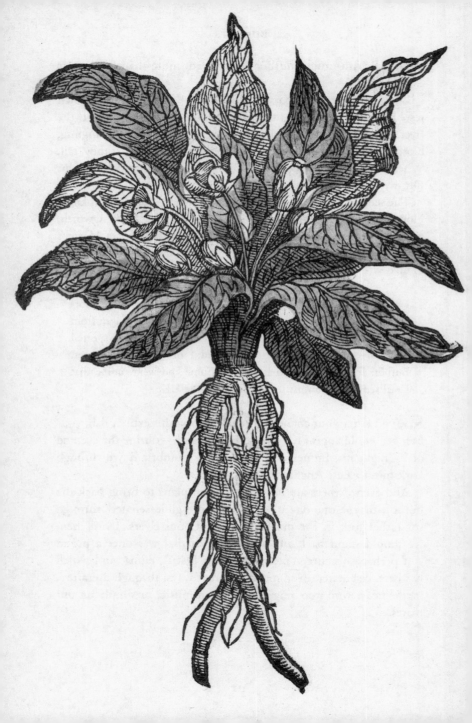

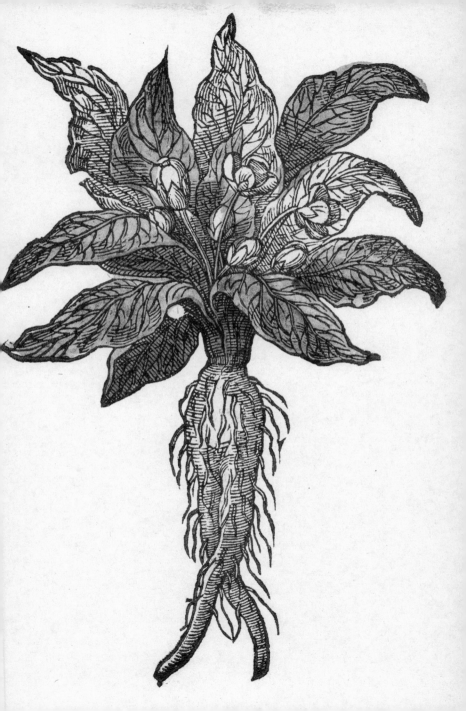

Were such things here as we do speak about?
Or have we eaten of the insane root
That takes the reason prisoner?

William Shakespeare, *Macbeth*, 1: 3

7

Nightshades

Enchantment and Chips

In a memorable scene from the film *Harry Potter and the Chamber of Secrets*, we see Harry and his classmates in a Hogwarts conservatory. Everyone is wearing earmuffs, because they are practising extreme botany. Harry and his fellow students are repotting mandrakes and the mandrake, as every wizard knows, can kill with the screams it produces when uprooted. Under the supervision of Professor Sprout, they gingerly pull the wriggling roots from their pots as the plants scream in protest, wrinkling their wizened faces and waving their twiggy arms.

By including mandrakes in her Harry Potter stories, J.K. Rowling was propagating a very old myth indeed. The mandrake's roots are anchored in classical folklore and this relatively obscure plant has spawned a vast unnatural history, including a 1968 track by the heavy metal rock band Deep Purple, entitled 'Mandrake Root'.

And it's not alone. Mandrakes are members of the *Solanaceae*, a huge family of around 2,500 species of plants whose influences are rooted in most areas of our lives. They can enchant us, feed us, poison us and send us out of our minds. They include toxic plants like deadly nightshade, a handful of whose shiny black berries could finish any of us off, and henbane, which was implicated in the disappearance and suspected murder of Dr Crippen's wife in 1910. But they're not all consorts of killers: the *Solanaceae* have many faces. Sandy Knapp, Head of the Plants Division at the Natural History Museum, has spent her life working on these fascinating plants:

> I think the reason I've stayed working on the *Solanaceae* is that they are so varied and fascinating. On one side there are mandrake and henbane – another poisonous plant; there's tobacco, one of the drugs most used by human beings; and on the more benign side of the family there are potatoes, tomatoes and aubergines. So we eat them, *and* they can kill us.

When the music-hall artiste Belle Elmore ordered potatoes from her local grocer, she had no suspicion that one day a close cousin of these harmless tubers would be her nemesis. Belle Elmore was only a stage name: her real name was Cora Crippen and her death allegedly at the hands of her husband remains one of the most notorious murders of the twentieth century. As Hawley Harvey Crippen was a homeopath, his buying quantities of hyoscine, a toxic compound of henbane that in dilute form was used as a powerful narcotic, raised no eyebrows. Until that is, he and his mistress panicked and fled the country when questioned about the mysterious disappearance of his wife. And then the police found human remains buried under the brick floor of the basement. Hyoscine, which comes from henbane, causes agitation and delirium followed by drowsiness and paralysis. More than a quarter of a grain normally kills within twelve hours. In the remains of what many believe to be the body of his wife, more than half a grain was traced.

From staple diet to outlandish end, it's a powerful illustration of the allure of this contradictory family of plants, which can both sustain and destroy us. And they do need to be treated with care. In 2008 the TV chef Antony Worrall Thompson, writing in *Healthy and Organic Living*, recommended henbane as a 'great' addition to the salad bowl. What he'd meant to say was fat hen, a harmless annual weed, but consternation ensued when the magazine issued a retraction and apology, with newspaper reports of 'Crippen weed'. Sensation and *Solanaceae* are seldom far apart.

*

The supreme example of the power of this family as a lightning conductor for superstition is the mandrake, *Mandragora officinalis*, a low-growing plant of stony soils, untilled fields and olive groves in Mediterranean countries. It's a kind of baleful 'anti-primrose' because it has a primrose-like rosette of large crinkly leaves surrounding single-stalked, purple, bell-like flowers, which turn into orange berries. The plant contains hallucinogens which can induce a coma. But it's what lies underground that inspired our ancestors to invest the mandrake with unearthly powers.

Mandrakes have a long, thick root, which they use to locate water in the dry stony habitats where they grow. This root can be forked once or more, to maximise the surface area available for the plant to obtain moisture, so that it often ends up resembling a human figure with limbs, as Sandy Knapp explains: 'The reason they are called mandrakes is that, just as when you plant carrots in stony soil, often the root will branch and they begin to look a bit like people. So in many medieval herbals the mandrakes were drawn with heads and their "legs" crossed.'

But looking like a manikin was only part of the mandrake's appeal. The plant, like its relatives the nightshades, contains chemical compounds known as alkaloids, which can have a dramatic effect on us. They can produce a combination of symptoms such as dilation of pupils, dizziness, faster heart rate, powerful dreams and a supposedly increased libido. Combine these physical and psychological effects with the humanoid look of the mandrake root, and you see why the plant became surrounded by a hotbed of hocus-pocus.

With this human shape, complete with mock genitalia, the plant inevitably acquired a reputation as an aphrodisiac; a property well appreciated in ancient Egypt, as this erotic poem from the Turin papyrus, dating back to 1500 BC, reveals:

> Surely she would bring
> A bowl of mandrake fruits
> And when she holds it in her hand

She would breathe from it,
Thus offering me her entire body.

It was also seen as an aid to fertility. In the Old Testament book of Genesis, Rachel – who is childless – asks her sister Leah to lend her the mandrake or 'dudaim', which Leah's son Reuben has found in the fields. The mandrake was later also supposed to have magical powers, and would be worn as a talisman to make the wearer richer, or allow them to become invisible.

The mandrake root's resemblance to a human being was further enhanced by its reputation for screaming as it was uprooted. These screams were said to be so loud that they could drive their excavators mad – sometimes even killing them. Josephus (c. AD 37–100) suggests using a dog to pull it up:

A furrow must be dug around the root until its lower part is exposed, then a dog is tied to it, after which the person tying the dog must get away. The dog then endeavours to follow him, and so easily pulls up the root, but dies suddenly instead of his master. After this, the root can be handled without fear.

Pliny recommended drawing circles around the plant with a sword-tip, facing west and reciting sexual verses as you uprooted the plant. Other, more practical, folk advocated a blast from a horn at the appropriate moment, to drown out the screams of the plant.

As time went on, mandrake tales became increasingly lurid. The plants were alleged to spring up where the semen of hanged men was spilled beneath the gallows – a belief alluded to in Samuel Beckett's play *Waiting for Godot*. There were rules about when to gather it: midnight, the 'witching hour' was predictably popular. But collecting mandrake was a dangerous business because the plant didn't only scream; its roots were also packed with poison. In common with many of the nightshade family, mandrake is laced with compounds known as tropane alkaloids, including hyoscine and scopolamine. Like other toxic plants, in small doses the plant could be used as an anaesthetic, and the Greek physician Dioscorides mentioned its use in the first century AD. But these compounds are capable of much more, according to Sandy Knapp: 'They change the chemical firing of the synapses in your brain and can give you the sensation of flying. They also make you feel rather sick if you take too much of them.'

It's a short leap from the sensation of flying to medieval witchcraft. Joyce Froome is Assistant Curator of the Museum of Witchcraft and Magic at Boscastle in Cornwall: 'Mandrake is probably the most magical of all plants. It was sacred to the ancient Egyptian goddess Hathor, and a drink made with mandrake was used at her festivals, so its hallucinogenic and trance-inducing properties have been known and valued for thousands of years.'

In 1518 Machiavelli wrote a play called *The Mandrake*, which centred on the use of a mandrake potion to seduce a woman. Shakespeare was also quick to realise its dramatic potential: 'Would curses kill, as doth the mandrake's groan,' cried the Earl of Suffolk in *Henry IV Part II*. And Romeo poisoned himself when he realised Juliet had drunk Friar Lawrence's potion, a mandrake infusion or 'Death Wine'.

No surprise, then, that many witches used the mandrake to perform their otherworldly deeds. Taken in large quantities, or by mistake, it could kill. But in skilled hands, it was believed to reveal great truths and allow mortals to converse with the spirit world. Long before the emergence of modern medicine in the nineteenth and twentieth centuries, the boundaries between food, drugs and magic were far more blurred than they are today, and there were more practical reasons for trusting to such folk remedies, as Joyce Froome explains:

> People simply couldn't afford to go to the more educated physicians, who charged a lot of money for treatment, so they would go to the village wise-woman or cunning-man, who had a good knowledge of herbal remedies, and would always accompany the medicine with some kind of ritual that evoked the idea of spiritual energy – the life-giving energy found in the natural world.

One of the properties of mandrake was its ability to make you remove yourself from your body, so to speak – to fly away in a trance – and escape the troubles of this earth. And so it was often used as an anaesthetic. But before mass-produced medicines, everything you needed from the natural world was collected locally, which meant that knowledge was localised too – centred on what grew around you, as Alain Touwaide, a historian of botanical medicine at the Smithsonian Institution in Washington DC, describes: 'A herbalist in ancient times was the equivalent of a modern pharmacist, procuring the remedies and giving them to people. Very often they were someone within the patient's family: a grandmother, for example, who had been told the remedies by her own mother, and transmitted it down the generations.'

But performing this role could be a risky business: the properties of these plants would have been discovered over time by trial and error – or, as the Australian aborigines put it, 'trying and dying'. Kill or cure was not exactly an ideal method, so gradually a formal guide to what might be a useful plant was developed. The Doctrine of Signatures was first defined by Paracelsus, the Swiss-German botanist and physician in the early sixteenth century, as Michael Heinrich from University College London recounts:

> The Doctrine of Signatures is in essence a concept where you say that something is treatable by a plant that looks similar to the medical condition. So if you have a hepatic disorder, you treat it with a plant where the leaves look like the liver; if you have a kidney disorder, you use something that looks like a kidney, and so on. In the case of the mandrake, because the root looks like a human being, you can say it must be a powerful medication for the whole body.

Observing the signs that God had placed in plants to show their healing qualities was also a clear demonstration of piety. But exactly how the mandrake was used is not easy to divine. Folklore was often passed down by word of mouth alone. Small wonder, then, that the Christian Church had ambivalent attitudes to the plant. Even owning a part of a mandrake could be dangerous. In 1630 three women were tried and hanged in Hamburg as witches for harbouring the roots. One of the accusations of heresy levelled at Joan of Arc was that she possessed mandrakes, a claim she denied.

Nonetheless, mandrake roots became an important talisman, so much so that in the British Isles, where they don't grow wild, the native white bryony, a member of the cucumber family with a thick root, was often gathered as a substitute. Such botanical skulduggery didn't impress the sixteenth-century herbalist William Turner, who railed in his *New Herball*, published in 1568, against the selling of 'little puppettes and mammettes . . . in boxes with hair and such forme as man hath, and nothing else but folishe fened trifles and not naturall'.

By the late sixteenth century, the mandrake's influence had begun to wane. Writing in 1597, the British herbalist John Gerard suggested that the powers attributed to the mandrake were possibly overblown, and that he and his servants had dug them up with no ill effect. His scepticism marked a decline in interest in the mandrake's powers. It was finally removed from the English pharmacopoeia at the end of the eighteenth century, superseded by less risky remedies.

Mandrakes may have taken centre stage, but other members of the *Solanaceae* were also proving useful in European culture and medicine. The deadly nightshade's scientific name, *Atropa belladonna*, highlights its bizarre relationship with humanity. *Atropa* comes from the Greek name for the Fates, the three goddesses who decided the moment a man should die by cutting the thread of his life. The plant has always been a popular poison, with at least two Roman empresses rumoured to have used it. Its other name, *belladonna* (from the Italian meaning 'beautiful lady') is because it has been widely used for centuries by women seeking to make themselves more alluring: they drop a tincture into their eyes which dilates the pupils. The plant is native to the British Isles, where it grows on chalky banks and wooded clearings on limestone. Its cup-shaped, bruise-coloured flowers are replaced by shiny black poisonous berries, as few as three of which can kill. Small wonder, then, that it has acquired such warning names as 'devil's berries', 'devil's rhubarb' and, from Somerset, the splendid 'naughty man's cherries'.

Once every hospital had its own garden, where the plants vital for its medicine were grown. Deadly nightshade is a persistent perennial, and now acts as a clue to the location of former physic gardens. Perhaps that is the explanation for its discovery growing at Guy's Hospital in central London as recently as 1978: because, for all its lethal qualities, it is still a useful plant. Before the Middle Ages it was used as an anaesthetic. The powers of its compound, atropine, were harnessed in the Second World War, when it was the sole known antidote to paralysis caused by a lethal nerve gas threatened by the Germans but fortunately never used. Among its many medicinal uses, atropine can alleviate tremors and paralysis caused by Parkinson's disease and, until relatively recently, it was used by eye doctors to dilate their patients' pupils. It has also been employed in Mexico as an antidote to the insecticide parathion, which people have sometimes inadvertently consumed in bread made from sprayed cereal. No wonder it is on the World Health Organisation's List of Essential Medicines.

In 1676 a number of British soldiers were sent to quell the Bacon Rebellion in Jamestown, Virginia, and gathered some local plants to use in a salad. Their culinary mistake was mentioned in Beverley's *History and Present State of Virginia* (1705). According to Beverley, the soldiers 'turned natural fools upon it for several days': blowing feathers in the air, sitting naked and grinning like monkeys or pawing at their companions. This good-natured, dream-like state lasted eleven days after which they returned to normal, as if nothing had happened. The plant responsible was thorn apple *Datura stramonium* and to this day is known in North America as Jimson weed, in honour of Jamestown.

Thorn apple still has the power to thrill, and is seldom over-looked when it turns up unexpectedly on waste ground and among crops. In the British Isles its long-necked, pleated flowers sometimes stand out as crop contaminants in potato fields. The flowers were a favourite of the American artist Georgia O'Keeffe, who admired their virginal white funnels and pinwheel shape when closed. However even they are topped by the evil-smelling spiky fruits, which look like medieval maces.

Thorn apples are survivors, originally from South America, the ancestral home of many *Solanaceae*, but we have spread them around the globe in fertilisers and foodstuffs, even in birdseed. Their seeds can remain fertile for a century or more, so the plants often pop up on disturbed soil on waste ground or allotments. Like deadly nightshade, thorn apple contains more than its share of mind-altering alkaloids, especially scopolamine and atropine. Accidents are rare, but it is still used as a hallucinogen by American teenagers, a risky business. The effects are said to make you 'red as a beet, dry as a bone, blind as a bat, and mad as a hatter'. In small doses, it raises the heartbeat, dries the skin and can invoke euphoria. In larger quantities, it can cause hallucinations and even cardiac arrest. On the credit side, in carefully controlled doses, it can alleviate the symptoms of asthma, stomach cramps and even bed-wetting. Crafty seventeenth-century women would use it as a means of seduction, as reported by John Petchey in 1694: 'And Wenches give half a dram of it to their Lovers, in beer or wine. Some are so well skill'd in dosing of it, that they can make men mad for as many hours as they please.'

Thorn apple has a glamorous relative, the angel trumpet or *Brugmansia*. These showy South American beauties have enormous hanging tubular white, yellow, pink or orange flowers, which can be 60 centimetres or more in length. They are horticultural favourites and often a centrepiece of conservatories. Fall asleep under one, though, and you may wake up with a headache. *Brugmansia* is a toxic plant containing hallucinogenic alkaloids such as scopolamine and in Peru its leaves are smoked or turned into infusions or suppositories. Like thorn apple it has anti-asthmatic qualities, and as a poultice or steam bath it can alleviate burns or swellings, or it can be used to control the spasms of Parkinson's disease.

In parts of South America, angel trumpets are shamanic plants, taken to bring on visions and help with divination. In Colombia they were given by the Chibcha people to the wives and servants of dead warriors to induce a stupor before they were buried alive. *Brugmansia* can also bring on deep, trance-like sleep, after which the recipient wakes up having conversed with ancestors or having seen dream-like visions. The effects vary depending on the strength and amount of plant used, but if not administered by a healer or *curandero*, they can be fatal: the perfect marriage of beauty and danger.

Finally, back to 'Crippen weed', the plant that probably did for Belle Elmore. Henbane, *Hyoscyamus niger*, is an annual plant found on disturbed ground, downs and sandy soils in Europe including the British Isles, where its folk names include 'devil's eye', 'hogbean' and, curiously, 'stinking Roger'. Its attractive cream flowers have a tracery of violet veins and its seed cases linger long after the plant has died, hanging like teats along the stem. Henbane was a convenient home-grown mandrake for British herbalists and alleged witches, offering a cure for rheumatism and gout, and giving the same sensations of flying and otherworldliness.

The sensations it induced were well known to Shakespeare, who refers in *Hamlet* to the 'cursed Hebenon' poured into Hamlet's father's ear to curdle his blood. Henbane is chock-full of hyoscine and hyoscyamine, which cause hallucinations or a coma. Sir Hans Sloane, whose collections formed the basis of the British Museum, writes of four children who mistook henbane seeds in their enclosing capsules for hazelnuts and fell into a deep sleep for two days and nights. But in the right doses, extracts from this contrary plant can also relieve bladder pains, control spasms and calm nerves.

The original 'Jaws', the jawbone of a great white shark, the inspiration
for Peter Benchley's novel and Steven Spielberg's famous film,
which has terrified generations of swimmers

A male mandrill, the world's largest monkey. Its lurid facial markings prompted Charles Darwin to write in his classic work, *The Descent of Man*, that 'no other member in the whole class of mammals is coloured in so extraordinary a manner'

A series of pinned specimens of Wallace's golden birdwing butterfly, one of the most dazzling of the world's insects

A boy looking through the glass at Archie, the world's best-preserved example of the legendary giant squid – the classic monster of the deep

The skull of a Barbary lion – a now-extinct race of the 'king of beasts' from North Africa – found in the Tower of London and dating back to the late thirteenth or fourteenth century

The burbot – surely the most obscure wild creature featured in this book – a member of the cod family now thought to be extinct in Britain. It inspired Chekhov and a Finnish death metal band

A hand-coloured copperplate engraving of one of our most poisonous plants, the deadly nightshade. Also known as *belladonna*, an extract from the plant was dropped into the eyes of Renaissance ladies to dilate their pupils, thereby augmenting their beauty

'Dippy', the best-known diplodocus in the world: a replica skeleton
presented to the natural history museum in 1905

Rocks falling from the sky: a sixteenth-century woodcut
showing the terrifying consequences of a meteor fall

A colourful coral reef may look remarkably like plants in a
garden yet, in fact, it is made up of tiny animals

A reconstruction of the Ilford Mammoth, a woolly mammoth named after the Essex town where it was unearthed in 1864

The Gaboon viper has the largest fangs and injects more venom into its unfortunate victim than any other snake on earth

Wild daffodils in bloom in early spring: the flowers that inspired
William Wordsworth to write his most famous verse

Even at the height of its popularity, though, some were sceptical: John Gerard warns against credulous acceptance of its apparent powers to cure dental problems:

> The seed is used by Mountibank tooth-drawers which run about the country, to cause worms to come forth of the teeth, by burning it in a chafing dish of coles, the party holding his mouth over the fume thereof: but some crafty companions to gain money convey small lute-strings into the water, persuading the patient, that those small creepers came out of his mouth or other parts which he intended to ease.

The sinister side of the *Solanaceae* enfolds the poisonous thorn apples and mandrakes, the nightshades and the henbanes, but most of us use other – more benevolent – members of this diverse family on a daily basis. This includes a group of far more familiar plants, coming from the New World, rather than the Old. For as we explored the Americas in search of precious gold and jewels, we found other treasures, with very different qualities, as Sandy Knapp explains: 'In Europe, *Solanaceae* – nightshades, mandrakes, henbane and so on – are baddies, not to be touched, not to be eaten and not to be meddled with. In the Americas, we have potatoes and tomatoes – the good guys.'

Tomatoes, potatoes, peppers, aubergines (and one of the 'bad guys', tobacco) are all related to nightshades; and thanks to us they have travelled the globe and provided incalculable benefits to our economies: in places they have changed the course of history. Who can imagine an Italian meal without tomatoes, or a British fish and chip shop without potatoes? Where would eastern Asian recipes be without peppers? And what of the millions of lives cut short because of the smoking of tobacco?

They may be widespread now, but the crucible of the *Solanaceae*'s evolution is South America. Locals had been using various types of *Solanaceae* for generations. Some were medicinal, some were conduits for contacting the spirit world, and some were foods. To Europeans, it must have been astonishing to see people eating potatoes and tomatoes which resembled the toxic nightshades back home and not going round the bend with delirium. The tomato is native to the continent's west coast and was already in cultivation there when the first Spanish colonists brought the plants to Europe in the early sixteenth century. But according to Sandy Knapp, these didn't exactly get a warm welcome when they first arrived on our shores: 'The tomato and potato were first characterised by the early herbalists as a kind of mandrake. So people understandably weren't very keen on eating them, and you can understand why.'

The tomato's modern scientific name, *Solanum lycopersicum*, means 'wolf-peach', a name loaded with suspicion. In North America, once the hurdle of its edibility had been vaulted – and it took time and the efforts of Thomas Jefferson's family cookbook to convince the populace that it wasn't poisonous – there were arguments about its status as a fruit. In 1893 the US Supreme Court ruled that it was a vegetable. A New Jersey importer had refused to pay import duties on the grounds that tomatoes were fruits and so were not liable to tariffs levied on vegetables. Although the court couldn't deny the botanical fact, it ruled that tomatoes were regarded by most people as vegetables and so fiscally speaking, that's what they were, a decision no doubt swayed by the fact that this helped swell the country's coffers.

Tomatoes are now an essential ingredient in salads and recipes around the world and the UK market is worth around £175 million a year. Here they're grown in glasshouses where, according to the charity Bumblebee Conservation, the flowers are pollinated by 2 million bumblebees recruited and bred especially for the purpose.

The value of the tomato may reach beyond the kitchen: the plant is also being heralded as a potential wonder-cure. As their fruits ripen, the green chlorophyll breaks down to reveal reddish pigments known as carotenoids, including lycopene, an antioxidant, which has been claimed to reduce hardening of the arteries, lower cholesterol levels and reduce the risk of pancreatic and colon cancer. It's a long way from ketchup bottle to cancer cure, but whether or not tomatoes live up to their role as a potential panacea, they are firmly entrenched as a global food, whose Andean origins are for most but a distant memory.

In 2013, according to the Food and Agriculture Organisation, we produced nearly 370 million tonnes of potatoes globally. The humble spud is a staple in Europe, and increasingly grown in India and especially China where about a third of the world's potatoes are harvested. It's a far cry from the Andean mountain slopes of Peru and Bolivia where wild potatoes were first cultivated around 8,000 years ago on terraces carved into the hills near Lake Titicaca. There are some 4,000 different varieties of potato in the Andes, all developed to suit the local terrain and climate. When the Spanish conquistadors overran the Inca Empire in the early sixteenth century, they exported a number of plants to Europe including maize, tomatoes and potatoes. Their arrival in Elizabethan England is widely (although probably wrongly) attributed to those great Elizabethan explorers Sir Walter Raleigh and Sir Francis Drake.

Initially there was resistance from people who recognised the frill of petals and cone of yellow stamens in the plant's flowers as being similar to nightshades. Eventually, though, the benefits of potato growing became obvious and they soon replaced root crops such as turnips as a staple food for working people. They provided plenty of dietary bulk and could easily be grown in a backyard or on a smallholding, so that farm labourers, coalminers and factory workers had access to a cheap and easy source of food. If an army marches on its stomach, then it's probably no exaggeration to say that the mills and presses of the new Industrial Age were fuelled by the potato, leading Friedrich Engels to claim that the vegetable was as important as iron in promoting the revolution.

But even as the potato influenced industrial change, there was a biological spanner in the works. Very few varieties of potato – perhaps just one – had been introduced from South America, which meant poor genetic diversity and lower resistance to disease. In 1845, when potato blight arrived in Ireland, a third of the country's arable land was under the crop. The blight is a fungal relative known as *Phytophthora infestans*, which may have been imported from North America and soon swept through the country, reducing leaves and tubers to a blackened pulp.

Although the blight also infested European crops, many Irish people were especially vulnerable because of the fraught political and social relationship with Britain, the role of absentee landlords and the impact of the Corn Laws, which kept prices high. Together with a heavy reliance on potatoes in their daily diet, these factors had a devastating impact. One and a half million Irish people died of starvation, poverty and disease: a million more emigrated or were despatched by landlords to North America. It was a turning point in the country's history and is credited by many as sparking the beginnings of Irish republicanism, as well as having an enormous influence on the history and development of the emigrants' new homeland, the USA.

The potato's subterranean tubers may not share the wolf-peach's glamour, but they are a vital part of our diets and our economies. As a more dependable crop, the potato is currently embarking on a further spurt of growth. Unlike grain, whose price can fluctuate widely in world markets, the potato is a reliable and locally grown source of fibre and carbohydrates, together with vitamins A and C. As a result, this humble vegetable is now taking eastern Asia by storm.

If the idea of the potato underpinning global economies is a little stodgy – not unlike the potato itself – then you may like to reflect on the first toy to be advertised on television. In 1952 the latest must-have craze hit American toyshops: Mr Potato Head. It had been invented by George Lerner in 1949, and comprised a selection of plastic and felt features – spectacles, noses, eyes and wigs – that children could attach to a real potato. Eventually a plastic potato body was supplied and a family of characters emerged. They are still being produced, a far cry from the mandrakes of

Harry Potter, but bizarre proof of the enduring fascination of the extraordinary nightshades. Half a century after he first appeared, Mr Potato Head (and his loyal wife) recently regained popularity among a whole new generation of children thanks to the *Toy Story* trilogy of films, in which he plays a small but memorable supporting role.

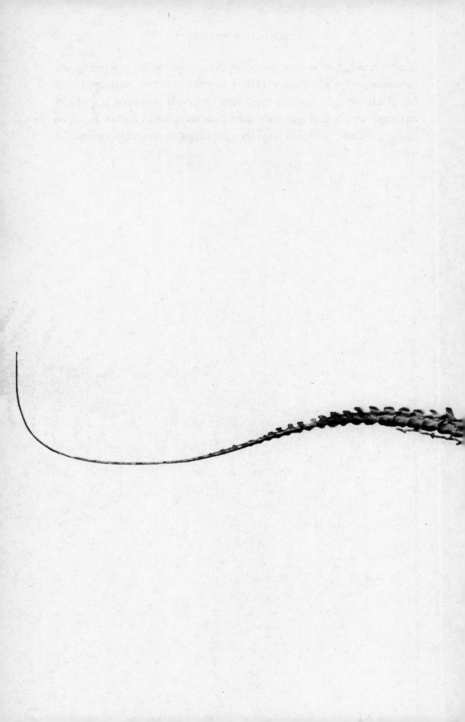

Television Host [*played by Graham Chapman*]: Good evening. Tonight – dinosaurs. I have here sitting in the studio next to me an elk. Aaagghhhh! Oh, I'm sorry, Anne Elk, Mrs Anne Elk.

Miss Elk [*John Cleese, as a very prim lady*]: Miss . . .

Host: Now, Miss Elk – Anne – you have a new theory about the brontosaurus.

Elk: Could I just say, Chris, for one moment that I have a new theory about the brontosaurus?

Host: Er . . . exactly. What is it?

Elk: Where?

Elk: Oh, my theory that I have follows the lines I am about to relate. [*Coughs*] Ahem. Ahem. Ahem. Ahem. Ahem. Ahem.

Host: Oh God.

Elk: Ahem. Ahem. Ahem. Ahem. Ahem. Ahem. Ahem. Ahem. Ahem. Ahem. Ahem. Ahem. [*Impatient noises from host*] The Theory, by A. Elk. That's A for Anne, it's not by a elk.

Host: Right . . .

Elk: This theory which belongs to me is as follows. Ahem. Ahem. This is how it goes. Ahem. The next thing that I am about to say is my theory. Ahem. Ready?

[*Host moans*]

Elk: The Theory by A. Elk brackets Miss brackets. My theory is along the following lines.

Host: Oh God.

Elk: All brontosauruses are thin at one end, much MUCH thicker in the middle, and then thin again at the far end. That is the theory that I have and which is mine, and what it is too.

Host: That's it, is it?

Elk: Right, Chris.

> **Monty Python**, 'Theory on Brontosauruses, by Anne Elk',
> *Monty Python's Flying Circus*

Dinosaurs

The End of the World – Or Is It?

The great dinosaurs of bygone ages have been on quite a journey through our minds, shape-shifting as we have uncovered their lives and chipped away at the mysteries surrounding them. From the time people first set eyes on dinosaur bones, they've been a huge influence, seen today in science, literature, film and comedy. If you want proof of (Miss) Anne Elk's theory you need go no further than the Natural History Museum. For 110 years Dippy the Diplodocus, or at least a replica of its skeleton, has been in residence, in recent times greeting visitors entering by the main entrance. Diplodocus was a close relative of Anne's Brontosaurus, as Paul Barrett, the museum's Curator of Dinosaurs, is happy to explain: 'Her theory about dinosaurs being thin at one end, thick in the middle and thin at the other end is pretty accurate – at least about Dippy. Diplodocus is a sauropod dinosaur, and they do have an incredibly long neck, small head, barrel-shaped body, four stout legs and a very long tail.'

The diplodocus itself is one of the best known of all the large dinosaurs. It was first identified in 1878, and for some time afterwards was considered to be the longest dinosaur that ever lived: large specimens may have been as much as 35 metres long, and weighed between 10 and 15 tonnes.

The most obvious feature of the diplodocus is its huge tail: up to 14 metres in length, and made up of more than eighty connected vertebrae. This gave the species its name: diplodocus means 'double beam', which refers to the unusually shaped tail bones. Originally it was thought to have been an aquatic animal, but more recent studies have disproved this theory, as it is now thought that the water pressure on its chest would have been too strong to allow it to breathe through those relatively small nostrils. Like today's largest land animal, the African elephant, diplodocus was a vegetarian, feeding on pine needles, ferns and other plant material, which it stripped from trees using its blunt teeth.

The body type of Dippy – looking rather like an obese giraffe – is just one example of the very diverse shapes and sizes of the different dinosaur species that dominated life on earth for so long. Dinosaurs existed for 150 million years, and Dippy lived in the middle part of the Age of the Dinosaurs. The big, scary T-Rex, that enormous predator that scares us half to death when we see it animated in films like *Jurassic Park*, however, lived at the end of the era of these giants, just before they suddenly disappeared off the face of the planet, roughly 66 million years ago.

Mike Benton is Professor of Palaeontology at the University of Bristol and a dinosaur specialist:

> If you look at the range of dinosaurs they start out about the size of a turkey, but over their time on earth they diversified fantastically. The largest plant-eaters were animals like diplodocus and brachiosaurus, which may have weighed as much as 50 tonnes. Many of the meat-eaters were actually very small, relatively speaking. The largest of the carnivores was T-Rex, which weighed about 5 tonnes – rather like an elephant perched on two legs.

The very largest of these giant creatures were at the biomechanical limits possible for a land-based animal – up to seven times the weight of the world's current largest living terrestrial animal, the African elephant.

*

They may have varied wildly in size and diet, but there is one characteristic common to all dinosaurs. From the very smallest to the very largest, all dinosaurs laid eggs, which is something we still see in living dinosaurs today. Birds are living dinosaurs, and reproduce in the way we'd expect dinosaurs to: dinosaurs laid hard-shelled eggs within nests, and they probably looked after their young while they were in the nest at the very least.

From the robin at your doorstep to the chicken in your freezer, all the birds we see around us today are now believed to be directly descended from dinosaurs, providing us with a tantalising link back to these unimaginable beasts. And the reason we think that birds and dinosaurs are so closely related is that they share a number of characteristics.

When Monty Python's Anne Elk proclaimed her theory in the early 1970s, the consensus view among palaeontologists was that dinosaurs had been slow, cold-blooded and reptilian – rather like giant versions of the world's largest lizard, the Komodo dragon. (The very name 'dinosaur' comes from the Greek words for 'fearfully great lizard'.)

Yet forty years later, we now know that dinosaurs were, like great white sharks, 'mesothermic' – a state between warm-blooded and cold-blooded that allowed them to maintain their bodies at a reasonably constant temperature (something most reptiles cannot do). Some were also feathered and even colourful. Our shift in knowledge and understanding is down to close examination of newly discovered fossils, which are so well preserved that scientists can see the feathers and the structures that would have formed colour, allowing them to draw new and exciting conclusions, as Mike Benton explains:

> We studied a dinosaur called *Sinosauropteryx*, and we found evidence of light and dark stripes around the tail, and in the darker stripes we found evidence that they were ginger-coloured, so we know it had a barber's pole of a tail with regular stripes of ginger and white. Another dinosaur, named *Anchiornis*, had black and white stripes

on its wings and over its body and a nice reddish crest on the top of its head.

Multicoloured dinosaurs take some getting used to, as does the notion that they were warm-blooded. After all, they look like reptiles, so surely they needed to bask in the sun like lizards to warm up. Mike Benton points out that we don't know exactly how they generated their internal heat, though we can suggest ways they may have done so:

> The example of turtles and tuna fish – so-called 'cold-blooded' animals that are actually warm-blooded – suggests that it was 'muscle-shivering'; that they had mechanisms that could change their temperature when needed. So it may be that in the morning dinosaurs would have a quick shimmy around to get themselves going – like a bumblebee on a cold day; and then once that temperature was up, just by virtue of their being so huge it would be maintained.

A shimmying dinosaur makes an arresting image. The other obvious things that birds have – that stick out – are feathers. It's hard to imagine Dippy sporting a soft covering of down or T-Rex a jaunty tuft of plumes, though as Mike Benton confirms: 'Many dinosaurs had feathers. The evidence is unequivocal in those flesh-eating species that are evolutionarily close to birds. It's possible that T-Rex and other giant meat-eating dinosaurs had shed the feathers by the time they got to adult size.'

All this is a far cry from the early days of dinosaur discovery when giant bones stuck out of the ground and spoke of a mysterious era when titans walked the earth.

Early discoveries were lost to later civilisations, but in 1836, in the Connecticut Valley in western Massachusetts, a geologist called Edward Hitchcock was mesmerised by the fossilised tracks of a three-toed creature that had once walked the desert sands, countless aeons ago. In those days these were thought to be the footprints of a giant bird, something like an ostrich on steroids. We can imagine Hitchcock sitting by the track in the hot sun, musing on the creature that left the mark of its existence in solid rock – and so he wrote this haunting poem, 'The Sandstone Bird':

> Footmarks on stone! How plain and yet how strange!
> A bird track truly though of giant bulk,
> Yet of the monster every vestige else
> Has vanished. Bird, a problem thou hast solved
> Man never has: to leave his trace on earth
> Too deep for time and fate to wear away.
> A thousand pyramids had mouldered down
> Since on this rock thy footprints were impressed;
> Yet here it stands unaltered though since then,
> Earth's crust has been upheaved and fractured oft.
> And deluge after deluge o'er her driven,
> Has swept organic life from off her face.
> Bird of a former world, would that thy form
> Might reappear in these they ancient haunts.
> Oh for a sorceress nigh, to call thee up
> From they deep sandstone grave as erst of old
> She broke the prophet's slumbers. But her arts
> She does not practice in this age of light.

The poem goes on to describe the bird appearing from out of the rock and staring around at a changed planet, so different to the days when it had been alive. It is dismayed that puny, quarrelsome, dissatisfied mankind, barely six feet tall, now rules where once giants had proudly walked. And with a cry of despair the bird speaks to the geologist.

> Sure 'tis a place for punishment designed,
> And not the beauteous happy spot I loved.
> These creatures here seem discontented, sad:

They hate each other and they hate the world,
I can not, will not live in such a spot.
I freeze, I starve, I die: with joy I sink,
To my sweet slumbers with the noble dead.
Strangely, and suddenly the monster sank,
Earth op'ed and closed her jaws, and all was still.

Those tracks in the desert sandstone turned out to be those of early dinosaurs, but the confusion surrounding these giant fossils continued. Slowly more pieces of evidence were assembled, and as the nineteenth century continued, dinosaurs emerged, blinking out of the darkness, to stare modern humanity in the eye.

That is at least what sculptor Benjamin Waterhouse Hawkins and the renowned palaeontologist and anatomist Richard Owen envisaged when they designed the first 'Jurassic Park' at Crystal Palace in south-east London. Following the Great Exhibition of 1851, Hawkins was commissioned to create more than thirty life-sized models of dinosaurs, cast in concrete, and placed in the park around the glass exhibition hall after its move from Hyde Park. He worked closely with Owen, the leading dinosaur expert of his time, to ensure that the size, shape and posture of the animals were accurate and, as far as could be determined, realistic. The two men even held a dinner party inside the mould used to make the iguanodon, to celebrate New Year's Eve 1853.

Most of the dinosaurs have survived to this day, and are still on display in the park, to the delight of visitors. Ellinor Michel is an evolutionary biologist at the Natural History Museum, and chair of the Friends of the Crystal Palace Dinosaurs:

The landscape itself tells a story. The islands on which the dinosaurs now stand were constructed to represent geologic time, and the dinosaur models were placed at the correct position that you would find them in the geologic record. So the older ones are at one end, the younger ones at the other. And when you walk on these islands, and underneath these sculptures, you can't help but be afraid.

Hawkins and Owen made huge efforts to make the sculptures anatomically accurate but, as Ellinor Michel says, sometimes the knowledge at the time just wasn't good enough to allow them to be definitive:

> If you look at the iguanodons, they present the controversy on how the animals were perceived at the time. Scientists were not in agreement as to whether these creatures stood with four legs underneath them, like a rhinoceros or an elephant, or had a sprawling gait like an iguana or a crocodile, with their legs out to the side. So Hawkins reconstructed these animals in two alternative forms.

Ironically, since then, our view of iguanodons has changed completely, and we now believe that they walked essentially on two legs, using their smaller forelegs for support.

By attracting so many visitors to the site, Hawkins's lifelike models helped to raise the profile of dinosaurs. This was the age when upright citizens improved their minds and everyone was encouraged to benefit from colonial expansion and the discoveries that accompanied it. The first books for children on prehistoric animals appeared around this time, first in America, when *The Mastodon* was published in 1839, and then in Britain, as Melanie Keane, a historian of science at the University of Cambridge who specialises in the history of science for children, explains: 'From the 1850s onwards we get really quite imaginative books that talk about these monsters coming back to life. In his 1859 book *The Fairy-Tales of Science*, John Cargill Brough opens with a chapter called "The Age of Monsters".'

In 1854 another author, John Mill, wrote *The Fossil Spirit: A Boy's Dream of Geology*, to fill what he saw as a gap in children's knowledge when it came to this fascinating subject. The book took the reader through the actual world of dinosaurs, and proved very popular, blending, in a favoured phrase of that time, 'instruction with amusement' to win over its young audience. Works such as this also paved the way for later nineteenth-century writers such as Jules Verne.

As science grew more confident in its view of dinosaurs, so their role in literature changed, and the precision on which Victorian writers prided themselves began to give way to more imaginative – and anatomically far less accurate – portrayals of dinosaurs, mostly in cartoons aimed at children. One of the very earliest animated films, the 1914 short *Gertie the Dinosaur*, used pioneering techniques to create something that now seems rather crude, being just a jerky series of line-drawings, but which at the time was revolutionary. Later cartoons included *The Flintstones*, made from 1960 to 1966, still being repeated today to successive generations of children; and Barney, a T-Rex-like dinosaur who was the lead character in *Barney and Friends*, a US children's TV series first broadcast in 1992.

Soft, smiley and bright purple with lime-green splodges, Barney does not resemble any dinosaur as far as we know – but as more colour is found in fossils, perhaps in the future he won't appear so far-fetched. One thing Barney does share with more scary representations of dinosaurs, however, is his size. In popular culture dinosaurs are always big – really big – and have enormous teeth and a bad attitude.

And of all the modern representations of dinosaurs, the most famous and influential is surely Steven Spielberg's 1993 blockbuster *Jurassic Park*. John Ó Maoilearca is Professor of Film and Television at Kingston University: 'There has to be a T-Rex as the central protagonist because it is the iconic dinosaur – the "terrible lizard" – so it has to be large and terrifying. The velociraptors are entertaining, but if there had only been those smaller-scale dinosaurs, and nothing huge and monstrous, I think the audience would have felt short-changed.'

But despite its great success, the dinosaurs in *Jurassic Park* reflect our older view of these lumbering beasts. Now that we know that many dinosaurs were feathered and colourful, will their portrayal in films be more accurate in the future? John Ó Maoilearca thinks not: 'I don't know if Hollywood would permit that: these are a genre of horror film after all, and perhaps there's something about feathered creatures, and their association with birds, that takes away from the edge, and makes the horror turn into something closer to comedy.'

He may well be right: the idea of Raquel Welch in the 1966 blockbuster *One Million Years BC* being chased by a massive dinosaur feathered up like a giant blue tit doesn't really work. It seems that even as science makes more amazing new discoveries about dinosaurs, we stubbornly cling on to the older view. And even though the original word 'dinosaur' was coined by Richard Owen as a purely scientific term, today it can have a very different connotation, meaning a person or attitude from a bygone age, as Kelvin Corlett from the *Oxford English Dictionary* points out:

> The first hint we have of this transformation taking place comes around 1935, when you start to see people using phrases such as 'like a dinosaur' to mean old-fashioned. By 1952 you start to see the word dinosaur taking on this meaning directly – one of the earliest examples is the US President Harry S. Truman talking about 'the dinosaur school of republican strategy', which he describes as expressing a desire to undo everything instituted since the New Deal in 1933. So in using the word 'dinosaur' he really is making the very firm point that these people are from a long-distant age, and not relevant today.

Dinosaurs are perhaps most famous, though, for their extinction when a huge meteorite crashed into the earth (see Chapter 9: Meteorites). The resulting mayhem cleared space for the start of a new era for life on earth – the age of the mammals – us. This should provide a salutary lesson, argues Paul Barrett:

> Dinosaurs are often regarded as icons of failure – icons of extinction – because having been so large, successful and prominent they were then wiped out by one single event in earth history. That

helps emphasise just how fragile the nature of existence can be. We have a group of animals that were successful for around 150 million years, and then suddenly they disappeared in a blink of an eye in geological terms. So there's a real lesson for humans, who currently occupy the position of being the dominant life forms on the planet, but are always vulnerable to one major global catastrophe.

The nearest link we are ever going to get to living dinosaurs now is birds. This is a prominent theme in *Jurassic Park*, in which maverick mathematician Dr Ian Malcolm (played by Jeff Goldblum) espouses the theory that dinosaurs are still with us, having simply evolved into birds. This notion is made explicit at the close of the film when, gazing out of the helicopter window after his traumatic experiences with the reconstructed dinosaurs, he sees a flock of brown pelicans – one of the most superficially dinosaur-like of the world's 10,000 or so bird species – flying in formation below.

The march of the dinosaurs through time has been a fascinating one. They had their stint on earth and left us with gigantic reminders, postcards in stone, of how fragile life can be. We will probably never get bored with speculating about them, reconstructing them – literally and metaphorically – and allowing them to roam our minds. And you can see dinosaurs in all their jaw-dropping skeletal splendour in the Natural History Museum in London, where they still rule some of the galleries. These 'terrible lizards' will always have a place in our lives.

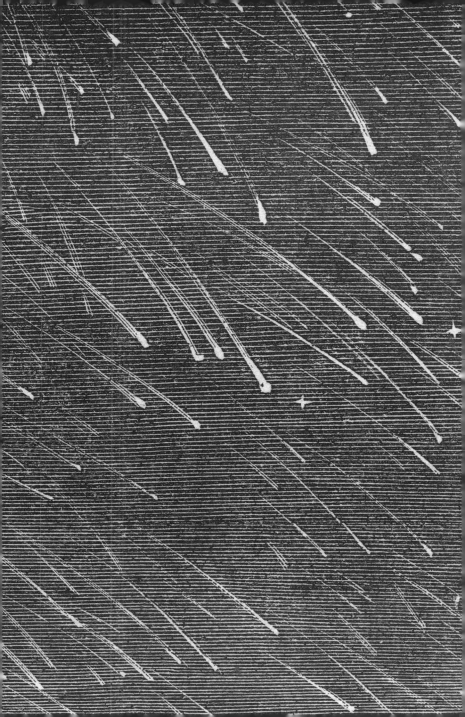

Among the hills a meteorite
Lies huge; and moss has overgrown,
And wind and rain with touches light
Made soft, the contours of the stone.

C.S. Lewis, 'The Meteorite'

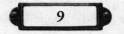

Meteorites
Messages From Heaven

These lines by C.S. Lewis conjure up a rather poignant image of earth quietly absorbing an alien fragment of rock that has come from the unknown, from outer space. It's just one example of how the mystery of meteorites has inspired art, religion, philosophy and poetry. As these unearthly objects have crashed their way into our lives, we have struggled to make sense of them in many ways. It is not just their physical presence as lumps on the ground that intrigues us. They fall so fast through our atmosphere that they often burn and glow, flashing across the heavens as streaks of light or shooting stars. Sometimes they are even accompanied by loud bangs. But what exactly are meteorites – and where do they come from?

Like frogs or butterflies, meteorites are known by different names according to which part of their life cycle they are in. They start their lives as parts of asteroids, the moon or Mars, millions of miles out in space. They are what astronomers sometimes call 'space debris', and orbit the sun, just as the earth and the other planets do.

While these objects are still in space, having detached from their parent body, they are called meteoroids, but once one enters the earth's atmosphere it briefly becomes a meteor. Only once the meteor – or if it has broken up before impact, its fragments – has actually hit the earth is it finally known as a meteorite. Meteorites can vary hugely in size, from minuscule – many just a few centi-metres in diameter, while 'micrometeorites' are microscopic – to very large indeed: the world's largest known example, the Hoba meteorite which lies buried in the ground in Namibia, has been estimated to weigh about 60 tonnes.

Normally, when a meteoroid enters the earth's atmosphere, the friction and pressure from the air turns it into a fireball – what we call a 'shooting star' – so much so that much of it burns up before it has the chance to reach the surface. Others are small enough to simply fall to the ground under the force of gravity. But a few are so large they explode when they hit the ground.

A fireball that streaked through the early morning sky, a dazzling white light that burned brighter than the sun, and a surge of heat were all followed by a huge explosion and shockwave that shook buildings and blew the glass out of windows.

Those who witnessed this event, in Russia's Ural Mountains on the morning of Friday, 15 February 2013, must surely have thought there had been a terrorist attack or major nuclear explosion, or perhaps even that the end of the world had come.

The event was captured in the many ways the modern world can offer: some took pictures of the glowing ball of fire on their smartphones, while other videos came from dashboard-mounted cameras designed to provide evidence in the case of a car accident. This footage was distributed around the world at astonishing speed, for everyone wanted to see science fiction become fact for themselves.

For the Natural History Museum's Dr Caroline Smith, it was one of those events when you remember exactly where you were and what you were doing:

I heard them say there had been a large explosion in a part of Russia that I knew had links with the atomic weapons programme, so my first reaction was 'Oh my goodness – not another Chernobyl!' I then looked over at the TV screen and saw the video of this amazing fireball; and I knew straight away that this was not some kind of fake; this was a real, spectacular meteorite. The hairs stood up on the back of my neck and I nearly spilled my coffee. For someone in my field this was simply amazing.

Astonishingly, nobody was killed, although almost 1,000 people were injured (mostly from flying glass and other debris), and over 7,000 buildings were badly damaged by the blast. Fortunately, the meteorite and its fragments had landed in a lake just outside a town in one of Russia's less populated regions, Chelyabinsk, about 1,500 kilometres east of Moscow and close to the border with Kazakhstan. President Vladimir Putin thanked God that no one had been killed, although one ultra-nationalist Russian politician claimed that the impact was caused by an American weapons test that had gone horribly wrong.

In fact the truth was even stranger. The meteorite was later estimated to have weighed between 10 and 13 tonnes, and measured 17–20 metres in diameter. It entered the earth's atmosphere at a speed of 65,000 kilometres per hour, and then exploded at an altitude of about 30 kilometres above the earth's surface, generating a bright flash and a massive shockwave as it broke up into dozens of much smaller fragments.

The Chelyabinsk meteor was the largest natural object to have entered our atmosphere for more than a century. The last had been the 'Tunguska Event' in June 1908. This fortunately also occurred in a depopulated part of central Russia, and thus also avoided human casualties, though it did destroy an estimated 80 million trees over an area the size of Leicestershire. The Tunguska meteor was even larger than the Chelyabinsk one: an estimated 60–190 metres in diameter and equivalent to roughly 10–15 megatonnes of TNT (a thousand times greater than the Hiroshima bomb), making it the largest impact event in recorded history. So the earth appears to have had two fortunate escapes in remarkably quick succession – geologically speaking in less than a blink of an eye.

*

Such cataclysmic events can happen anywhere – even much closer to home. The most famous British example is the 'Wold Cottage Meteorite', named after the place in Yorkshire where it fell to earth, at around three o'clock in the afternoon on 13 December 1795. It came to rest on the land of Major Edward Topham, a local landowner, playwright and newspaper proprietor, and just missed hitting a young farm boy called John Shipley, who was showered with dust and mud from its impact. He was not the only witness: others talked of a dark object whizzing through the air and hearing explosions.

Although the Wold Cottage Meteorite remains one of the largest ever recorded in Britain, it was considerably smaller than the far more destructive Russian examples, weighing about 25 kilos and making a crater less than a metre in diameter. A few years after it fell, analysis showed it to be in two parts: a soil-like compound rather like kaolin (china clay), containing silicon, magnesium, iron and nickel; and a more malleable mixture of iron and nickel.

To commemorate the event, in 1799 a 7½-metre-tall, brick-built monument was erected on Topham's land, with a plaque proclaiming:

> Here
> On this Spot, Dec. 13th, 1795
> Fell from the Atmosphere
> AN EXTRAORDINARY STONE
> In Breadth 28 inches
> In Length 36 inches
> and
> Whose Weight was 56 pounds.

The meteorite was bought in 1804 by the naturalist and illustrator James Sowerby for his collection of natural objects, and later acquired by the Natural History Museum, where it remains today.

Very occasionally, meteorites do hit people. In 1954 in Sylacauga,

Alabama, a meteorite the size of a rugby ball crashed through a roof, bounced off a radio and hit Anne Hodges as she sat in her living room. Luckily she got away with just bruising, and the dubious honour of being the first person on record to be struck by an extraterrestrial object.

Meteorites of varying size can be found on land all over the world, and who knows how many lie under the sea. Hot and cold deserts are good places to look for them, as the meteorites are easy to spot and the climate and geography of these regions are such that they are preserved for longer periods. A sixteenth-century woodcut shows a group of farmers and their livestock prostrate on the ground as a shower of stones falls all around and over them.

Occasionally, though, we have managed to track a meteorite all the way from space to earth. Brother Guy Consolmagno, a Jesuit and an astronomer, was for twenty years the keeper of the meteorite collection at the Vatican Observatory:

> The most exciting case of a meteorite that was seen to fall to earth happened in the Sudan in 2008. The meteorite was actually seen in space by a telescope, and when they calculated how close it was going to pass, they realised that its orbit was going to pass closer than a single radius from the centre of the earth – which meant that it was going to hit the earth.

But not all sightings are so trustworthy. He meets a lot of people who honestly believe they have found a meteorite: 'There are a lot of false alarms – I'm brought rocks all the time from people who claim, "I saw this fall out of the sky and I'm sure it's a me-teorite." And you look at it and you know it's a terrestrial rock – we don't call these things meteorites, but "meteor-wrongs".'

It is very unusual for an individual to see both the meteor's fireball streaking across the sky and then find the exact piece of rock that caused it, simply because of the scale on which the devastation would occur: 'These things move so fast and they are so bright that we want to say they are closer and slower than they really are. People say, "I saw something about the size of a hat and it fell behind the barn." In fact it's probably the size of a house and fell more than 200 miles away.'

And yet many people continue to believe that they have found a meteorite, even when the evidence against (sometimes including clear evidence that the object is man-made, such as a screw or printed writing) is overwhelming. That may be because the idea of an object arriving from outer space – from 'beyond the surly bonds of Earth' – has always been such a tantalising one.

No wonder, then, that the sudden appearance and dramatic consequences of falling meteorites have fired our imaginations over the ages. Ever since we have known about meteorites, we have tried to understand how it is that rocks can possibly fly through the air. The Greek philosopher Aristotle, in the fourth century BC, tried to make sense of them. He reasoned that because the heavens were perfect, the idea that they would cast giant objects down upon the earth was simply absurd. Having ruled out this possibility, he wrongly assumed that they must be some kind of meteorological phenomenon: vapours in the air that had coalesced into solid form, which were then somehow blown across the surface of the earth.

Due to his profound influence on later thinkers, Aristotle's mistaken belief in the terrestrial origin of these heavenly bodies persisted for many centuries. As late as the eighteenth century the French scientist Antoine Lavoisier, known as the 'father of chemistry', confidently announced: 'Stones cannot fall from the sky, because there are no stones in the sky!' Yet meteorites are mentioned in the Old Testament Book of Joshua, when the Amorites, enemies of the people of Israel, are killed as they flee: 'The Lord cast down great stones from heaven upon them.'

Meteorites had long been part of the ancient Egyptian culture, perhaps because there are many examples scattered across the desert, where they are easier to find than those in the heart of forests or jungles, or ones that fall into lakes or seas. In 1911 nine tube-shaped objects were discovered in a 5,000-year-old tomb being excavated south of Cairo. They appeared to be beads, strung together with gold and jewels to make a necklace for the teenage boy buried there. Soon afterwards, tests revealed that the objects contained an unusually high concentration of nickel; but it wasn't until more than a century later, in 2013, that scientists revealed these objects were in fact made from meteorites.

The ancient Egyptians had a single hieroglyphic symbol for 'iron', which encompassed all hard metallic objects, but around 3,500 years ago this changed, when a new symbol emerged. Dr Diane Johnson, from the Department of Physical Sciences at the Open University, explains: 'From soon after the death of Tutankhamun [in 1342 BC], we see a new term for iron, and this literally means "iron from the sky". One possible explanation is that there has been a big dramatic event like a fireball, which would make iron and the sky synonymous, with an impact crater or meteorite fragments.'

Although we cannot link this change to a specific meteorite, there is an impact crater about 45 metres across in southern Egypt, very close to the border with Sudan. The Kamil Crater was caused by an object weighing roughly 1.5 tonnes, which would have been easily observable, with a fireball accompanied by sonic booms. It has been dated as being less than 5,000 years old, which would fit with the timing of the new hieroglyph.

In such superstitious times, it is hard to overestimate just how major an impact the landing of a meteorite would have had on ordinary people, as Brother Guy Consolmagno points out: 'In ancient times there was certainly the sense that meteorites – things that fell out of the sky – might be some kind of message from the gods.'

So were these flashes in the sky and huge, deafening bangs a sign of heavenly displeasure, or some other kind of messenger from beyond the clouds? Was earth being used as target practice by unpredictable gods? After all, stars falling from the heavens were supposed to be a sign of the end of the world, as in this chilling verse from the Second Epistle of Peter: 'The heavens shall pass away with a great noise, and the elements shall melt with fervent heat, the earth also and the works that are therein shall be burned up.'

As human learning progressed, however, such long-held beliefs were often dismissed as 'superstitious nonsense'. These ideas about rocks hurtling from the heavens were not something that sat easily with the rational minds that dominated European thinking during the period from the middle of the seventeenth to the end of the eighteenth centuries, known as the Age of Reason, or simply the Enlightenment.

It is not hard to understand why, as scholars began critically to examine beliefs that had held sway for so long, and to apply a rigorous analysis based on rational thinking, many ancient truths were simply swept away. And we can hardly blame the Enlightenment thinkers for dismissing what appeared to be fanciful tales of blazing rocks hurtling down from the heavens.

This was a time when seeing was believing, and evidence, usually in the form of the results of an experiment or a reliable observation, ruled. If you didn't actually see a meteorite hit the ground, then it didn't. People who claimed to see rocks fall from the sky were viewed in the same light as those who believed in plagues of frogs or rain made of blood. They were unreliable witnesses – usually regarded as uneducated peasants – who had let drama cloud their rational thoughts.

But meteorites don't play by the usual rules of science, and it would be hard to imagine an experiment that might recreate the effects of a meteorite impact. So for a considerable time, they were consigned to the realm of mythology and old wives' tales. Even Isaac Newton refused to believe in their existence, maintaining that small rocky objects simply couldn't exist in the vastness of interplanetary space.

But one event changed all that. One day in late April 1803 the inhabitants of the commune of L'Aigle in Lower Normandy, France, heard loud crashes, as more than 2,000 rocks fell from a 'serene spring sky'. The Académie Française, who until then had been highly sceptical of such claims, concluded, to its amazement (and some embarrassment) that the rocks had indeed come from outer space. They did so mainly because of the evidence provided by Jean-Baptiste Biot, a young physicist and astronomer who had been sent to the village to investigate this strange phenomenon. His report noted that: 'At a time when we were . . . still discussing the degree of authenticity of ancient and modern stories, L'Aigle's inhabitants and from a large area thereabout witnessed the phenomenon . . . with circumstances most appropriate to strike them with wonder and bewilderment.'

Following this incident, the evidence for meteorites became incontrovertible; nineteenth-century scientists simply had to face the fact that the earth was being bombarded from outer space. Accepting that grapefruit-sized meteorites fell to earth was one thing, but even as recently as the late twentieth century it has proved hard for many scientists to accept that the impact of a meteorite could wreak havoc on a truly apocalyptic scale.

But if there is one event that is, above all else, associated with meteorites, it is the extinction of the dinosaurs. These giant beasts first appeared around 230 million years ago, became the dominant life form on the planet about 200 million years ago, and ruled the world for more than 135 million years. Then, in an infinitesimally short time by geological standards, around 66 million years ago they simply vanished.

Many theories have been put forward to explain their sudden and catastrophic demise: an event that allowed birds, larger mammals and eventually human beings to thrive and become the dominant life forms on earth. Early palaeontologists – working before the advent of Darwin and Wallace's theory of natural selection – wondered if this calamity could have been the result of the biblical Flood (especially when other cultures also turned out to have similar flood stories), while other hypotheses included volcanic explosions, rising sea levels and the shifting of the continents.

But none of these could adequately explain why the dinosaurs (and perhaps two-thirds of all the other life forms on earth) had disappeared so suddenly; nor could they account for the comprehensiveness of the catastrophe, which extended across the whole globe.

Then, in 1980, US scientist Walter Alvarez and his colleagues at the University of California, Berkeley, proposed a radical new theory to account for the extinction event itself, which also helped to explain its suddenness and global scale. They had discovered that a layer of clay near the surface of the earth, dating to the same time period as the dinosaurs' extinction, contained unusually high levels of iridium, a metallic element very rare on earth but common in asteroids. This, they suggested, could be evidence that a massive meteorite had hit the planet.

Meanwhile, almost 4,000 kilometres to the south-east, in the Yucatan Peninsula, two geophysicists working for the Mexican state-owned oil giant Pemex had made an extraordinary discovery: a huge underwater arc which, along with a second arc on land, formed a ring roughly 180 kilometres in diameter, centred on the village of Chicxulub. It appeared to be evidence of a cataclysmic geological event – but what could have caused it?

Eventually the two groups of scientists stumbled across each other's findings, and after careful detective work concluded that the Yucatan crater was indeed the site of a meteorite impact; an event so huge that it could have led to the extinction of the dinosaurs. The meteorite itself would have been roughly 10 kilometres in diameter, and produced the energy equivalent to 100 million megatons of TNT – roughly 200 million times as great as the 2013 Russian meteorite, and 2 million times as powerful as the biggest human bomb ever detonated.

Professor Mike Benton, a palaeontologist from the University of Bristol, believes that the impact of this massive meteorite would have been truly cataclysmic. First, there would have been a massive 'megatsunami', enough to flood many of the world's low-lying coastal regions. Then, the clouds of dust and gases created by the impact would have shrouded the entire atmosphere, blocking out the sun. This would have stopped photosynthesis almost immediately, killing plants, which would mean that herbivores starved, with carnivores disappearing soon afterwards. Temperatures would also have plummeted, making the planet a very hostile place for creatures like the dinosaurs. What's truly incredible is that the whole process may have taken place in a matter of days or even hours.

The effects of that asteroid impact on the Mexican peninsula 66 million years ago have lingered ever since, changing the course of evolution and marking the extinction of about 60 per cent of life on earth – not just the dinosaurs. Large groups of animals such as ammonites – a group of giant marine invertebrates – also disappeared at the same time.

Yet the Yucatan meteorite crater is by no means the biggest of its kind. Scientists have recently discovered twin scars in Australia's outback which mark the impact of a truly enormous meteorite. It may have split in two before it hit the earth more than 300 million years ago and left a crater 400 kilometres wide, the largest ever found, though there is still some debate over the interpretation of these results.

For anyone still unconvinced about the power of the meteorite, the briefest look at the pockmarked face of the moon offers conclusive proofs that large and damaging rocky missiles are flying around us. This has not gone unnoticed by science-fiction writers. The vulnerability of our tiny earth, with its fragile inhabitants whirling in the dark vastness of a hostile universe is just too good a theme to ignore. H.G. Wells's 1897 short story 'The Star' was written nearly a century before the effects of the Yucatan meteorite were understood. It describes the near impact of a huge meteor that streaked past earth, heating it up and causing all kinds of mayhem:

And then the clouds gathered, blotting out the vision of the sky, the thunder and lightning wove a garment round the world; all over the earth was such a downpour of rain as men had never before seen, and where the volcanoes flared red against the cloud canopy there descended torrents of mud. Everywhere the waters were pouring off the land, leaving mud-silted ruins, and the earth littered like a storm-worn beach with all that had floated, and the dead bodies of the men and brutes, its children. For days the water streamed off the land, sweeping away soil and trees and houses in the way, and piling huge dykes and scooping out titanic gullies over the country side. Those were the days of darkness that followed the star and the heat. All through them, and for many weeks and months, the earthquakes continued.

As Mike Benton has shown, H.G. Wells wasn't far off the mark. Even though today we know considerably more about meteorites, it doesn't stop our imaginations working overtime. Scientists now generally accept that a meteorite played a major part in the extinction of the dinosaurs, and therefore, by default, in our current dominance of the planet. But could a meteor one day also be the reason our own species disappears from earth?

The idea that the end of the human race will come about as the result of an object from outer space has long been a staple of Hollywood disaster movies, from *When Worlds Collide* in 1951, through *Meteor* in 1979, to two blockbusters in 1998 – *Deep Impact* and *Armageddon*. And yet the events of 15 February 2013, when the Chelyabinsk asteroid was not even detected until it was close to the ground (partly because it came out of the same sector of the sky as the sun), serve to remind us that meteors can and do hit the earth from time to time. Just because there were no fatalities then doesn't mean that next time we will be so lucky. And as the events of 66 million years ago show, the effects of a meteor hitting the earth can, if it is big enough, change the course of history.

In spite of all we have learned about them, some people would still like to believe that meteorites are personal messages from a huge, dynamic universe, or, at the very least, the bearers of extra-terrestrial life forms. Modern myths are still being propagated, including one related to a very unworldly-looking plant, the carnivorous Venus flytrap. This unusual species feeds entirely on small insects that are caught by the closing of the hinged 'jaws' of the plant's modified leaves, where they are gradually dissolved and subsumed. Like other carnivorous plants such as our own native sundew, the Venus flytrap evolved to survive in boggy areas with low amounts of nutrients – especially nitrogen. Eating insects was a viable way to obtain what it needed to survive.

But confronted with the Venus flytrap, with its odd appearance and even more bizarre habits, our ancestors formulated a myth that it came from another world, as Nick Johnson, from the Royal Botanic Gardens at Kew, explains:

> There are stories that suggest that these plants were some kind of 'cosmic hitchhikers', cadging a lift on a meteorite. This probably arose because Venus flytraps do admittedly often grow on the edge of depressions, between boggy areas and grasslands, which may have led our ancestors to jump to the conclusion that these were craters left by meteorites.

However, as Nick Johnson points out, when you examine the DNA evidence then this theory soon falls apart, as the Venus flytrap is closely related to other members of the sundew family.

Even in the face of scientific progress, however, we do like to maintain a little mystery. The late Terry Pratchett used meteorite iron in his hand-made sword, and if you fancy forging your own weapon, you may be interested to hear that many people do buy fragments, believing in their healing properties. Beth Holtum and her husband Graham run a shop selling all kinds of crystals and meteorites in Wadebridge in Cornwall. The various meteorites and tektites, the glassy rocks usually found some distance from an impact crater, are claimed to have different properties from increasing spiritual awareness to aiding healing.

When we interviewed her, Beth was wearing a necklace of green tektites, gathered from a meteorite crater, which she described as:

'A very active stone from a crystal healer's point of view. It will raise one's spirits; one feels lighter, which may be because of the contrast with the heavy meteorite.' Today's belief in the healing properties of meteorites is, she says, a continuation of ancient beliefs going back hundreds of years. 'For many centuries, different civilisations have looked at stones that have landed from somewhere else, and realised that by holding an item you can actually pick up on the past events it has experienced, in a process known as "vibrational healing".'

Scientists may dismiss this as 'New Age nonsense', but our fascination with meteorites lingers. Steven Spielberg, director of *E.T.* and *Close Encounters of the Third Kind*, recalls a childhood event that cemented his fascination for extraterrestrial objects:

> My dad took me out to see a meteor shower when I was a little kid, and it was scary for me because he woke me up in the middle of the night. My heart was beating; I didn't know what he wanted to do. He wouldn't tell me, and he put me in the car and we went off, and I saw all these people lying on blankets, looking up at the sky.

Spawning speculation and sensation throughout the centuries, meteorites will always hold us in thrall. They are literally other-worldly, visitors from an alien realm. They may heal us – or they may not – but their bigger relatives may determine no less than the future of our planet and its inhabitants.

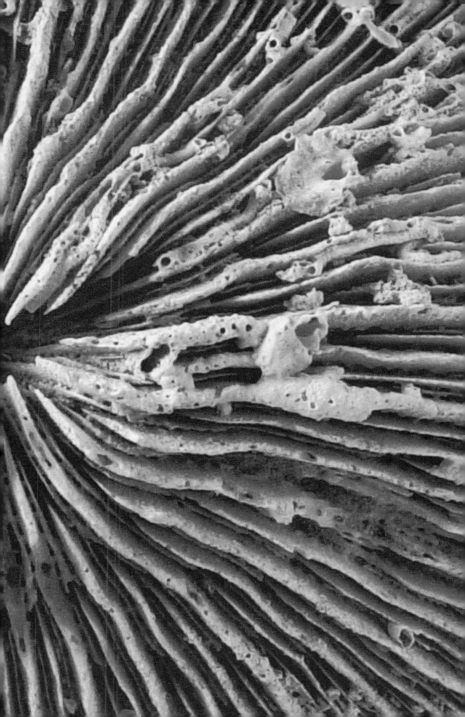

Full fathom five thy Father lies;
And of his bones is coral made;
Those are pearls that were his eyes,
Nothing of him that doth fade
But doth suffer a sea change
Into something rich and strange.

William Shakespeare, 'Ariel's Song', *The Tempest*

Corals

Paradise – Lost?

At last we came among the Coral Islands of the Pacific, and I shall never forget the delight with which I gazed, when we chanced to pass one, at the pure, white, dazzling shores, and the verdant palm-trees, which looked bright and beautiful in the sunshine. And often did we three long to be landed on one, imagining that we should certainly find perfect happiness there!

R.M. Ballantyne's children's classic *The Coral Island* perfectly captures the magical quality of coral reefs – natural phenomena evocatively described by American oceanographer Sylvia Earle as 'a jewelled belt around the middle of the planet'. For those of us who happen to live on a wet, windy and decidedly untropical archipelago off the north-west coast of Europe, coral reefs really do evoke an image of paradise, even though slow-growing corals can and do occur in cooler waters off Britain and north-west Europe.

Few natural phenomena are quite as beautiful, or extraordinary, as a coral reef. Even the name evokes bright blue seas and warm tropical breezes, and remote atolls in vast oceans. And then diving beneath the surface of the sea, you enter a new and silent world, shimmering with shards of sunlight.

It's like floating over a forest canopy, with branching trees and open clearings; but here, instead of birds, tight shoals of fish swim through the foliage, flashing alternately light and dark as they twist and turn to evade predators. Ken Johnson, Coral Researcher at the Natural History Museum, is still mesmerised every time he swims over one: 'Coral reefs make me feel very happy: they're beautiful places, you're underwater, you're flying over the reefs – complex, three-dimensional structures with all this diversity of life beneath you.'

Many corals look like trees, their branches reaching towards the sky through a layer of clear blue water. But they are double-edged beauties, for the very nature of corals is ambiguous. They look like plants, but are actually animals. They appear to be individuals, but live in colonies, made up of thousands of individual creatures that can only function as part of a greater whole. Those colourful fish patrolling round the reef may be beautiful, but many are also poisonous, while sharks lurk in the shadows, waiting for their chance to grab a passing meal.

Once there were coral reefs throughout the warmer parts of the Mediterranean. Coral (especially red) was highly sought after. A Greek myth explained how Perseus had used the severed head of Medusa (the Gorgon with snakes for hair, whose gaze turned people to stone) to slay a sea monster. An unexpected side effect was that her head turned the surrounding plants and seaweed into coral. The Roman poet Ovid took up the story in his *Metamorphoses*:

The fresh plants, still living inside, and absorbent, respond to the influence of the Gorgon's head, and harden at its touch, acquiring a new rigidity in branches and fronds. And the ocean nymphs try out this wonder on more plants, and are delighted that the same thing happens at its touch, and repeat it by scattering the seeds from the plants through the waves. Even now corals have the same nature, hardening at a touch of air, and what was alive, under the water, above water is turned to stone.

The official name for coral still echoes this today: 'Gorgeia', meaning 'of the Gorgon'. Over the centuries coral reefs have inspired authors and artists, naturalists and scientists, poets and filmmakers – everyone from Charles Darwin to David Attenborough – and they have been celebrated in works ranging from *Robinson Crusoe* and *The Coral Island* to *Finding Nemo*. So what exactly are corals? And what does our obsession about them tell us about our concept of paradise – and its opposite – a heaven or hell here on earth?

Corals are part of the largest group of animals on the planet: invertebrates. They belong in the group Cnidaria, which comprises more than 10,000 marine or freshwater creatures, characterised by their jelly-like structure; within this they are in the class *Anthozoa* (deriving from the Greek meaning 'flower animals'), which includes sea anemones as well as corals.

The vast majority of corals consist of colonies of many genetically identical polyps, each only a few millimetres in diameter and several centimetres long, but collectively making up some of the largest superorganisms on the planet. Each of these tiny creatures consists of a set of tentacles around a single opening (used both for feeding and excretion), with a hard exoskeleton beneath. Over aeons of time, these hard structures have combined to form what appears to be a single assemblage, creating a coral reef.

Given their static lifestyle, corals must feed on whatever comes close enough: some stinging small fish and plankton with their tentacles. However, most corals get their energy from microscopically tiny, single-celled organisms known as dinoflagellates, which actually live inside the tissues of each individual polyp. To survive, most must live near the surface in shallow seas, usually within 60 metres of the surface, so that they are able to take advantage of sunlight.

Corals may be individual creatures, but they also function at two much larger scales: as treelike colonies, and as entire coral reefs. These can be vast: Australia's Great Barrier Reef – the largest in the world – comprises almost 3,000 separate sections, and stretches for more than 2,300 kilometres over more than one-third of a million square kilometres – an area almost as large as Germany.

The Great Barrier Reef could arguably be considered the world's biggest living entity, and can even be seen from outer space.

Coral reefs are the most diverse ecosystems in the sea, with more than 25 per cent of all oceanic species living there. They are full of colour and movement, not just because of the corals but also from all the other creatures that make their home there. Yet as Erica Hendy, lecturer in the School of Biological Sciences at Bristol University, points out, the reefs themselves are mostly dead: 'Coral reefs are made up of skeletons of corals and calcareous algae – organisms that are forming limestone – that are now dead and have been washed ashore to form islands.'

And as she goes on to explain, this means that we may not quite realise what we are looking at when we gaze at a coral reef:

> What we are actually looking at is a veneer: the living part might be just a few millimetres, whereas the skeleton can be metres and metres thick. It's just the very thin layer of tissue on the top that's living – the rest is the skeleton, laid down incredibly gradually at a rate of just a few millimetres a year, and over time taking over more and more real estate on the reef.

Many human analogies have been used to describe a coral reef: they have frequently been described as underwater cathedrals and gardens, for example. But Ken Johnson sees them more as a kind of farm: 'Reef-building corals are special because they are an animal, but inside their bodies are small single-celled algae. So corals are farmers, growing their crops inside their bodies.'

The algae are plants, so they use sunlight to photosynthesise, creating food for the coral. In return the coral makes waste products that fertilise the algae. Much of the colour we admire when we look at reefs comes not from the corals but actually from the algae within. But what appears to be a city of colour and light is, in reality, a ferocious, competitive warzone, where it's every polyp for itself, as Erica Hendy notes:

A reef is also a wall of mouths, with coral tentacles ready to capture any small creature that lands on them. Corals can also release mucus, like a kind of fishing-net, enabling them to capture even smaller particles such as bacteria to feed on. But what's really striking is there is a constant warfare going on, as they try to take over their neighbours by extruding their stomachs and digesting them alive. So when we look at this beautiful reef, what we're actually looking at is a battlefield.

And the warzone extends beyond the edge of the reef as corals themselves are also fighting against a variety of enemies: UV radiation produced by the tropical sun, a range of marine predators, and longer-term issues such as pollution and global climate change. The Victorians were particularly fascinated by coral. James Gates Percival tried to capture their beauty in his poem 'The Coral Grove':

> Deep in the wave is a coral grove,
> Where the purple mullet, and gold-fish rove,
> Where the sea-flower spreads its leaves of blue,
> That never are wet with falling dew,
> But in bright and changeful beauty shine,
> Far down in the green and glassy brine . . .

The industrious nature of corals appealed to a society obsessed with progress. They marvelled especially at the way so many organisms came together to build a coherent, functioning ecosystem; one on which they could perhaps model their own rapidly growing empire. Ralph Pite is Professor of English Literature at the University of Bristol: 'The way in which coral reefs grew could be seen as an emblem of a perfect, harmonious society, in which every tiny polyp contributed to the greater good, and the reef gradually developed from the toil of each individual polyp; just as the British Empire developed out of the toil of individual workers.'

This connection was often made explicit, as in this 1827 poem by James Montgomery, 'Pelican Island':

> Millions and millions thus, from age to age,
> With simplest skill, and toil unweariable,
> No moment and no movement unimproved,
> Laid line on line, on terrace terrace spread,
> To swell the heightening, brightening, gradual mound,
> By marvellous structure climbing towards the day . . .
>
> Each wrought alone, yet all together wrought,
> Unconscious, not unworthy, instruments
> By which a hand invisible was rearing
> A new creation, in the secret deep.

And once religion got involved, the comparison of the nature of coral reefs with our human life went still further – the reef was viewed as a physical and material analogy for our own ability to escape from sin. This was because at low tide, when the sea has retreated, the reef looks just like any other rocky place; but as soon as high tide covers the coral again with water, life immediately returns. As Ralph Pite describes: 'All the coral creatures start to feed, and the flowers grow; and this sense that beneath what appeared to be dead were living creatures was taken as an allegory for the presence within us of a living soul; that even in people "locked within sin", as Montgomery would have called it, there was the potential for life.'

But it was undeniable that coral reefs had a darker side too. Their jagged, sharp rocks lurking unseen under the water were notorious for tearing wooden hulls to shreds. Coral reefs were the scene of many shipwrecks and responsible for the deaths of thousands of sailors, who drowned amid the warm seas. The familiar image of coral islands as an earthly paradise competed all the time with a sense of their menacing danger.

Charles Darwin first encountered corals when on the *Beagle*, one of whose tasks was to map coral reefs, because they presented such a threat to shipping. He'd been intrigued by them long before he saw one for himself.

When the *Beagle* set out in 1831, the formation of coral atolls was a scientific puzzle. In 1824 and 1825 French naturalists Quoy and Gaimard had observed that the coral organisms lived at relatively shallow depths, but the islands appeared in deep oceans. Darwin set out to test their theory that the atolls formed on the top of dormant volcanoes. He couldn't actually see the reefs underwater, but he still managed to work out how they formed, hopping from top to top with the aid of a 'leaping stick'.

Such formations surely rank high amongst the wonderful objects of this world. It is not a wonder which at first strikes the eye of the body, but rather after reflection, the eye of reason. We feel surprised when travellers relate accounts of the vast piles & extent of some ancient ruins; but how insignificant are the greatest of these, when compared to the matter here accumulated by various small animals. Throughout the whole group of Islands, every single atom, even from the most minute particle to large fragments of rocks, bear the stamp of once having been subjected to the power of organic arrangement. [Charles Darwin, *Diary from the Voyage of the Beagle*, 12 April 1836]

Darwin became so fascinated with them that they formed the subject of his first book, *The Structure and Distribution of Coral Reefs*, published six years after the voyage, in 1842. He proposed a new – at the time, revolutionary – theory for their origin, suggesting that the different types of reefs and atolls were shaped by the movements of the earth's crust, way beneath the oceans' surface. Darwin went on to win the Royal Society's coveted Royal Medal for his work, and more than 180 years after he first conceived his speculative theory – before he had even seen a coral reef for himself – he has now been proven right.

In 1857 the Scottish children's author R.M. Ballantyne wrote

The Coral Island: A Tale of the Pacific Ocean. His heroes are three boys, who like Robinson Crusoe are marooned on a desert island – in this case a coral reef – after a shipwreck. Brave and resourceful, they thoroughly enjoy their experience. As one of the characters, Peterkin, says, 'There was indeed no note of discord whatever in that symphony we played together on that sweet coral island.' The book was an instant success, appealing to boys eager for colour and adventure amid the regulations and dullness of Victorian schools.

The Coral Island is far more than a *Boys' Own* adventure story. It deliberately touches on a wide range of themes that, although they might have passed over the heads of many of its readers, would have appealed to their parents and teachers. These include British imperialism, the civilising influence of Christianity, and the importance of strong leadership. Ballantyne was a deeply religious man who felt he had a duty to educate Victorian youth in the 'codes of honour, decency and religiosity'. The novel's setting – on an untouched, pristine coral island – was no accident; it served as a metaphor for the paradise from which all mankind had fallen. According to the literary critic Frank Kermode, the novel is 'a document in the history of ideas', taking Darwin's original theory and shaping it to the Victorian ideology of the superiority of white, western civilisation over the savages. As Ballantyne himself described it: 'Britons at the top of the tree, savages and pigs at the bottom.'

And as such, *The Coral Island* was ripe for subversion. William Golding's *Lord of the Flies*, published in 1954, took a much more Darwinian approach to the idea of the desert island and twisted Ballantyne's paradise into a horrific dystopia, in which evil triumphs over good.

From his experience as a teacher, Golding was convinced that the idyllic events of *The Coral Island* could never exist in real life. So he wrote a novel that explored the darker side of human nature starting from the same basis of boys stranded on a desert island, away from all civilising influences. Things start going wrong immediately. Golding deliberately inverts Ballantyne's moral code; even the book's title is a literal translation of the name Beelzebub, another name for the devil. On *this* coral island, paradise has turned into hell. When the naval officer who comes to the rescue of the survivors at the end of the novel congratulates the boys on a 'Jolly good show. Like the *Coral Island*', what Golding was slyly suggesting was how badly we could misread evidence if we'd already decided on the story we wanted to hear. As Darwin pointed out in his monograph on coral reefs, while coral is beautiful, it remains a living organism, amorally determined to survive at all costs: 'In an old-standing reef, the corals, which are so different in kind on different parts of it, are probably all adapted to the stations they occupy, and hold their places, like other organic beings, by a struggle one with another, and with external nature.'

Meanwhile, coral reefs have, like other natural phenomena, long been used and abused by advancing human civilisations. During the Spanish conquest of Central America in the late sixteenth and early seventeenth centuries, the Spanish built fortifications to defend themselves against what they regarded as 'English pirates' (the English preferred to refer to themselves as 'privateers'). They did so by taking advantage of an abundant local resource: the coral reefs lying just offshore.

Known as 'sea stones', this hard, durable material proved ideal for construction, which continued for a further 200 years. One settlement in Panama, Portobelo, has been estimated to have used almost 13,000 cubic metres of coral, while the total amount of coral mined during the period has been estimated at more than 70,000 cubic metres. But along with the environmental damage, there was a human cost too, as Erica Hendy explains: 'When they wanted to build the customs house at Portobelo slaves were sent out in canoes to the local reefs. Can you imagine grabbing these really sharp coral boulders the size of large crates out of the reef? Just as they can destroy a ship, they destroy your skin – it must have been a hellish job.' The destruction of the reefs continued well into the twentieth century: during the construction of the Panama Canal, which opened in 1914, and during the 1960s, when roughly 5 million cubic metres of coral reefs were dredged to provide infill material for the construction of an oil refinery.

Over the centuries, coral reefs have been exploited for human gain in many other ways. Early coastal and marine civilisations benefited hugely from the abundance of fish around reefs, while collecting corals to make into jewellery also has a long pedigree. While these activities were only carried out on a small scale, they were sustainable; but even as early as Roman times there was a profitable trade in coral. Pliny the Elder observed that the Gauls were known to use it to decorate their helmets and weapons, while superstition led to Romans putting coral necklaces around children's necks to keep them safe from danger; coral was also used as a cure for various diseases.

Coral continued to be harvested throughout the Middle Ages and afterwards, but it was only when big business became involved during the twentieth century that the damage to many reefs accelerated, in many cases becoming irreversible. One particular group, the red corals, have now become very scarce because of over-harvesting for jewellery, especially along the coastlines of Italy and other Mediterranean countries.

On a more positive note, chemicals extracted from corals are used in medicine, both traditional and modern forms; reefs have been described as 'the medicine cabinets of the twenty-first century'. Compounds found in coral – which the corals themselves use as defences against predators – have been used to develop treatments for cancer, arthritis, heart disease and Alzheimer's disease, among many others. Corals are even bred in captivity, either simply for pleasure, or as part of reef restoration programmes, in which specially grown corals can be used to repair damaged areas, or to 'replant' areas where the existing reef has been destroyed.

Perhaps the most fascinating tale of corals is that of Bikini Atoll, a group of twenty-three tiny islands covering an area of just 8.8

square kilometres in the Marshall Islands, roughly 2,000 kilometres north-east of Papua New Guinea, in the western Pacific Ocean. Bikini was catapulted into public attention in 1946 when the United States government chose this as the site to test its nuclear weapons.

The project, known as Operation Crossroads, aimed to test the effects of a nuclear explosion on ships and also on a range of animals placed within the blast zone, including guinea-pigs, mice and rats. Unfortunately the US authorities appeared to have ignored the fact that human beings also lived and worked on and around the reefs: so when the first blast went off, soon after dawn on 1 March, a boatload of Japanese tuna fishermen (whose craft was, ironically, named the *Lucky Dragon*) were within range of the explosion. Not sure what to do, the crew continued fishing for several hours afterwards, but by 10 a.m. extremely radioactive particles of coral dust were falling from the sky on to the deck of their boat.

They set off back to their home port, but on the way they began to suffer the effects of the nuclear fallout, including nausea, bleeding gums and headaches. They were immediately admitted to hospital, where the doctors – some of whom had treated survivors from Hiroshima and Nagasaki just a year earlier – diagnosed them as suffering from acute radiation poisoning. However the US authorities denied this. Less than a decade later, the *Lucky Dragon*'s radio operator, Aikichi Kuboyama, was dead at the age of just forty.

During the following twelve years, as the Cold War got into its swing, twenty-three nuclear bombs were detonated at the test site: some in the air, others on the ground or beneath the sea.

Since then the islands – which also, incidentally, gave their name to the two-piece swimsuit, rather tastelessly described by its creator Louis Réard as being 'like the bomb . . . small and devastating' – have remained uninhabited, as even after almost six decades the levels of radiation remain too high to be safe for permanent residents. However, scientists (and well-heeled scuba divers prepared to bring all their food with them and pay thousands of dollars for the privilege) are still able to visit the atoll where, despite the destruction caused by the bombs, corals are now flourishing in the mile-wide crater left by the biggest device. Ironically the reason the corals and sea life are doing so well is as a direct result of the lack of human interference here. UNESCO has now named Bikini a world heritage site:

> Bikini Atoll has conserved direct tangible evidence that is highly significant in conveying the power of the nuclear tests, i.e. the sunken ships sent to the bottom of the lagoon by the tests in 1946 and the gigantic Bravo crater. Equivalent to 7,000 times the force of the Hiroshima bomb, the tests had major consequences on the geology and natural environment of Bikini Atoll and on the health of those who were exposed to radiation. Through its history, the atoll symbolises the dawn of the nuclear age, despite its paradoxical image of peace and of earthly paradise.

Elsewhere in the world's oceans, corals have not been enjoying such protection. Although some have demonstrated an ability to 'shift' to deeper or cooler waters, many corals are unable to do so. As a result, roughly 10 per cent of the world's coral reefs are now beyond saving, with many others – including large parts of the Great Barrier Reef – under threat. Sea temperature rises of just one to two degrees Celsius are enough to cause permanent destruction; so with some projections suggesting temperature rises of as much as four degrees by the end of this century, the future for the world's coral reefs is looking bleak. In the worst affected region, South East Asia, four out of five reefs are now endangered, while globally it has been estimated that more than half the world's coral reefs could be destroyed by 2030.

People are at least now far more aware of the beauty and fragility of coral reefs than they used to be, and this is thanks in no small part to a film. *Finding Nemo*, which first appeared in 2003, is an animation that tells the story of a young clownfish who, in an attempt to gain independence from his over-protective father, ends up leaving the safety of his home reef and gets lost in the vastness of the world's oceans. Ralph Pite suggests that the success of *Finding Nemo* is because of the way it restores our original, primal view of coral reefs as an earthly paradise:

> One of the striking things is that it goes back to the idea of the paradisal that we find in nineteenth-century accounts of coral reefs. There are moments in the film where the coral reef provides a kind of illuminated and sacrosanct space of safety and security. This is absolutely contiguous with the way authors such as R.M. Ballantyne wanted to portray coral islands.

Despite its good intentions, the film has had a mixed influence on the fate of coral reefs and the creatures that live there. On a positive note, it has raised awareness of the plight of this unique habitat. But another side effect of the film's popularity led to a huge increase in demand for clownfish as pets.

This had two major environmental impacts. First, these dazzling orange fish with their black and white stripes were removed in vast numbers from their native reefs, with unscrupulous traders sometimes using cyanide to stun and capture them, causing the deaths of many other species left behind. Then, as a response to concern aired in the media, some aquarium owners decided to release their clownfish back into the wild. Unfortunately, they did so in entirely the wrong place, and as a result clownfish have now become a problematic invader, especially in Florida and California, where they can spread diseases and compete for food with native species.

Such is the tangled web we humans weave when we interact with the natural world. But the last word goes to Ralph Pite, who sees in corals and coral reefs something fundamental to our human need for a paradise here on earth:

> So much of nature now is portrayed as a place of predation and cruelty and violence, with species warring with one another. This

creates in us a sense of worry and danger, and the coral reef provides us with some counterweight to that. The science doesn't bear that out – it suggests that there, as elsewhere, there is competition, predation and scarcity of resources – but what we see is something that fills us with that sense of reassurance that nature is full of beauty and comfort.

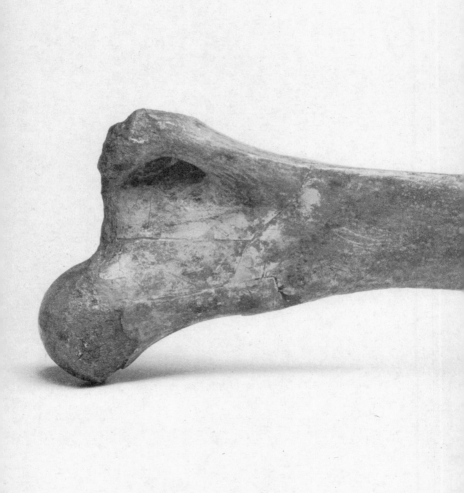

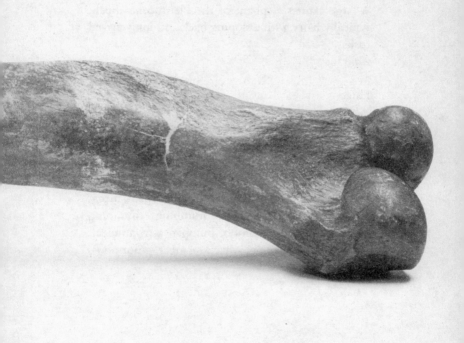

Mammoth
Noun
1.
A large extinct elephant of the Pleistocene epoch, typically hairy with a sloping back and long curved tusks.
Adjective
2.
Huge.
'A mammoth corporation'
Synonyms: huge, enormous, gigantic, giant, colossal, massive, vast, immense, mighty, stupendous, monumental, Herculean, epic, prodigious, mountainous, monstrous, titanic, towering, elephantine, king-sized, king-size, gargantuan, Brobdingnagian, mega, monster, whopping great, thumping, thumping great, humongous, jumbo, bumper, astronomical, astronomic, whacking, whacking great, ginormous.

Mammoths

Trade and Protection

The sound of a flute floats through the air, ethereal and mysterious. But as well as travelling through space, it is also moving through time: back more than 30,000 years to a period when much of northern Europe – including what we now call the British Isles – was blanketed with a thick layer of ice. For this flute made from a woolly mammoth tusk is the closest we'll ever get to hearing the sound of the Ice Age.

There are no written records this far back, so we will never know who made these instruments, and why – whether it was for a special ceremony, or simply for pleasure – but its makers were highly skilled, producing different types of flute to produce a range of sounds. Their singing, chanting and clapping are not available, so those sounds stay in the past with the bones of the people. But their instruments give us a tantalising glimpse of our ancestors' lives, a fragment of sound from an otherwise silent world.

Today, the Ice Age – specifically that of North America, with its particular suite of creatures – has been packaged and marketed as a series of highly popular animated films. But the reality of this period in our history is in many ways very different. Packs of wolves, fierce sabre-toothed cats, huge ground sloths and giant deer wandered through the cold and windswept landscapes of the north. But without doubt the creature that still sums up this bleak period in the earth's history is the mammoth.

The name 'mammoth' derives from a Siberian word for the animal which was brought to western Europe in an account by a seventeenth-century Dutch traveller. It was introduced into general use by Hans Sloane, founder of the British Museum, writing about the elephant remains in his collection for his lecture to the Royal Society, when he became its president in 1727. Sloane recognised these large fossilised bones belonged to an elephant from a different climate before the time of the Flood, rather than the biblical human giants they were previously assumed to be, but nevertheless it is as a giant that this animal has entered our language as a metaphor. As John Simpson, editor-in-chief of the *Oxford English Dictionary*, notes, like the word 'monster', 'mammoth' is now shorthand for anything larger than life.

Apart from the use of the word as a synonym for something almost unbelievably huge, it would be easy to assume that the mammoth – a creature that became extinct around 4,000 years ago – has little relevance to our modern-day world. And yet mammoths still loom large in our lives – if we just know where to look.

Mammoths formed the now extinct genus *Mammuthus*. They were close relatives of the elephants that today are the largest land animals on earth. They lived alongside our ancestors, and may well have heard that flute music, for their lives were closely inter-twined with that of the human population. Woolly mammoths were hunted for food, while their skins were used for clothing, their tusks were carved into ornate sculptures, their ribs were used as tent poles, their skulls were made into drums to make music, and their images were painted on cave walls. They were vital to our ancestors' survival.

The common image we have is of shaggy elephantine beasts roaming across the icy wastes of Siberia and Arctic North America; yet in fact the places where they lived were fertile grasslands. They were not the only species that existed. Many thousands of years before the Ice Age, and before the mammoth got woolly, our own ancient ancestors lived alongside a less hairy species. If you want to see the jaw-dropping skull of this monster mammoth, it can be seen on display in the Natural History Museum. It is known as the Ilford Mammoth, after the location in suburban Essex where it was unearthed in 1864. Adrian Lister is the museum's specialist in mammoth evolution:

> This really is one of the most spectacular fossils ever discovered in Britain. The tusks on this specimen are about 2½ metres long, and the skull as a whole – including the tusks – is at least 4 metres long. A mammoth tusk takes two strong men to lift it off the ground, and yet this animal was walking around with two of them sticking out the front of its head.

At about 200,000 years old, the Ilford Mammoth represents an early stage of the evolution into what today we recognise as a woolly mammoth. It would have been about 3.5 metres tall at the shoulder, weighing about 5 or 6 tonnes – roughly the same size as a bull African elephant, though other species did grow much larger. Its hunting grounds would have been around the banks of the River Thames, whose course at that time ran further north than it does today. These huge beasts, sporting their simply enormous tusks, didn't live alone; mammoths were part of a rich fauna that lived in east London, and indeed across much of Britain and Europe. You can imagine predator pitched against prey, the roars and screams, the fights and the blood as they battled it out in the endless struggle for survival – they were the original East Enders.

The lifetime of this beast coincided with one of the warmer periods between Ice Ages, known as an 'interglacial', which also allowed human beings to thrive, as Adrian Lister explains:

> There were people in Britain at the same time as the Ilford Mammoth: early Neanderthals, who used stone tools, and left bone remains. Their role is still unsure: they were certainly eating meat,

but to what extent they were hunting animals or scavenging carcasses is a longstanding debate amongst archaeologists. I would presume that by this time – about 200,000 years ago – they were doing both.

For a few thousand years after the Ilford Mammoth finally sank into the riverside mud, the climate remained similar to today. But then, about 190,000 years ago, it began to get really, really cold. Apart from a brief warm interglacial period for about 15,000 years, Britain and Europe endured an ice age for many millennia. As the ice took its grip across Europe, those species that preferred warmer climes began to retreat southwards or disappear, and those better suited to life in the freezer gradually took over. The Neanderthals – heavily built, squat and rugged, a species of human very closely related to us, but particularly well adapted to life in cold environments – thrived. But then, 45,000 years ago, an important change took place: one that would have major consequences for all Ice Age wildlife, including the mammoth. Modern humans arrived in Europe.

Coming into Europe from Africa, via the Middle East, *Homo sapiens* was not at first well suited to living in cold climates. But these early humans were nothing if not adaptable: their intelligence enabled them to learn to stitch animal skins together to make very warm and effective clothing, and tents where they could live through even the coldest winters. For the next few thousand years, modern humans and Neanderthals managed an uneasy coexistence, alongside the wild animals that could also survive this bitter, bone-chilling cold. One of these was the mammoth – now evolved into an altogether hairier beast. Stomping into our lives – massive and shaggy – the woolly mammoth and our ancestors braved the Ice Age together.

We know a lot today about the woolly mammoth thanks to one crucial factor: when the animals that roamed across Siberia died they froze solid and were then buried in the permafrost. Adrian Lister has been able to describe their lifestyle:

They lived in what is essentially an open landscape: there were very few trees, because that far north it was too cold for tree growth. What you did have was a very rich growth of vegetation such as grasses, flowering plants and small shrubs. So there were not only very large numbers of mammoths – remember, these were animals that lived in herds – but also rhinoceroses, horses, bison and so on. It's a mistake to think of the Ice Age as some desperately difficult time with only a few animals managing to eke out a living. Although it was colder than today, it was very productive: there was a lot of vegetation and food growing to support these herds of large animals. There had to be, or they wouldn't have been there.

The 30,000-year-old flute that opened this chapter comes from the middle of this icy time. The people who carved it from mammoth tusk and played those haunting melodies were the same as us – they loved music for a start – but they lived in a land that is far removed from anything we can imagine in the twenty-first century. They were hunter-gatherers living in small bands and dependent on the creatures of the Ice Age. Jill Cook specialises in Palaeolithic culture at the British Museum:

They're the same sort of people as us: fully modern humans, with the same brain. They express themselves in complex language and, brought forward in time, they could drive cars, use mobile phones, and so on. Back then, they were part of an environment with plains teeming with game, amongst which they were the least numerous of the species. So amongst this extraordinary animal kingdom here we were as humans, taking all this in; aware that we were part of this, but also different, because we're thinking, we're communal, we have the use of fire. We did lots of things that are different yet we were still part of this world.

Being surrounded by so much rich life soaked into their minds, into their culture and into their art and beliefs.

They saw mammoths almost every day; they recognised particular individuals and may have even named them. And this really comes out through the representations of these animals that they made. And right from the earliest sculptures about 40,000 years ago, right up to the end of the Ice Age about 12,000 years ago, mammoths are ever-present in their art.

Just as more modern human beings used elephant tusks to create ornate works of art, so our ancestors used mammoth ivory, as Adrian Lister explains: 'The use of ivory for weapons, ornaments and works of art goes back more than 40,000 years. These are both functional objects and also artistic ones: we have beautiful sculptures of animals including the mammoths themselves.'

The British Museum collection has a 20,000-year-old weapon carved from a reindeer antler in the form of a mammoth, as well as an exquisite sculpture of a pair of reindeer made from the tip of a mammoth tusk. The weapon, a spear thrower, is one of only two known examples depicting a mammoth. Although essentially caricaturing the beast, it captures the mammoth's defining characteristics. Just a few centimetres long, it is unmistakably a tiny mammoth, beautifully observed with that characteristic hump on the head and the sloping back. The obvious care and attention that went into these sculptures and paintings tells us about the people who made them, as Jill Cook points out:

They're thinking about the animal that they're looking at – and they're putting something of themselves into this creature. With the paintings, sometimes on a cave wall all you see is the hump, the feet, the line of the back and the tail. It's enough to tell you instantly 'mammoth'. Like a cartoon, you don't need the full detail to know what it is. At other times they did go into detail: depicting the trunk, with its fantastically delicate end that would enable this beast to pick up a buttercup. So these creatures made a very important impression on artistic expression, and are also providing all sorts of raw materials and food.

Sculpting or sketching a mammoth from a distance is one thing – actively hunting it for food is quite another. Remember, some of these animals were the height of a double-decker bus and the hunters would only have had wooden spears with a sharp point made of stone. Adrian Lister is not convinced that the usual image we have of hunters chasing down the mighty mammoth is the true picture:

> My view of mammoth hunting is that it was a relatively rare occupation. There were lots of easier animals to hunt: horses, bison and deer, whereas a mammoth would have been a very dangerous animal. But we do have evidence that at least on occasion people did hunt mammoths: there's a mammoth skeleton found in Siberia, which has been carbon-dated to about 14,000 years ago, with the tip of a flint spear-point embedded in the vertebra.

Jill Cook speculates on a deeper relationship between the hunters and their different kinds of quarry:

> They need these animals to survive, and yet they do things that enable them to overcome them. So it's a developing relationship, and these early humans may have seen the supernatural represented within that system too. These animals may have been ways in which they could connect with different realms of the cosmos; part of a religious, as well as an everyday, life.

So from roughly 200,000 years ago we see early humans living with mammoths in balmy conditions on the edge of what is now London. Then, during the Ice Ages, modern humans developed a complex and intimate relationship with the woolly mammoth, relying on it for all kinds of things from food, tools and clothing, to art and spiritual expression. This tension with an animal that supplied so much became a wellspring of creativity. Fast-forward thousands of years to the present day, and the human–mammoth tension provided the foundation for the storyline for the first of the hugely popular *Ice Age* films, which appeared in 2002.

The story of *Ice Age* revolves around a Neanderthal baby, Roshan, who is rescued by a massive, grumpy and unsociable woolly mammoth called Manny, and ultimately returned to his father. Yet at first, Manny is very reluctant to help the infant, as he understandably holds a grudge against the people who try to hunt and kill him. Michael J. Wilson, the film's writer, explains why he chose a grumpy mammoth as his lead character:

> I placed the mammoth at the centre of my story because during my research at the library I found out that during the Ice Age, Neanderthals and mammoths actually coexisted. The Neanderthals were using the mammoths for everything – shelter, food, jewellery and so on. If you were a mammoth and you saw a Neanderthal you would be like a deer in the headlights; you would be looking at your biggest fear and your mortal enemy. If you were a mammoth and trying to teach your family the ways of the world, the first thing you would point out to your children would be 'stay away from the humans'. It just struck me as a fantastic thing if we could find a situation where a Neanderthal actually owed a mammoth something: that instead of seeing a mammoth and killing it, they would want to protect it and thank it for saving a member of their family.

In reality events did not turn out so well for the woolly mammoth – nor, indeed, for the Neanderthals (who, incidentally, being confined to Europe, would never have come across sabre-toothed cats and much of the other fauna in the film). The Neanderthals eventually disappeared somewhere around 40,000 years ago. Mammoths survived much longer, though most populations had become extinct by the end of the last Ice Age, roughly 12,000 years ago. Yet some did manage to survive far longer – only finally dying out surprisingly recently, as Adrian Lister reveals:

We've realised in recent years that some did survive on islands, such as St Paul Island off the cost of Alaska, where they lived until about 6,500 years ago; we've also got Wrangel Island off the north coast of Siberia, where we have the very last population of mammoths, and the radiocarbon dates from there show they survived until about 4,000 years ago. So these 'prehistoric' animals survived into the beginnings of civilisations such as the Egyptians.

They may have gone, but their frozen bodies, many still with skin and hair, remained locked in icy wastes until they appear, eerily, out of the frozen soil, or are dug up by people. What on earth did new settlers on the now ice-free areas make of these huge creatures emerging whole from the ground? Adrienne Mayer is a researcher in the Classics Department of Stanford University:

The entire creature has been frozen – naturally preserved, mummi-fied if you like – in the permafrost from which they eventually erode out. So indigenous people of the Arctic came up with theor-ies about these being burrowing animals that lived underground, avoiding the sunlight; and that all died when they emerged into the bright sunshine. That would explain why you find them coming out of the icy ground, looking as if they had just died.

A giant burrowing beast is an extraordinary thought, but people didn't just create myths. In some areas where the mammoth died out only in the last few thousand years, hunting them may have been a genuine memory, passed down through generations and still being passed on today: 'There are some stories I [Mayer] found amongst the Abenaki people of north-east Canada, who had an oral tradition that in the remote past their ancestors used to hunt a gigantic elk-like creature with a long, arm-like appendage stretching from its head. That sounds a lot like a mammoth.'

Other people folded the discovery of mammoth bones into the beliefs of their time, incorporating them into established religion:

In Europe during the Middle Ages, most people believed when they found the bones of mammoths that these were the giants who had been destined to perish in the Flood sent by God. The British naturalist William Catesby was visiting the Carolinas in the 1700s, and was there when a group of African slaves belonging to a plantation-owner ploughed up a huge tooth. Everyone came from miles around to see it, and everyone believed that this must have come from a giant who died in Noah's Flood. But remarkably enough, it was the African slaves who correctly identified the tooth as belonging to an elephant. They were the first people to correctly identify a mammoth fossil anywhere in the Americas.

Throughout the centuries we have pondered on the remains of woolly mammoths – and sometimes more than pondered. In 1872 the *New York Times* reported that some French adventurers heading for the North Pole found so many well-preserved mammoth specimens that for a time they 'lived entirely on mammoth meat, broiled, roasted and baked' – though this claim has never been proven. But true or not, these accounts of people digging up mammoths from the great freezer of the north and making dinner intrigued the writer Hilaire Belloc so much that he wrote a poem called 'The Frozen Mammoth':

This Creature, though rare, is still found to the East
Of the Northern Siberian Zone.
It is known to the whole of that primitive group
That the carcass will furnish an excellent soup,
Though the cooking it offers one drawback at least
(Of a serious nature I own):
If the skin be but punctured before it is boiled,
Your confection is wholly and utterly spoiled.
And hence (on account of the size of the beast)
The dainty is nearly unknown.

But nowadays, when people discover a woolly mammoth carcass or skeleton some are more interested in the tusks. For thousands of years, while the beasts still roamed the earth, mammoth ivory was carved into beautiful objects. But this didn't end with their extinction. Because the mammoth carcasses came out of the ground in such good condition, they seemed as fresh as the ivory from living elephants – and in some ways easier to obtain. The carving of ivory is of course hugely skilled and the American poet George Henry Boker wrote about his wonder at seeing a figure emerge from the carved tusk of a mammoth in his 1857 poem 'The Ivory Carver':

> Yet even earthly natures may beget
> Grand ends, and common things be wrought
> To holiest uses. I in thought
> Have seen the capability
> Which lies within yon ivory:
> This rough, black husk, charred by long age,
> Unmarked by man since, in his rage,
> A warring mammoth shed it. Lo!
> Whiter than heaven-sifted snow,
> Enclosed within its ugly mask
> Lies a world's wonder; and the task
> Of slow development shall be
> Man's labor and man's glory. See!
> His foot-tip touched it; the rude bone
> Glowed through translucent, widely shone
> A morning lustre on the palm
> Which arched above it.

The trade in ancient mammoth ivory continues to this day, fuelled by the tens of thousands of mammoth carcasses still buried throughout the Arctic tundra, as Adrian Lister explains:

It's still legal to trade in mammoth ivory, so you can still buy little ivory objects in shops in Russia. In Siberia the mammoth tusks are now being commercially dug out of the ground, and that is feeding an industry producing very beautiful carved objects. The smaller ones are popular with tourists, but you can also purchase – if you have the wherewithal – magnificent carved tusks that have taken years of work for a craftsman to produce. These are traded internationally, and that's all legal because the mammoth is an extinct species.

One issue with the current situation is the potential to substitute a legally produced carving in mammoth ivory with an illegal one made from elephant tusks. A cross-section of both elephant and mammoth ivory reveals a criss-cross pattern; the angle is subtly different between the two but only experts can tell the difference.

Esmond Martin and Lucy Vigne produced a report on the mammoth ivory trade for Save the Elephants and the Aspinall Foundation in 2014:

> We don't know an exact figure of how much mammoth ivory is traded, but we do know where the major markets are. Much of it – about 70 tonnes a year – is exported directly from Russia to Hong Kong and China. We don't know the trade in elephant ivory, but we can estimate the number of elephants being poached each year – perhaps 25,000 animals – producing about 100 tonnes of ivory.

Lucy Vigne takes an ambivalent view of the current situation:

> The mammoth ivory trade is a double-edged sword. In one way it's an opportunity for someone to buy a piece of ivory legally; but elephant ivory also can be confused with mammoth ivory, especially for smaller items. When trading the raw material – the tusks – it is easy to distinguish mammoth from elephant ivory, but when it is carved, and the outer layer removed, it can be easily confused. So mammoth ivory can act as a cover for elephant ivory.

The figures, though hard to pin down exactly, show that up to 50 per cent of the trade in ivory into China is mammoth ivory, and the demand is increasing every year, despite attempts by the government to stop it. Adrian Lister believes that all trade in ivory (apart from certified antiques) should be banned, not just from elephants, so that mammoth ivory carvings are not able to keep the demand going. And he has an unusual suggestion to make this happen: 'I think there's actually an argument for making the mammoth the first ever extinct species to be listed by CITES [the Convention on International Trade in Endangered Species]. Both of the living elephant species are listed by CITES, which means that international trade in elephant ivory for the most part is banned.'

If you'll forgive the terminology, it looks as though putting mammoths on the CITES list of endangered species may well prove to be something of a mammoth task. Which brings us to the question: when did that expression, and others like it, first enter the English language? Kelvin Corlett works on the *Oxford English Dictionary*:

The earliest example we have of the word 'mammoth' being used to describe something huge is 1801, in a letter written by Thomas Jefferson [the third President of the United States], where he discusses a 'mammoth cheese'. And around this time there are lots of examples, including an entry in a private diary, which rather unkindly describes dancers in a theatre production as having 'mammoth legs'. So this expression really caught on very quickly, and became part of our culture.

Mammoths, woolly or smooth, have lumbered their way into our lives and are staying put, in our minds and hearts, if not in the flesh. And we still have the wonderful Ice Age art and sculpture to remind us of just how truly extraordinary these animals once were.

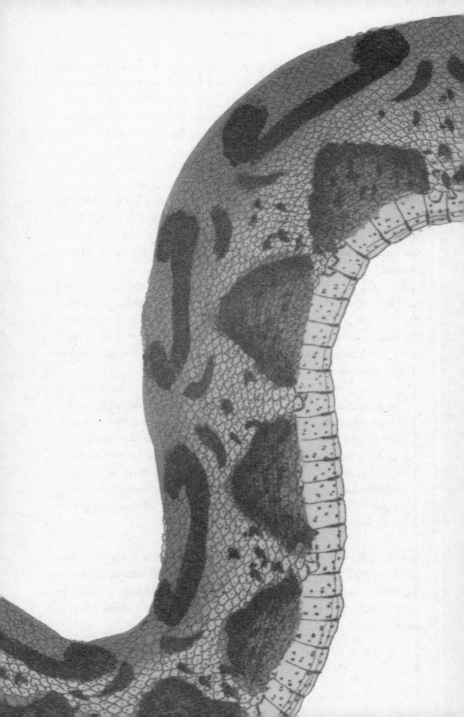

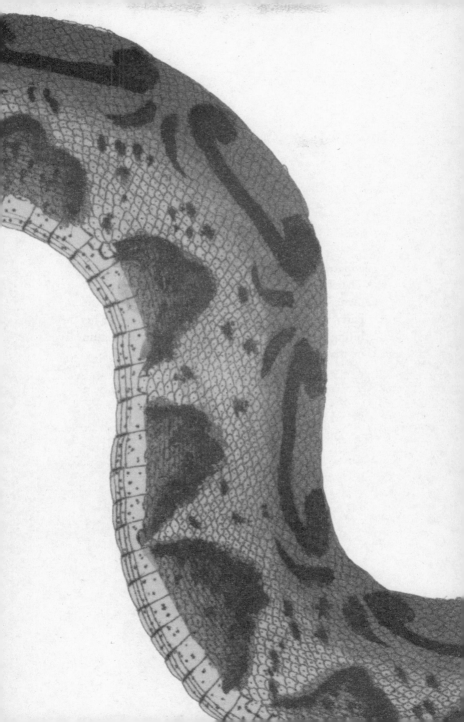

Cleopatra: Hast thou the pretty worm of Nilus there,
That kills and pains not?

Clown: Truly, I have him: but I would not be the
party that should desire you to touch him, for his
biting is immortal; those that do die of it do seldom
or never recover.

Antony and Cleopatra, v: 2

Snakes

Venom and Antidote

The snake makes his first appearance in the Bible in the third chapter of the Book of Genesis; and it would be fair to say that he doesn't make a very good impression: 'Now the serpent was more crafty than any of the wild animals the Lord God had made. He said to the woman, "Did God really say, 'You must not eat from any tree in the garden'?"'

Using all his arts of persuasion, in Adam's absence, the crafty snake coaxes Eve to take a bite of the forbidden fruit. She does so, and as a result Adam and Eve – and the whole of the future human race – are cast out of the Garden of Eden. It all goes downhill from there. Eve blames the serpent for deceiving her, and from that moment on, the sly and sinister snake takes the blame for our Fall from Grace, and will for ever be considered untrustworthy and – for many – evil. The wrathful Old Testament God leaves us in no doubt as to how we should regard these duplicitous creatures:

> Cursed are you above all livestock
> and all wild animals!
> You will crawl on your belly
> and you will eat dust
> all the days of your life.

And I will put enmity
>between you and the woman,
>and between your offspring and hers;
>he will crush your head,
>and you will strike his heel.

But perhaps this version of the story isn't quite as cut and dried as it might at first appear. Richard Kerridge is a nature writer and lecturer at Bath Spa University, who has a lifelong fascination with reptiles, especially snakes:

In that story there is a deep ambivalence, because the Fall was a catastrophe that produced a world dominated by Original Sin. Because of the Fall, human beings became mortal, capable of evil and treachery, and subject to the randomness of fate; but because of it they also became creatures that could be responsible for their own redemption, their own salvation from damnation. And without the Fall there would have been no intercession by Christ. So paradoxically the snake is at once an object of terror and loathing and one of gratitude. And thus our ambivalence about our whole condition then focuses on the snake, and becomes our ambivalence about snakes.

Nevertheless, this story has had serious consequences: in many cultures it's considered sensible to kill any snake on sight. Snakes are among the most persecuted creatures on earth: during the pioneering conquest of the Wild West in nineteenth-century North America, rattlesnakes were virtually wiped out.

Even when we don't subscribe to snake genocide, the word is always used in a loaded way: from expressions such as 'snake in the grass' (a metaphor first used, incidentally, by the Roman poet Virgil) to 'snake-oil', meaning a fraudulent health product or unproven medicine. Comparing someone to a snake is almost always an insult, unless, of course, you are referring to their hips or sinuous dancing. But as with the serpent in the Garden of Eden, it's not always as black and white as that.

One case in point is one of the most popular and enduring children's board games, snakes and ladders. The premise of the game is simple: it's a race to get to the end. The board is a grid of squares with snakes and ladders on them. Each player throws the dice in turn, and if they land on a square with the bottom of a ladder on it, they go up it; but if they land on a snake's head, they slide all the way down its body to the tail. The moral couldn't be clearer: good children succeed and are rewarded; naughty ones fail and are not. The early versions of the game, which first appeared in Britain towards the end of Queen Victoria's reign in 1892, made this message much more explicit. The vices of Cruelty, Covetousness, Unpunctuality and Avarice were written on the snake squares, and the virtues ranging across Patience, Kindness, Forgiveness and all the way to Self-denial were on the ladder squares, often accompanied by self-explanatory illustrations. Catherine Howell, the Collections Manager at the Victoria and Albert Museum of Childhood, explains the rationale behind the design of the board:

Victorian morality at the time is shown really well: Pride coming before a Fall is portrayed as a man in a top hat walking along with a peacock behind him (as a symbol of Pride); and going all the way down the snake, he has literally fallen over, as the peacock flies away. [At the top of another snake] you have a little child being selfish by eating an extra slice of cake; and you go down that snake and the child has ended up at the bottom with toothache.

However, it turns out that as usual the Victorians were borrowing the idea from elsewhere and that the game is very old indeed. The original Indian game – hence all those snakes – was played by adults, not children; and before the nineteenth century it did not feature ladders, instead showing two kinds of snake: good and evil. Under the name Moksha Patam, it has been played in India for hundreds of years. It too was a moral exercise that was designed to make the players aware of the role of karma or fate. Both the Hindu and Jain religions had their own separate versions.

Deepak Shimkhada is Professor at the Claremont School of Theology in California:

The idea of such a game existed perhaps at the time of the Buddha [between the sixth and fourth centuries BC], but since then, over the centuries it has had many modifications. The black snake – a cobra – stands for evil, and if you land on its head the snake swallows you and you end up at its tail, whereas the red snake, or naga (a mythical serpent), brings goodness, prosperity and good luck, and is worthy of worship. So it serves as a ladder.

The Indian version also had a higher purpose: Moksha Patam was used as a tool for teaching the effects of good deeds versus bad. The board was covered with symbolic images, the top featuring gods, angels and majestic beings, while the rest of the board displayed pictures of animals, flowers and people. The morality lesson of the game was that a person can attain salvation (*moksha*) through doing good, whereas by doing evil one will be reborn into a lower form of life. The number of red snakes was less than the number of black as a reminder that a good path is much more difficult to tread than a path of sins. 'The game was to measure one's level of karma, like a measuring rod. Someone who has good karma would be able to reach his destination, and those with bad karma would not be able to progress and obviously would be the losers. It's a karma barometer,' says Deepak Shimkhada.

By the nineteenth century the good snakes had been replaced by ladders – perhaps because to our Victorian forebears, the idea of a 'good snake' was something they couldn't understand – and the game appealed to the sturdy Christianity of the British colonials stationed in India. They saw it as a Game of Life: if you behaved badly you slid down the snakes to hell; but if you behaved well you went straight up to heaven.

Snakes and ladders is not just an enjoyable way to pass a rainy afternoon, or to improve your moral tone; it also fascinates mathematicians because previous moves have no influence on current and future ones – unlike chess or draughts – the odds of moving to the next square being fixed and finite. On average, on a board with 100 squares and nineteen snakes or ladders, a player will take about forty moves to reach the last square. And the first player also has a marginal advantage – they are likely to win 50.9 per cent of the time.

One feature of snakes and ladders – the ability to be close to victory and then go right back to the beginning by landing on the head of a snake – is thought to have introduced the phrase 'back to square one' into the English language.

The original version of snakes and ladders highlights the complex relationship we have with snakes. They can be both good and bad, evil and helpful, in our journey through life; and this duality slides through our culture and winds its way – rather like a snake itself – through art, literature and religion. Time, perhaps, to take a closer look at the reality – rather than the myth – of snakes.

Snakes are long, legless, carnivorous vertebrate animals that, together with lizards, belong to the order Squamata, or 'scaled reptiles'. There are almost 3,000 different species, found on every continent bar Antarctica, and from the Arctic Circle to the southern part of South America. They can live at below sea level, in the case of the world's sixty or so species of sea snakes, which live in the Pacific and Indian Oceans, and as high as 4,900 metres above sea level, in the Andes and Himalayas. They are, however, absent from many islands, including New Zealand, Iceland and famously Ireland, due to the inability of terrestrial snakes to swim across even narrow stretches of sea, rather than because kindly saints like St Patrick banished them.

They are known to have evolved from lizards; but there is some controversy as to which route they took: were their ancestors burrowing lizards, found on land, or did they evolve in the sea, from marine lizards? At present the jury is out, but we do know that they first appeared on earth roughly 150 million years ago, during the Jurassic period, and began to diversify into the different groups we see today around 60 million years ago.

Snakes can still be confused with legless lizards such as the slow-worm, but have several key differences, including their inability to blink – a snake's eyes are always open. Their exterior is made up of a series of tightly overlapping scales, creating what appears to be a smooth surface. Their bodies have several crucial adaptations as a result of their unusually elongated shape: notably organs such as their kidneys are not placed side by side but one in front of the other; they completely lack front limbs and have only rudimentary 'spurs' instead of hind limbs; and their skeletons are basically a long, extended ribcage, with up to 400 vertebrae. They lack external ears and, instead, detect vibrations from the ground via their jaws. Most famously of all, snakes have an incredibly flexible jaw structure, enabling them to open their mouths wide enough to swallow prey much larger than you would imagine – usually live and whole.

Snakes vary considerably in size. There is the tiny Barbados threadsnake, a blind, wormlike creature endemic to that Caribbean island, whose adults measure just 10 centimetres long. At the other end of the scale two species vie for supremacy: the reticulated python of South East Asia, which can reach a length of almost 7 metres; and the South American anaconda, which although 'only' 5.2 metres long, tips the scales at almost 100 kilos. But these are dwarfed by the largest snake that ever lived: *Titanoboa cerrejonensis*, which roamed South America about 60 million years ago, and was 13 metres long.

Today's snakes are excellent hunters, using their acute sense of smell to track down their prey; and then their forked tongue to both taste and smell, and to work out the direction of their victim. Although their eyesight differs a great deal between species, some snakes (such as rattlesnakes) have a very special sense: the ability to perceive infrared rays through special receptors on their upper lips, enabling them to detect the heat given off by any potential prey – a useful asset given that many snakes hunt after dark.

Being constantly in contact with the ground means their skin needs to be both tough and flexible; hence the need for snakes to shed their skin from time to time – up to four times a year for some individuals, and even more frequently for baby snakes.

The most obvious characteristic of snakes – one that every child knows – is their venomous bite. Except that the majority of snakes are not venomous; and even those that are, do not habitually attack or bite humans – the venom is normally used to paralyse their prey. Non-venomous snakes either use constriction techniques to kill, or, if their victim is small enough, swallow it alive.

Yet sufficient numbers of snakes are venomous to explain the long-running enmity between people and snakes. This distrust isn't purely a cultural artefact: modern psychological research has shown it is hard-wired into our neurones too. Gordon Orians is a Professor of Biology at Washington State University:

> It's not surprising that we have an inborn fear of snakes, because until fairly recently our ancestors lived in small hunter-gatherer groups, and were in constant contact with nature, 24 hours a day and 365 days a year. They had to deal with the many challenges that nature posed; and among the challenges were dangers – things that could hurt us. Throughout the history of primates snakes have been a very important cause of mortality, and in areas of the tropics they still are today. So learning how to detect and avoid snakes would have been very important for our ancestors.

We are not the only species hard-wired to fear snakes: monkeys raised in captivity, that have never seen a snake, show extremely strong responses when they are confronted with one. Human eyesight even shows a special sensitivity to that distinctive tessellated pattern along the backs of many snakes – a pattern very rare in the rest of nature.

It is of course sensible to avoid snakes, especially those that may be venomous: about 720 species worldwide, of which roughly one-third can kill a human with a single bite. Although the number of human deaths from snakebites is mercifully rare in the developed world, the same is not true elsewhere. In India alone it is thought that as many as 50,000 people die each year from snakebite.

The vaults of the Natural History Museum contain millions of preserved animals, including the head and gaping jaws of an African Gaboon viper. According to Ronald Jenner, researcher in the Department of Life Sciences, among herpetologists this particular snake is renowned for having the largest fangs and injecting the most amount of venom into its victim:

> If you look at the animal you can already infer something about its biology: it looks like a dried leaf, pale with darker brown spots; and this is perfect camouflage for when the snake lies in wait for its prey on the forest floor. It's actually quite docile, and can spend a lot of time without moving; but then when the prey comes near, it strikes in the typical manner of snakes, with its mouth wide open, with its two very large fangs – about 5 centimetres long – through which the snake injects its venom.

Rather than paralysing, the venom of the Gaboon viper works differently: once the prey is bitten it starts to bleed internally, the blood vessels relax, and its blood pressure drops very rapidly. This causes shock, and that's how the snake prevents its victim from escaping. The other difference with this species is that unlike most snakes, which bite their prey and then let go to avoid being injured as the victim struggles, the Gaboon viper keeps a tight hold with those fearsome fangs, until its quarry finally becomes immobile and is ready to eat.

It's a gruesome – though fairly quick – death, but as well as providing a suitable horror story to terrify newcomers to the African bush, the effect of the snake's venom is also of great interest to scientists. Venom is a highly complex cocktail of different chemicals, all of which do specific damage to the body. And in a neat reversal of expectations, this can be harnessed to save life as well as cause death, as Ronald Jenner explains:

Venom components have been shaped by evolution to do one specific thing very carefully – for instance they will knock out one pathway, with which two nerve cells communicate, with almost no side effects. Those abilities can be exploited to develop drugs; and there are already several different drugs derived from snake venom available, and being used for treatment for blood clots, and also for the opposite use, to stem bleeding during operations. So snake venoms have been developed into very useful tools.

Venom from all kinds of animals, not just snakes, is now used in medicine to control pain, to slow the heart rate, to treat cancer and lower blood pressure. Snake venom is even used in anti-wrinkle cream, because it can stop the skin from contracting.

The connection between snakes and health is not a modern phenomenon. The Rod of Asclepius – showing a snake wrapped around a long staff – has been the symbol of healing for over 2,000 years. Asclepius was the Greek god of healing, and he had two symbols: the snake and the staff. The staff represents support, helping someone to walk; the snake, knowledge – and if you think about the serpent in the Garden of Eden you can understand that in classical times the snake was very much associated with the acquisition of knowledge. It's also an animal that sheds its skin and so can rejuvenate itself. So when you put those two together – the rod and the serpent – they have come to symbolise medicine.

In classical Greece, temples established in the name of Asclepius became centres of healing – you might even call them the first medical schools – and Hippocrates was a graduate of one of them. But aside from being places where people went to be healed or learn about healing, the temples would also have been places where, because of their symbolism, snakes would be allowed to live and roam free. There is even a species of snake in the eastern Mediterranean called the Asclepian snake, named as a result of this tradition.

Oddly, the Asclepian (or as it is sometimes known, the Aesculapian) snake can be found living wild in the middle of London: along the banks of the Regent's Canal near London Zoo, where a small, self-sustaining population was released and became established during the 1980s. Fortunately for passing Londoners, this particular species of snake is not venomous, but is a constrictor, squeezing the breath from its victims; so apart from striking terror into the local rodent population, it does no harm.

Since the time of ancient Greece the symbolism of the Rod of Asclepius has spread globally; a process that began when Alexander the Great conquered much of Asia, carried on through the Roman Empire, and continues to this day. The symbol crops up in many places, with hundreds of different organisations – including the British Medical Association, ambulances and some commercial pharmacy chains – using it as an instantly recognisable shorthand for medical care.

Despite these benevolent associations, snakes continue to terrify most people, as the success of the 2006 action thriller movie *Snakes on a Plane*, starring Samuel L. Jackson, bears witness. The plot, as anyone suffering from ophidiophobia (a fear of snakes) would appreciate, is pretty terrifying: hundreds of these venomous creatures are released on a passenger plane in an attempt to kill a witness to a crime. Although highly exaggerated, the film is loosely based on a real event, when Indonesian brown tree snakes (one of those species that is venomous but not enough to threaten humans) climbed aboard a cargo plane during the Second World War.

J.K. Rowling used snakes as a dark theme throughout her Harry Potter novels. Voldemort, the villain so terrifying that most characters refer to him as 'You-Know-Who' rather than dare say his name, has a special affinity with snakes and is one of the few characters who can speak their hissing sibilant language, Parseltongue. D.H. Lawrence, a poet and novelist never afraid of celebrating a phallic symbol, wrote a fascinating poem that explores our contradictory relationship with snakes. Lawrence is mesmerised by the majesty of a snake – which he comes across by chance on a hot summer's day in Sicily:

> He lifted his head from his drinking, as cattle do,
> And looked at me vaguely, as drinking cattle do,
> And flickered his two-forked tongue from his lips, and mused a
>   moment,
> And stooped and drank a little more,
> Being earth-brown, earth-golden from the burning bowels of the
>   earth . . .

While Lawrence is intellectually fascinated by the snake, he cannot override his teaching that it is his ancient enemy:

> The voice of my education said to me
> He must be killed,
> For in Sicily the black, black snakes are innocent, the gold are
>   venomous.

Lawrence is unable to go through with actually killing the reptile, and ends up throwing a log in the water-trough where the snake is drinking to scare it away:

> And immediately I regretted it.
> I thought how paltry, how vulgar, what a mean act!
> I despised myself and the voices of my accursed human education.

So what is it that the snake represented that made Lawrence's educated self want to kill it? Sometimes this is interpreted as being about sexuality, about a kind of innocent joy in sexuality that is suddenly interrupted by fear and a kind of panic-stricken recoil. But it doesn't only have to mean that. Perhaps what Lawrence is also looking for is some sort of world in which we really do not need to be dominated by our very traditional attitudes towards these creatures; by the old morality play that we traditionally impose upon the non-human world. Richard Kerridge argues that we should understand it differently: we can see a snake as part of its environment, as another manifestation of life, an essential part of the whole ecosystem; we can even find it beautiful. Lawrence says, 'I missed my chance with one of the lords of life', and that phrase returns the snake to being regarded as an amazing natural phenomenon rather than representing it as a villainous, treacherous outsider as it has so often been portrayed.

Although we have an inbuilt fear of snakes hard-wired into our brains, we do have a choice as to how we respond to that fear, as Gordon Orians explains:

> There certainly is a tremendous variability in how strong the snake fear is: some people have it very powerfully, while others have it very weakly. But this is not surprising: we are a sexually reproducing, highly variable species, and so any particular trait can also be highly variable – anyone who has raised kids knows this – and that's the way it is with every response that we have.

So while many people – probably the majority – are fearful of snakes, at the other end of the scale are a few who simply love them. For these rare ophidiophiles, snakes are simply beautiful, compelling creatures they have to get close to. Nigel Marven, naturalist, animal-wrangler and TV presenter, is one such person, who has kept snakes since he was a child. His enthusiasm for his favourite snake, a four-year-old bull snake named Bully, is infectious:

> This is a magnificent snake: I've had him since he was a tiny hatchling, and he's now longer than I am tall – nearly 2 metres. He's been specially bred for his colour: he has lovely pink blotches, and orange scales – he really is one of my favourite pets. They are so beautiful: when I was a boy and kept my first snakes as pets I used to admire their patterns, as every snake seems to be different; they really are things of beauty.

So whether you are terrified or passionate about snakes, one thing cannot be denied: that since Eve was first tempted by the serpent in the Garden of Eden, these fascinating creatures have wound their way intricately through our lives.

> yes, in spite of all,
Some shape of beauty moves away the pall
From our dark spirits. Such the sun, the moon,
Trees old and young, sprouting a shady boon
For simple sheep; and such are daffodils
With the green world they live in;

Keats, *Endymion*

Daffodils

Narcissistic Poetry

It's late March and a rapier wind is doing its best to deny spring. We're being tugged westwards, after checking Met Office reports and calendar to catch the flowers at their fleeting best. Our goal is a corner of Gloucestershire where the M50 burrows through oak and fir woods east of Ross-on-Wye. Get the timing right and they are obvious even at speed from the car, pale yellow stars over-brimming the coppice and spilling down the motorway embankments as if the wood were too full to hold them: wild daffodils.

Wild flowers have always nourished our senses as well as providing more tangible comforts in the form of herbal remedies and foods, but few have the daffodil's power to get under our skin. Poets have famously fallen under their spell. Their charm may lie in the impertinence of their sudden appearance in the teeth of a March gale.

There's also a disbelief, perhaps, that such a flamboyant flower is at large in our countryside: daffodils are as blowsy and exotic as the finest orchids. We can also measure our lives against their appearance. Like a spring snowfall, the delights of daffodils are short-lived, a bittersweet reminder of the year's turning. They appear as blue-green stubs as early as January, pushing through the packed winter earth or snow, and as winter wanes the green pod-shaped flower buds extend beyond the leaves. Shaking off the dry papery sheath, the flower unfurls, a halo of half petals/half sepals called tepals surrounding the corona, better known as the trumpet. The sweet scent attracts pollinating insects, especially bumblebees and some hoverflies that cross-fertilise the flowers. For some people it's the quintessence of spring, but for others it has a whiff of animal waste, because of chemicals known as indoles which not everyone can detect. Some even go as far as to warn of the risk of placing a vase of daffodils in a bedroom at night: a nasty headache in the morning. Happily daffodil hangovers aren't a serious problem, but they are a reminder of the origins of its name. Narcissus derives from the Greek *narcao*, to numb.

Once native wild daffodils were common throughout the British Isles. The herbalist John Gerard described them as 'having narrowe leaves, thicke, fat, and full of slimie juice; among the which riseth up a naked stalke smooth and hollow, of a foot high' and noted that in the late sixteenth century they grew 'almost everywhere through England'. They spread rapidly by seed and especially by division of the bulbs, leading to natural clumps as new plants arise around the parents.

Heading towards Gloucestershire, gardens are already bright in every shade of yellow, but these are cultivated plants. Along with the rose, the daffodil is probably the most malleable British wild flower. Over centuries, we have hybridised daffodils of many species, subspecies and forms to produce a stunning array of varieties. Daffodils are naturally variable and growers have harnessed and hand-pollinated these variations to produce over 27,000 named varieties and hybrids. Our native daffodil has been crossed with Mediterranean varieties including *Narcissus cyclamineus* and *Narcissus tazetta* to produce large and colourful trumpets, from fiery orange to salmon pink, petals of cream, yellow and white, and multi-flowered and double varieties. On the way, the real wild daffodil has become increasingly marginalised in the modern countryside. Its bolder, brasher cultivars are now big business for florists and the horticulture trade. Planted in battalions on verges and village greens, they overshadow the wild plants, but in places the native is thriving thanks in part to poetic protection and, as we shall see, an increasing affection for its place in the landscape.

Our wild native daffodil (*Narcissus pseudonarcissus*) is disarming en masse or alone. Singly, the flowers are small and delicate, butter-and-cream-coloured, the outer tepals paler than the deep yellow trumpet. The poet Gerard Manley Hopkins noted the glistening quality of the tepals: 'the bright yellow corolla is seeded with very fine spangles which give it a glister and lie on a ribbing which makes it like a cloth of gold'. In sunlit meadows, they grow in dense sheaves, colouring the whole pasture. In shady woods and dingles, where the light is filtered through the tree canopy, the flowers are sparser and scattered among the blue-green grasslike leaves, in a constellation rather than a solid carpet.

The way each flower faces slightly downwards, and the fact that they can often be found growing along the edge of rivers and lakes, could well have inspired the story of Narcissus in classical mythology. In Ovid's version of the story in *Metamorphoses*, Narcissus became notorious for cruelly rebuffing all suitors. When one rejected lover prayed 'may he love like me and love like me in vain', the goddess of vengeance made him fall in love with himself and beautiful Narcissus wasted away, entranced by his own reflection in a pool. The ruddy pinks of his healthy complexion turn to a jaundiced yellow and he dies. After death his body changes into a beautiful flower, a narcissus or daffodil: 'when looking for his corps they only found / A rising stalk with yellow blossoms crown'd'.

Pliny the Elder, such a strong believer in empirical evidence that his death was the result of his inability to pass up the opportunity of personally cataloguing the volcanic eruption at Pompeii, argued that the plant's name *Narcissus* rather derives from the numbing, narcotic qualities of their bulbs and leaves, rather than from the story of Narcissus.

From benumbing to entrancement is a small step and daffodils have always entranced poets. In the corners of north Gloucestershire and south Herefordshire, wild daffodils put on a more spectacular display but they are always associated with Cumbria, thanks to William Wordsworth's celebrated poem. But their first literary appearance was in this diary entry, written by William's sister Dorothy on 15 April 1802:

> When we were in the woods beyond Gowbarrow park we saw a few daffodils close to the water side, we fancied that the lake had floated the seed ashore & that the little colony had so sprung up – But as we went along there were more & yet more & at last under the boughs of the trees, we saw that there was a long belt of them along the shore, about the breadth of a country turnpike road. I never saw daffodils so beautiful they grew among the mossy stones about & about them, some rested their heads upon these stones as on a pillow for weariness & the rest tossed and reeled and danced & seemed as if they verily laughed with the wind that blew upon them over the Lake, they looked so gay ever dancing ever changing. This wind blew directly over the lake to them. There was here & there a little knot & a few stragglers a few yards higher up but they were so few as not to disturb the simplicity & unity & life of that one busy highway.

Two years later William, who had seen them with her, wrote his best-known poem:

> I wandered lonely as a cloud
> That floats on high o'er vales and hills
> When all at once I saw a crowd
> A host of golden daffodils
> Beside the lake, beneath the trees
> Fluttering and dancing in the breeze.

Dorothy's observations of the flowers had been turned into something deeper. The poem's popularity, according to Professor Sally Bushell of the University of Lancaster, lies in its rhythm and simplicity. Because it was easy to memorise and recite, it became a favourite in schools and among poetry groups. But within its simplicity, the principles of Romanticism are still strong. The famous first line of Keats's poem that opens this chapter runs 'A thing of beauty is a joy forever': here Wordsworth captures and holds the experience to remember and revisit:

> For oft, when on my couch I lie
> In vacant or in pensive mood,
> They flash upon that inward eye
> Which is the bliss of solitude;
> And then my heart with pleasure fills,
> And dances with the daffodils.

It's the thought that counts. The poem has been described by ex-Poet Laureate Andrew Motion as 'not a great poem, but . . . a poem of real charm'. It certainly brings in the tourists. When recording on location for *Natural Histories* on the shores of Ullswater, we were accompanied by a coach party, snapping away at the diminutive flowers at their feet, picking a path through the turf of glaucous leaves. There weren't exactly a host of golden daffodils, but enough to make a local impression in this strip of stony woodland, sandwiched between road and lake.

But to see wild daffodils really colour the countryside, you need to go to the borders of Gloucestershire and Herefordshire where around the villages of Dymock and Kempley they grow in ready-made bunches in the pastures, under orchard trees and in open woods. Even where fields have been ploughed, they hang on as a yellow tidemark under the hedges, peering out from the sheltering thorns. So frequent were the wild daffodils that the area was once known as the Golden Triangle.

These daffodils inspired another group of poets. For a brief period between 1911 and 1914, Dymock was the haunt of several poets including Rupert Brooke, Robert Frost and Edward Thomas. The best-known poem written there was Robert Frost's 'The Road

Not Taken'. It's since become a mantra for lifestyle 'gurus' who see it as a meditation on choice and outcomes, but Frost never intended it to be deeply philosophical. The poem was rather a comment on his fellow poet Edward Thomas. Thomas and Frost took long walks together to explore the local woods and fields. Thomas carefully contrived routes aimed at taking in particular views or special wildlife but at the end of the walk would sometimes regret not taking a more productive path:

> Two roads diverged in a yellow wood.
> And sorry I could not travel both,
> And be one traveler, long I stood
> And looked down one as far as I could
> To where it bent in the undergrowth . . .

Why a yellow wood? You only have to visit the woods around Dymock now to see that daffodils line the paths and flood the clearings before the spring greenery appears. When Frost was there in the last spring before the Great War, they would have been an arresting sight.

The Dymock daffodils were far more than a poet's fancy. They were valuable to local people because they provided hard cash at the start of the season before the orchards and fields produced their intended crops. In the 1930s a Daffodil Special train run by the Great Western Railway brought carriage-loads of spring-hungry Londoners to Ledbury and Newent, eager to stroll among the flowers and buy bunches. Daffodil picking was a national pursuit in many parts of Britain at Easter when the 'Lenten Lilies' were at their best, in demand for Mothering Sunday in March or for sale at London flower markets. In Yorkshire, Devon and Cornwall, they brought extra income to farmers, villagers and gypsies who hawked the flowers to tourists. Schoolchildren were often pulled out of school and pressed into service as daffodil pickers. Another local poet (this time from Ledbury), John Masefield, observed them:

And there the pickers come, picking for town
Those dancing daffodils: all day they pick.
Hard-featured women, weather-beaten brown,
Or swarthy-red, the colour of old brick.

Part of the charm of wild daffodils was where they were found. Although widespread before the Second World War, they were especially common in Cumbria, the south-west of England, Yorkshire and the Welsh Marches, often where the climate was damp and the soils moist. Picking didn't seem to diminish their numbers, but from the 1940s and 1950s onwards more damaging processes were at work. With the coming of agricultural mechanisation and industrialisation, many of the daffodils' old meadows were ploughed up and the bulbs destroyed, sometimes deliberately because they are poisonous to livestock. In places woods were coniferised to provide fast-growing softwood timber of fir, larch, pine and spruce, casting a dense shade in which the flowers would not grow and then the hedges, which were their last refuges, were grubbed out. The wild daffodil was in decline. In 1959 the Daffodil Special stopped running to Dymock, even though the area remained a more reliable stronghold for the plants.

But this story, unlike so many other modern tales of wildlife and agriculture, has a happy ending. In this rural corner of Britain, the pace of change proved slow enough to spare some of the flowers in woods, meadows and orchards. Perhaps their value as a wild crop also prolonged their existence here. Whatever the reasons, wild daffodils are once more celebrated as part of the local landscape and culture and are a tourist attraction again. There is now a 16-kilometre circular route known as the Daffodil Way, which follows public footpaths through yellow woods, meadows and orchards, linking the best spots to see them. Some of the finest daffodil meadows are now managed by the Gloucestershire Wildlife Trust and the villages of Dymock, Kempley and Oxenhall hold annual Daffodil Weekends with guided walks and other activities. At Kempley there's even a Daff-and-Ride bus service to bring the people to the plants. Thanks to its renewed popularity, the wild daffodil has been declared the county flower of Gloucestershire. There's just one difference between modern times and the wild daffodil's heyday in the mid-twentieth century: picking them is now illegal.

In Welsh the daffodil is called *cenin pedr*, 'Peter's Leek', perhaps imagining that in heaven leeks (St Peter was the gatekeeper) would transform into golden trumpets. Legend has it that St David, the patron saint of Wales, once commanded his soldiers to identify themselves in a battle that took place in a leek field by wearing one of the plants attached to their helmets. It is still worn on 1 March, St David's Day, but a daffodil, the national flower of Wales, was accepted as a substitute during the nineteenth century possibly because its upright bright green leaves have a slight look of the leaves of the leek, but more probably because it makes a more attractive, if still somewhat pungent, buttonhole: David Lloyd George, the only Welshman to become British Prime Minister, advanced its popularity even further by wearing one proudly in public on 1 March.

The wild daffodil with its circlet of pale primrose, enclosing a deep egg-yolk yellow trumpet is still common in Welsh woods and old pastures, but in the narrow and twisting lanes of west Wales lurks the botanical puzzle that some say may be the genuine Welsh emblem: the Tenby daffodil.

Brett stumbled on this rare flower by accident one wild March day, while travelling to see a very rare bird, a Pacific Diver from North America, which had turned up on a remote Pembrokeshire reservoir. Through a sleet-spattered windscreen, he saw a clump of small daffodils with bright yellow trumpet *and* tepals on a laneside bank. Thoughts of rare birds went by the board as he scrambled out for a closer look at this neat little flower, golden and beaded with raindrops.

It was sturdier and more compact than wild daffodils, with shorter rather rounded petals and a trumpet in perfect proportion. This plant has bemused botanists for generations since its first discovery in 1796 when it was said to be abundant around the

Welsh harbour town of Tenby. Because it looked so different from the native wild daffodil, it became sought after by collectors and, as a result, by the end of the nineteenth century was already very rare; the *coup de grâce* came with the ploughing up of meadows between the wars.

So where had these laneside daffs come from and why is the plant so common again in and around Tenby itself? In *Flora Britannica*, Richard Mabey traces the resurgence of this enigmatic plant. In the 1970s an Essex boy on holiday in the area asked the local tourist office if he could buy some Tenby daffodils to take home to his aunt. No one knew where to lay hands on any, but the boy's request sparked a search for bulbs in local nurseries. The Tenby daffodil took pride of place at the next Tenby in Bloom festival and went on to grab the municipal imagination of the town, where it was planted out on verges and traffic islands. A former rarity has now become part of the local identity, a botanical connection with town and nation. Many of the daffodils are popular in gardens from where they have re-invaded the wild, which may explain that laneside clump.

The Tenby daffodil was originally classified as *Narcissus obvallaris*, a daffodil unknown outside the British Isles. According to Mabey, it was said to have been brought by Phoenician traders, Flemish settlers or grown by monks, though there's no evidence of any truth in this. Now it is considered a subspecies of the native wild daffodil, properly known as *Narcissus pseudonarcissus* ssp *obvallaris* though why it is so localised remains a mystery.

The fortunes of the Tenby daffodil have been ruined and made by horticulturalists, a sign that daffodils and other narcissi such as jonquils are big business. The humble wild plant has been crossed with European plants to produce around 27,000 hybrids and cultivars including white flowers, double blooms, pink trumpets and all shades of yellow and orange. Because our mild Atlantic climate suits daffodils, the British Isles are the largest producer in the world of cultivated daffodils, bringing in £45 million to the economy. We export around 10,000 tons of bulbs every year.

If you want to get your spring fix of cultivated narcissi early, go to the Isles of Scilly, where narcissus growing has been an industry for generations. The mild, almost frost-free climate allows the Scillonian bulb industry to steal a march on competitors and here you can see the yellow Soleil d'Or or Paper White narcissus in flower as early as October. The bulb industry burgeoned here in the late nineteenth century so that by 1889 the flowers were generating more than £10,000 per year for the island economy, the modern equivalent of several millions. In the last few decades, the Scilly bulb industry has been reduced by competition but they are still grown in some sheltered places.

Daffodils are grown for more than their flowers. The bulbs contain a compound called galanthamine which is also found in the bulbs of their close relatives the snowdrops. The drugs containing galanthamine are marketed as Reminyl, which can be used to treat the symptoms of early onset Alzheimer's disease.

The most ubiquitous daffodil variety is King Alfred. First bred around 1890, its gaudy, flared trumpets appear each spring like vegetable Tannoys in gardens, parks and increasingly on road verges throughout the British Isles, where they are not always welcome. In April 2010 a spat unfolded in the *Guardian* when its leader suggested that we should welcome these bold blooms big enough to beautify our nondescript roadsides: 'It takes all the vigorous vulgarity of February Gold or Cheerfulness to be seen over the strips of tyre and the fast-food debris that would overwhelm the more fastidious natives.'

Ecologist Andy Tasker responded robustly:

The problem of planting garden daffodils everywhere is twofold. On the one hand they take up space, growing so closely together once established that they exclude all other plants. On the other they give that unnatural suburban feel to our rural landscape, with their gaudy colours outshining our native primroses and cowslips. It's like painting lipstick on the Mona Lisa.

Andy Byfield of the wild flower charity Plantlife agrees that there is a real danger of hybridisation with native daffodil populations which can lead to more robust, less 'true' wild plants. 'Planting cultivars should not be a substitute for wild flowers on our road verges, which simply require more sensitive management. The worst-hit counties have lost one native flower every year, on average, throughout the twentieth century. In the past 150 years, twenty-one native flowering plants have completely disappeared from our islands.'

Back where we began in the lanes and orchards of north Gloucestershire, the native wild daffodil remains king. Even here, though, there are a few roadside plantings, no doubt well intentioned, of cultivated varieties. In the presence of the real thing, it looks like gilding the lily.

Man has always been aware of birds, and they still supply material and inspiration for recreational, intellectual, and scientific pursuits, as well as fresh eggs for breakfast.

Austin L. Rand, *Ornithology: An Introduction* (1974)

Birds' Eggs

Mysterious Fragility

Like many other boys obsessed with nature back in the 1960s, Brett remembers the thrill of watching a blackbird fly back to its nest, then hearing the soft 'chuck' of the hen bird as she departed in a flurry of wings. There in the tightly woven nest lay a quartet of irresistible sea-green eggs, heavily freckled in reddish-brown. The act of breaching the sanctity of the nest was fraught with guilt: it was hard not to imagine the heavy hand of the local policeman falling on his shoulders as he reached to take an egg. But the possibility of being caught red-handed was part of the attraction. There was an unwritten code among schoolboys that only one egg should be taken from each nest: the removal of a full clutch could lead to temporary social exclusion from the informal collectors' club.

Once collected, the trophy was blown by piercing a hole in one end and expelling the yolk through a straw, then mounted on cotton wool in a small cardboard box. After a few days of covetousness, this egg was stored away and forgotten, a fragile reminder of one passion soon to be eclipsed by others, much longer lasting.

But for some, the lure of egg collecting lingered well into adulthood. These characters once had their own group, known as the Oological Club. Its activities were frowned upon by many members of their parent organisation, the British Ornithologists' Union, which in 1908 had passed a resolution condemning the taking of

birds and their eggs. In the *Spectator* of 11 August 1922 corres-
pondence appeared under the title 'The Eggs of British Wild Birds
and the Collector', referring to the large numbers of wild birds'
eggs exhibited at one of the club's regular dinners:

> It is made clear that most of the eggs – of the Red-backed Shrike
> and the Fly-catchers – had been collected over a long period, and
> that both the Oological Club and the British Ornithologists' Union,
> of which the Club forms a part, strongly deprecate the action of
> any member who disregards the Acts for the protection of wild
> birds.

And in the *Illustrated London News*, William Plane Pycraft of the
Natural History Museum commented:

> If the whole science of oology is not to be brought into disrepute,
> these all-devouring schemes must be abandoned. They are intem-
> perate and exasperating. They can only be carried on by flagrant
> breaches of the law, often possible only by the exercise of a low
> cunning disgusting to all reasonable men. That the collecting of
> birds' eggs is an essential part of the study of ornithology is beyond
> dispute. But the collector must exercise discrimination.

It wasn't until the passing of the Protection of Birds Act in 1954
that it became illegal to take the eggs of most British breeding
birds. The same year saw the publication of the *Observer's Book of
Birds' Eggs*, a pocket bible that went on to sell 1½ million copies.
Its itchy-fingered readers were meant to gaze fondly, but not to
touch. As it happened the Act didn't specifically outlaw taking the
eggs of common wild birds, and schoolboys' clutches remained
safe from those of bobbies on the beat, until the Wildlife and
Countryside Act finally closed that legal loophole in 1981.

Even so, a hard core of pernicious collectors remains, obsessed
with the natural variety in birds' eggs – not just between blackbirds
and song thrushes, but even within the same species, for patterns

can vary enormously from bird to bird and from year to year. Their determination to collect as many clutches as possible, and in particular of birds that nest only occasionally in Britain, still threatens the existence of very rare species. So when red-backed shrikes bred in Devon recently, the Royal Society for the Protection of Birds (RSPB) had to mount twenty-four-hour surveillance to protect the nest from egg thieves. Had anyone succeeded, theirs would have been a hollow victory, like stealing a Van Gogh or a Picasso, objects with provenance so notorious that the spoils can only be gloated over in private.

Sadly, these illegal egg collectors do a huge disservice to legitimate scientists, whose analysis of the variation in colour and shape of eggs, and their weight, helps them to study the way clutches and individual eggs vary from bird to bird within a species, and between different, though related, species. This is essential if we are to continue to learn more about the evolution of birds.

Pleasing to hold, beautiful to the eye, versatile in cooking, intriguing in nature, and wonderfully practical – eggs will always inspire us. Yet they are far more, of course, than scientific curiosities or collector's items. For every one of the world's 10,500 or so species of bird, from the bee hummingbird to the ostrich, eggs are their way of creating the next generation. Eggs are not, like feathers, unique to birds – fish, reptiles, invertebrates and two species of mammal (the duck-billed platypus and echidna) lay different kinds of eggs too – but few other creatures are so closely associated with this form of reproduction.

A bird's egg is a miracle of nature. Eggs have been described as 'a life-support system for the embryo', protecting it throughout its early developmental stage from a tiny, fertilised ovum until the chick finally hatches out from the shell. And as such, it contains within its hard outer casing everything the developing bird could possibly need to grow and develop, including fats and proteins in the yolk, to feed the developing embryo. The yolk and embryo are surrounded – and protected – by the white, or albumen, which acts as a shock absorber; and outside this, the hard shell.

For us, eggs serve two other crucial purposes: filling our stomachs and inspiring our souls. From the point of view of consumption, it is hard to imagine a world without a readily available supply of eggs. The egg is in some ways the perfect package: the yolk and white contain essential protein; it can be cooked and eaten in many different ways, used in recipes as varied as chocolate mousse, pastry and fried chicken; and its versatility and availability have made eggs from many different bird species a favoured food across the globe – ever since our prehistoric ancestors first stumbled across a bird's nest, and wondered if those strange ovoid objects might be good to eat.

Today, domestic chickens *Gallus gallus*, farmed for their meat and eggs, are by far the commonest bird in the world; indeed with an estimated population of around 25 billion, there are almost four times as many chickens as there are human beings. Of these, somewhere between 4.9 and 6.4 billion hens lay an estimated 62 million tonnes of eggs each year – roughly 1.2 trillion eggs, or 180 eggs for every man, woman and child in the world, though of course consumption of eggs varies considerably between individuals and especially between different cultures.

The original 'chicken' is a colourful and shy member of the pheasant family living in the jungles of Asia, from India and Nepal to south China, Thailand, Vietnam and Borneo. In the wild, the red junglefowl *Gallus gallus* is a fairly common and widespread bird, though with its golden-brown plumage, blue-green tail and red wattles just like a domestic cockerel it does look rather out of place in a dense forest habitat or wandering along the side of a dirt track.

Archaeologists suspect that the red junglefowl was originally domesticated not for food, but for sport: 'cock-fighting', a cruel but dramatic contest in which males use the sharp spurs on the back of their legs to attack – and often kill – their rival. However, once it was discovered that the hens were prolific layers, something encouraged and developed through selective breeding, the chicken soon became even more popular and widely kept.

When early chickens were domesticated is subject to debate, with some suggesting that it first occurred in southern China as early as 6000 BC (about the time that Britain became an island). They were certainly being kept in the Indus Valley (present-day Pakistan) in 2500 BC, and may have reached south-east Europe even earlier. Traders such as the Phoenicians took the chicken with them throughout the empires of the ancient world, and eventually they spread through Africa and the Americas.

One distinctive breed found in South America, the araucana from southern Chile, lays bluish eggs – a trait it shares with some Asian chickens. This has led to speculation that these chickens did not come to the Americas with Columbus and the European explorers of the late Middle Ages, but much earlier, brought from Asia by the Polynesians, across the vast Pacific Ocean.

Being large and tasty, and with a reliable and regular daily supply, domestic chicken eggs rapidly displaced many of the wild alternatives, though eggs from other bird species are still widely eaten throughout the world. These range from other domesticated birds such as ducks and geese, through to the harvesting of eggs from wild birds including seabirds such as gulls and puffins, gamebirds including pheasants, quails and guineafowls, and in Britain – at least until the introduction of the first comprehensive bird protection acts in the 1950s – 'plover's eggs', from lapwings. The latter featured in Evelyn Waugh's 1945 novel *Brideshead Revisited*, in which they became shorthand for the louche sophistication and privilege of young Lord Sebastian Flyte, as he consumes them in his rooms at Oxford, announcing: 'Mummy sends them from Brideshead. They always lay early for her.'

Once eggs had satisfied their appetites, our ancestors began to regard them in a less utilitarian way, turning to more spiritual, religious and cultural matters. Many ancient beliefs have tended to die away as the modern world becomes more and more sophisticated and far removed from our humble origins, but one particular aspect of eggs is still very much at the forefront of our annual calendar.

Easter eggs, whose origins embrace both Christian and pre-Christian cultures, are big business: about 90 million large chocolate eggs are sold in the UK each year: roughly nine per child.

The chocolate Easter egg tradition is a relatively recent development, originating in France and Germany in the early nineteenth century, and only coming to Britain via Fry's of Bristol in 1873. But eggs have been associated with the Christian festival of Easter (whose name derives from the pagan goddess of the dawn, Eostre) since the earliest days of the Church. The festival is linked both with pagan rites of spring and the resurrection of Christ, and so the egg – which represents both rebirth and transformation – is the perfect symbol for this twin celebration. However, the use of the egg as a symbol of life predates Christianity by a long way. Hindus believe that the world developed from an egg, while some of the earliest examples of primitive art ever found are on eggs; ostrich eggs decorated with engravings dating back 60,000 years have been discovered at Diepkloof, an archaeological site near Johannesburg in South Africa.

One plausible theory for the origin of the custom of decorating chicken's eggs at Eastertime (the original 'Easter eggs') is that each spring coincided with a glut of eggs, allowing some to be spared for decorating. In addition, there would be a surplus of eggs available because from the fourth century onwards the Church banned their consumption during the forty days of Lent.

These early Easter eggs would have been decorated using natural dyes such as brown from onion skins, black from charcoal, yellow, pink and violet from various flowers, and green from leaves. In some cultures, such as the Ukrainian tradition known as 'pysanka', these colours are symbolic: yellow for the sun and harvest, blue for the skies and good health, white for purity, green for new life in the spring, and red for the blood of Christ.

Decorated Easter eggs became especially popular during the Middle Ages: the household accounts of King Edward I for the nineteenth year of his reign, 1290, show that 450 eggs were purchased at a cost of 18 pence (7.5p, equivalent to roughly £55 today), which were then decorated with gold leaf and given as gifts for Easter. This custom had the backing of the Church, as in this traditional blessing: 'Lord, let the grace of your blessing come upon these eggs, that they may be healthful food for your faithful who eat them in thanksgiving for the resurrection of our Lord Jesus Christ, who lives and reigns with you for ever and ever.'

The link between eggs and the resurrection gains further strength when allied to the belief that the egg represents the stone that closed Jesus's tomb and was found rolled aside on the third day after his burial – a reminder to the faithful that Jesus rose from the grave.

This belief led to another Easter tradition. Egg-rolling – pushing decorated eggs down steep hills and then chasing them to the bottom – remains popular in parts of northern England and Scotland, while Easter egg hunts for children are still widespread throughout the United Kingdom and North America. Even the sixteenth-century German reformer Martin Luther is known to have held Easter egg hunts.

But when it comes to decorating eggs, one name reigns supreme: Fabergé. Peter Carl Fabergé was a Russian jeweller who in 1885 was commissioned by Tsar Alexander III to make an elaborately jewelled egg as an Easter gift for his wife, the Tsarina Maria Fyodorovna. Fabergé made a beautiful golden egg within another gold and white enamel egg, with a golden chicken and replica of the imperial crown at its centre. The delighted Tsarina commissioned similar eggs every Easter, a tradition continued by her son Nicholas II. However the custom came to an abrupt end – along with the rule of the tsars – with the outbreak of the Russian Revolution in 1917.

Of the original fifty made, roughly forty eggs have survived – so unsurprisingly they are highly sought after. One egg, given by Alexander III to his wife for Easter 1887, had been assumed lost, having last been recorded in 1922. A tantalising hope that it had survived surfaced in 2011, when researchers discovered a picture of what appeared to be the vanished egg in an auction catalogue from 1964. Enquiries revealed that it had been sold for less than £1,000 to a woman who had later died, and that the whereabouts of the precious object was no longer known.

Then, in 2012, a scrap-metal dealer in the American Midwest was idly wondering about the provenance of the ornamental egg he had bought a few years earlier, intending to sell it for its scrap value. Googling the name 'Vacheron Constantin', which he found etched on a timepiece inside the egg, he was astonished to discover that this might be the long-lost Fabergé egg. He contacted London jeweller Kieran McCarthy, a Fabergé expert, who flew over to the US to examine the find. On realising that it was indeed the lost egg, McCarthy said: 'I was flabbergasted – it was like being Indiana Jones and finding the Lost Ark.' At auction in 2014 the egg sold for £20 million – a record for a Fabergé egg – so far, at least.

The tradition of using eggs in art goes back long before Fabergé. But the most important use of eggs for artists was not as an object to decorate, or even as one to portray in their works, but as a medium for creating the artwork itself. Egg tempera – coloured pigment mixed with egg yolks and other ingredients such as vinegar or white wine – has been widely used by artists since at least the time of the birth of Christ, and probably earlier, as a convenient, flexible and fast-drying medium for painting.

During the medieval and early Renaissance period, up until about 1500, egg tempera (painted on to wooden boards) was the primary medium with which artists such as Giotto, Fra Angelico and Botticelli created their stunning works of religious art. As well as being flexible and ideal for making precise brushstrokes, and producing a smooth, matt finish when dry, egg tempera has one added advantage for posterity: unlike the oil paints that superseded it from the early sixteenth century onwards, which have faded and darkened over time, tempera has managed to retain its bright, vivid colours for centuries.

But perhaps the most unexpected use of eggs in art is found in an unusual tradition practised by clowns. This dates back to just after the Second World War, when London's International Circus Clowns Club (now known as Clowns International) began employing an oddly practical method to record its members' make-up: they copied each design on to an egg – or 'amazing boneless chicken', which was then placed in a registry that effectively trade-marked the identity of each member. Painted on real eggshells, with the inside emptied out, by Stan Bult, the first head of the Circus Clowns Club, these studies now form part of the Clowns' Gallery and Museum in north London. Though not an official registry, the collection is meant to preserve the uniqueness of each clown's face make-up. The Department of Clown Registry infor-mation sheet explains that 'it is an unwritten law among clowns that one must never copy the face of another'. In 1984 the new chairman of Clowns International, 'Clown Bluey', resurrected it, but instead of using (breakable) chicken's eggs, decided to employ a professional artist to paint the patterns on to china eggs, as a permanent copyright register of each clown's unique face. Today the collection – numbering 300 eggs in all – is on display at Gerry Cottle's Clown Museum, at Wookey Hole in Somerset. The custom has since spread to the United States, where the registry now contains more than 700 (goose) eggs.

On 27 September 1962 a modest book was published in the United States: one that would go on to change the course of history. It opened with an apocalyptic warning: 'It was a spring without voices. On the mornings that had once throbbed with the dawn chorus of robins, catbirds, doves, jays, wrens, and scores of other bird voices there was now no sound; only silence lay over the fields and woods and marsh.' The title of the book was *Silent Spring*; its author, a US scientist called Rachel Carson.

At the centre of Carson's book was her belief that chemical pesticides such as DDT, then widely used in the agricultural indus-tries of both North America and Europe, were killing millions of birds; hence the dramatic title of her book. For some – such as the smaller songbirds she mentions in the opening lines of the book – death came rapidly; they were poisoned by ingesting the chemical as they fed on seeds or insects in fields sprayed liberally with DDT. But in larger species the effects were slower and more insidious: it accumulated in their bodies as they fed on smaller birds, becoming more concentrated the higher up the food chain it went.

This made birds of prey, especially eagles, sparrowhawks and peregrines – sitting at the very top of the pyramid – uniquely vulnerable, especially because they live for a long time. But although some were poisoned directly, for most the effect of DDT revealed itself in something no scientist could have predicted: the thinning of their eggshells, caused by a lack of calcium. Thinner eggshells were obviously more vulnerable as the birds incubated. As a result, the populations of species such as the peregrine and sparrowhawk went into freefall.

Carson's claims caused outrage among the chemical and agricultural industries, for which the use of DDT, and other associated chemicals, was producing higher yields and far less loss to pests. Attempts were made to discredit her and her associates; but for the scientific community, who had already suspected that DDT might be to blame for the unusual phenomenon of eggshell thinning, *Silent Spring* fired the starting gun on new and crucial research to prove or disprove Carson's theory.

Within six years, two scientific papers had confirmed that DDT was indeed responsible. The first, 'Decrease in Eggshell Weight in Certain Birds of Prey', was published in the scientific journal *Nature* in July 1967. Written by Derek Ratcliffe, a researcher at the Nature Conservancy (now Natural England), it showed that the incidence of broken eggs in the nests of three key species – golden eagles, peregrines and sparrowhawks – had increased hugely since 1950, with peregrine and sparrowhawk eggshells collected after that date weighing on average between one-fifth and one-quarter less than those collected before, due to having thinner shells. He investigated the possibility that this might be due to some other environmental cause such as lack of food or radiation, but concluded that pesticides were in fact to blame.

A year later, in October 1968, the US journal *Science* published a paper that confirmed Ratcliffe's sensational findings. Its authors, Daniel Anderson and Joseph Hickey from the University of Wisconsin, concluded that: 'Catastrophic declines of three raptorial species [peregrine, bald eagle and osprey] in the United States have been accompanied by decreases in eggshell thickness that began in 1947, and have amounted to 19 per cent or more, and were identical to phenomena found in Britain.'

Gradually the theory that DDT was causing these problems for birds gained widespread acceptance, and in 1972 the chemical was finally banned in the United States; though it took another decade, until the early 1980s, for a similar ban to come into force in the UK. Since then, there has been a spectacular increase in the populations of these iconic raptors, and birds such as the peregrine have now colonised major cities on both sides of the Atlantic, including London and New York.

Back at London's Natural History Museum, twenty-two objects have been specially selected from more than 7 million in the museum's collection, to feature in a permanent exhibition aptly entitled Treasures. Alongside the first edition of Darwin's *Origin of Species*, a fossilised Archaeopteryx – probably the world's first bird – a stuffed great auk, a moon rock and two objects that feature elsewhere in this book – the Barbary lion skull and the Wold Cottage Meteorite – is a rather more modest exhibit: a large, pear-shaped egg measuring about 13 centimetres across, with a rectangular hole on one side. It belongs to an emperor penguin, the largest and most spectacular of the world's twenty or so species.

The hole in the egg was made by its finders in order to extract the embryo, which, it was hoped, would show an intermediate stage between birds and reptiles. This turned out to be a theoretical dead-end; and yet, as Phil Rainbow, former Head of Life Sciences at the museum, points out, the cultural significance of the egg has proved far greater than its biological one: 'We now consider it to be an icon of human endeavour in the name and pursuit of science.'

In an era when we can travel in ease and comfort to most parts of the world, it is hard to remember that only a little over a century ago some places were so difficult to reach that only enormous human endeavour, allied with pain, discomfort and the very real risk of death, were required to explore the remotest of the world's regions. And regions don't come more hostile and remote than Antarctica, where this particular egg was collected, in 1911, as part of Robert Falcon Scott's doomed expeditions to the South Pole.

The story behind its collection is one of almost unimaginable hardship in pursuit of a scientific dream; a story first told in *The Worst Journey in the World* (1922). A flavour of the book comes from this sardonic and much quoted line: 'Polar exploration is at once the cleanest and most isolated way of having a bad time which has been devised.'

The author was far from the cynical, hard-bitten hero those words suggest; Apsley George Benet Cherry-Garrard was perhaps the least likely polar explorer in history. Short-sighted to near blindness – especially in driving Antarctic blizzards – intellectual and academic rather than naturally adventurous, and suffering a litany of physical ailments and mental illness, he was only on Scott's expedition at all by chance. Back in 1907 he was visiting the home of his older cousin, Reginald Smith, when Scott and his long-time colleague Edward Wilson happened to drop in to discuss a new expedition to the Antarctic. Fired up by their tales of derring-do, the twenty-one-year-old decided then and there to volunteer.

Thus in 1910 Cherry-Garrard sailed on *Terra Nova* from Cardiff to Antarctica. At first he was not entirely welcomed by his fellow explorers, who suspected that his lack of experience and scientific knowledge (he had been given the title 'assistant zoologist') might prove inadequate to the daunting tasks they faced. But he was soon taken under the wing of Scott's second-in-command, Dr Edward Wilson (known to all as 'Uncle Bill').

Wilson himself was a man of many talents. An accomplished artist and naturalist, a qualified medical doctor and a passionate explorer, Wilson had a theory: that close study of the embryos of birds – especially 'primitive' birds such as the emperor penguin – might show an evolutionary link between birds and reptiles, and thus reveal the ancestry of modern birds. To prove his theory – known as 'recapitulation' – Wilson had to obtain an egg. Emperor penguins nest in one of the most remote parts of Antarctica, in the middle of the southern winter, when the whole continent is shrouded in darkness and temperatures plummet.

Few men would have even considered, let alone attempted an expedition, which Cherry-Garrard later referred to as 'a horribly dangerous and inhumanly exhausting feat'. But Wilson and Cherry-Garrard – and their companion Henry 'Birdie' Bowers – were made of stern stuff. And so, at the start of July 1911, the three men set off from base camp at Cape Evans to make the 100-kilometre trek inland to the penguins' breeding colony at Cape Crozier.

They trudged at a snail's pace in almost total darkness, in temperatures down to minus 57 Celsius – which must have been almost unbearably cold, given their primitive clothing and limited supplies. When they eventually reached their goal, a severe blizzard promptly carried away their tent, leaving them with just their sleeping bags. Thirty-six hours later the winds finally dropped, and to their amazement and great good fortune they discovered their tent, more or less intact, nearby.

They collected five eggs (two of which broke on the journey home) and then began the long march back to base, Cherry-Garrard's teeth chattering so violently in the intense cold that they shattered. The three exhausted men and their precious cargo finally reached Cape Evans five weeks later, on 1 August. But there was no time to rest: Wilson and Bowers then joined Scott for his final push to the South Pole, while Cherry-Garrard stayed back at base with the support team. A year later, with no news from their comrades, and fearing the worst, he went in search of them, finding only the frozen tent – just a few miles from safety – where Scott and his companions had perished.

On his return to London, Cherry-Garrard took the three surviving emperor penguin eggs, for which he, Wilson and Bowers had gone through so much suffering, to the Natural History Museum. It took far longer than expected to actually look at the three eggs. The embryos were removed and then sliced and mounted on to 800 microscope slides for examination, but the First World War intervened. Richard Ashton, the museum's specialist in embryology, then died, further delaying their examination. Eventually, when the study of the eggs was finally published in 1934 – almost a quarter of a century after they had been collected – Cherry-Garrard was told that this had not only failed to prove the (later discredited) theory of recapitulation, but that the eggs had not even taught the museum's scientists anything useful about penguin embryology. Their quest had, it turned out, been almost entirely in vain.

Cherry-Garrard concealed what must have been enormous disappointment beneath a veneer of British stiff upper lip. His book contains several memorable reflections on the nature of polar exploration, in particular its final lines, which highlight both the bravery and futility of his particular quest:

And I tell you, if you have the desire for knowledge and the power to give it physical expression, go out and explore. If you are a brave man you will do nothing: if you are fearful you may do much, for none but cowards have need to prove their bravery. Some will tell you that you are mad, and nearly all will say, 'What is the use?' For we are a nation of shopkeepers, and no shopkeeper will look at research which does not promise him a financial return within a year. And so you will sledge nearly alone, but those with whom you sledge will not be shopkeepers: that is worth a good deal. If you march your Winter Journeys you will have your reward, so long as all you want is a penguin's egg.

Cherry-Garrard went on to lead a long but quiet life, always silently reproving himself for failing to save his friends. He died, aged seventy-three, on 18 May 1959.

Since his death, Cherry-Garrard's reputation as both a polar explorer and a writer has gone from strength to strength. He himself, though, always saw things from a wry perspective, refusing to play the martyr, and pointing out that the bird whose egg they had collected suffered far more than any human visitor to the Antarctic: 'Take it all in all; I do not believe anybody on Earth has it worse than an emperor penguin.'

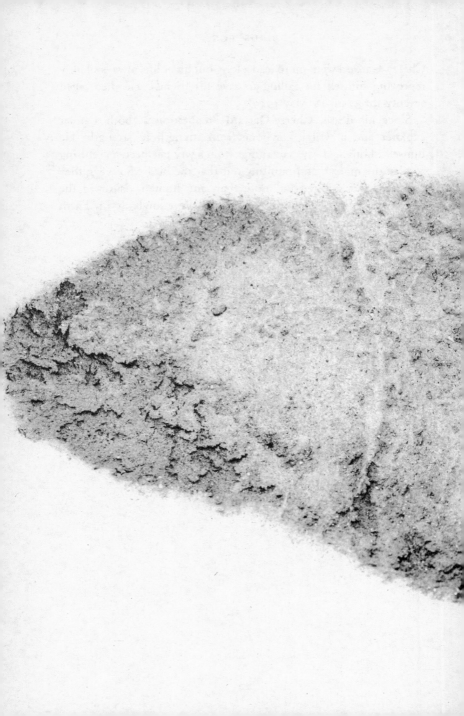

A bear is a shaggy, slothful, wild beast, in all respect like a man, and wishful to walk upright.

Anonymous (ancient Greece)

Bears

Beasts or Best Friends?

It had been a long day's hunting in the hot and muggy Mississippi Delta, and the guest of honour was becoming increasingly frustrated. Everyone else, it seemed, had managed to kill at least one animal. He risked having to return home to Washington embarrassingly empty-handed.

Then a shout went up: an animal had finally been cornered. But when the hunter arrived at the scene he found the unfortunate creature tethered, surrounded by baying hounds and whimpering pathetically. He refused to take a pot shot, reportedly saying: 'I've hunted game all over America and I'm proud to be a hunter. But I couldn't be proud of myself if I shot an old, tired, worn-out bear that was tied to a tree.'

The hunter was the US President, Theodore 'Teddy' Roosevelt, and although he may have thought little of the incident at the time, the story struck a chord. A few days later, in November 1902, a cartoon appeared in the *Washington Post*, featuring the President and the bear. Toymaker Morris Michtom then made two stuffed bears and put them in his shop window, accompanied by the newspaper clipping and a sign saying 'Teddy's Bears'.

Within a few years the craze for these toy animals had taken off: women and children carried them around the streets of New York; Roosevelt himself used a bear as his mascot during his successful re-election campaign in 1904 (despite loathing his nickname); and three years later composer John Walter Bratton wrote the popular tune 'The Teddy Bears' Picnic'. By the time Roosevelt stood down from the presidency in 1909, the teddy bear – and the billion-dollar industry that surrounds it – was well and truly on its way.

Natural historian and cultural expert Robert E. Bieder of Indiana University explains the sudden craze for bears at the turn of the twentieth century as a product of a growing enthusiasm for the natural world, along with fears of becoming disconnected from it: 'A growing involvement with nature was sweeping over America with the development of national, state and city parks. Psychologically, a growing sense of anxiety had crept in among the population as the industrial age accelerated, probably contributing to the acceptance of the teddy bear as a figure of comfort.'

Others link our love of bears to primal, mythological connections with the animals, deep in our subconscious minds, while US psychologist Paul Horton suggests the reason might simply be that bears and humans resemble one another just enough to allow a child to relate to a teddy bear without causing confusion.

Those early teddy bears did look fairly lifelike, whereas over time their features have softened to give them a more human appeal. Their faces are flatter, their eyes larger and their legs shorter – making them more like a human baby than a wild animal; a process of 'neoteny' similar to that followed by cartoon characters such as Mickey Mouse, who has also become more childlike in appearance over time.

The cult of the teddy bear feels like a uniquely twentieth-century phenomenon; and yet bears themselves have – perhaps more than any other animal – been the subject of cults, worship and veneration over many thousands of years, all the way back to our Palaeolithic ancestors. So what is it about bears that – uniquely among wild creatures – has inspired such devotion and passion?

The worship of bears is probably as old as human society itself, as the US anthropologist Joseph Campbell noted: 'the bear, the deer, the great eagle, these are our brothers'. This is hardly surprising, as bears are by far the largest and strongest animal found across most of the northern hemisphere; added to which, until only a few centuries ago the great apes were unknown to western civilisation.

Bernd Brunner, author of *Bears: A Brief History* (and whose own forename derives from the Old German meaning 'strong like a bear'), notes that bears were often regarded as intermediaries between the human and animal worlds. Ancient hunters would refer to a bear not by its name but by the term 'cousin', 'brother', or 'grandfather', suggesting a close kinship between their fellow species. Other names given to bears in various North American, European and Asian cultures include 'four-legged human', 'chief's son', 'fur father', 'old claw man', 'little uncle' and 'old man with fur garment'.

The way bears can stand up on their hind legs to feed, have forward-facing eyes, are omnivorous, opportunistic hunter-gatherers, eating more or less the same foods as us, and the extraordinary physical resemblance between a skinned bear and a human, all led to a close bond between these early humans and their wild animal peers. It was also thought by several cultures that bears had the power to hear and understand human speech.

Bears were useful, too: their skins kept our cave-dwelling ancestors warm, their meat was eaten, their fat was used for cooking, and their teeth, bones and claws were worn as ornaments – symbolically borrowing the strength of the wild animal for the wearer. But our connection with them was always somewhat ambivalent, as Brunner points out: 'Bears are much stronger than humans, so there was always a difficult relationship. They were hunted and seen as threatening human life. Bears and people did not live in harmony – they were opponents but humans still revered bears for their strength.'

Bear worship was especially common among the hunting tribes of the northern hemisphere, from North America across northern Europe and Siberia. Bears were often considered to embody the spirits of the ancestors, and several pagan deities took the form of bears. Remains have been found in archaeological excavations, the bears' skulls and bones arranged in such a way that anthropologists believe they were part of some sort of cult. And several cultures have myths about women who marry bears and produce half-breed children, perhaps told to children as a warning against wandering off into the woods, or breaking other social and cultural taboos.

We even see bears in the stars, with the two constellations of Ursa Major and Ursa Minor (or the Great Bear and Little Bear) constantly tracking their way across the heavens above our heads. Ursa Minor is home to Polaris, the North Star, around which Ursa Major passes, never setting over the horizon; a phenomenon the ancients compared to a bear walking round and round the stake it was tied to, never settling. The myth they told about the two constellations was that Juno was so outraged to discover that a nymph, Callisto, had borne her husband Jupiter's child that she turned her into a bear. Sixteen years later Callisto, still a bear, encountered her son Arcas hunting in the forest. Just as he was about to kill her, Jupiter stepped in, placing mother and son among the stars as Ursa Major and Minor, respectively.

Bears also feature prominently in early Chinese, Korean, Japanese and Finnish cultures; in fairy tales ('Goldilocks and the Three Bears', a traditional folk tale given renewed popularity when republished by nineteenth-century poet Robert Southey); and in many traditional European myths and legends. In some, the bear is portrayed as a rather slow, clumsy creature, pitted against the sly and cunning fox. Others, including 'Goldilocks', play with the idea that humans and bears are close cousins. Thus Goldilocks assumes from what she finds that the house in the forest is lived in by human beings; only when the bears return does she realise her mistake and flee. For Bernd Brunner, this sums up the paradox of the close yet always mutually antagonistic relationship between humans and bears.

Sometimes the bear is seen not simply as a dangerous wild creature but also as a protective figure, tamed by a saint. This goes back to the Old Testament Book of Hosea, which compares God to a mother bear fiercely defending her cubs against attack: 'I will meet them as a bear that is bereaved of her whelps . . . and there will I devour them like a lion: the wild beast shall tear them.'

The link between bears and motherhood is a profound one, and is perhaps linked to the habits of wild bears: they give birth during the harshest months of the year, then emerge with their cubs at the start of spring; the verb 'to bear' (as in children, fruit) is thought to derive from this. In northern cultures, bears are also closely associated with the changes in the seasons, again because of their annual cycle, in which they are most active during the spring and summer, and hide away, out of sight, in autumn and winter. The Romans believed that mother bears gave birth to formless lumps in the winter and then proceeded literally to 'lick them into shape' – this is the origin of the English expression – a theory that was obviously based on observations of the mother bear licking her newly born cubs. Pliny the Elder goes into more detail: 'Newborn cubs are a shapeless lump of white flesh, with no eyes or hair, though the claws are visible. The mother bear gradually licks her cubs into their proper shape, and keeps them warm by hugging them to her breast and lying on them, just as birds do with their eggs.'

This image of the fierce but protective bear lives on in modern culture: notably in the Russian bear, a widely used symbol that dates back to the sixteenth century. The Russians have, however, always been rather ambivalent about their national symbol, trying to defuse this image when, as the mascot of the 1980 Moscow Olympics, they chose a cute and cuddly bear cub named Misha, rather than a huge, fierce adult bear.

Though we may not realise it, bears are also embodied in common names among several northern European nations and cultures. The Germanic name Bernard (or Bernhard) means 'bold or brave bear', and the Irish surname McMahon signifies 'son of the bear', while the Swiss city of Bern and the Scandinavian name Bjorn simply mean 'bear'. But the best-known name associated with bears is Ursula, Latin for 'little female bear'.

An early Christian martyr, Ursula was a princess of late Roman Britain, who set sail to join her future husband, the governor of Armorica, in north-west France. Legend has it that she was accompanied by no fewer than 11,000 virginal handmaidens (later commentators have argued that this enormous figure must have been mistranscribed) and when they miraculously survived a terrible storm they pledged to go on a pilgrimage across Europe before the marriage took place. Unfortunately, just outside Cologne they ran into the Huns and Ursula's companions were all beheaded in a grisly massacre. When she chose virginity over survival she was also killed. It's an odd story that may well have benefited from its assumption of elements of existing folk stories and beliefs about bear worship. There was a cult of St Ursula around Cologne, a heavily forested area notorious for bears, in the Middle Ages.

Early Christians rejected the pagan veneration for bears; now they were regarded as 'little more than a wild beast in need of God's order'. Bears were seen as an impediment to the conversion of pagan peoples, as they still worshipped bears, which were then supplanted by the cult of another big, fierce, but far less familiar animal (see Chapter 5: Lions), as Bernd Brunner explains: 'The medieval Catholic Church tried very hard to eliminate the last remnants of the ancient bear cults, demonising bears. Slowly the lion – the king of beasts – replaced the king of the forest. The lion wasn't found in Europe so could be attributed with qualities that couldn't be questioned.' Meanwhile, during the same period, as Europe's human population grew, it expanded into areas where bears lived, felling forests and increasing contacts and conflict between bears and us.

So what of the bear itself? How does the natural history of the world's bears mirror or contradict the ways we regard them in myth, legend and popular culture?

Bears are easily recognisable: large and hairy, with thick legs, walking on the soles of their feet as well as their toes (like human beings and other primates) and with short, rudimentary tails. They are, along with the big cats and wild dogs such as wolves, classified as carnivores, and their closest relatives include dogs, mustelids and pinnipeds (walruses, sea lions and seals). However for most species (apart from the polar bear, which is almost exclusively carnivorous), much of their diet consists of plant matter, or even – in the case of black bears and some brown bears – ants or moths, which they consume by the thousand.

There are eight different living species of bear, found mainly in the northern hemisphere continents of North America, Europe and Asia. There is one outlying representative, the Andean or spectacled bear, found in the mountainous regions of South America. This, along with three other specialised species, the sun bear of South East Asia, the sloth bear of the Indian subcontinent, and the giant panda of China (recently reclassified as a true bear), each has its own monotypic genus; while the other four species – what we think of as the 'true bears' – are together in the genus *Ursus*.

They are the Asiatic black bear, the American black bear, the brown bear of North America, Europe and Asia (the American races are also commonly known as the 'grizzly bear') and the polar bear. The polar bear is the world's largest terrestrial carnivore, with big males reaching a shoulder height of up to 1.7 metres and weighing as much as 800 kilos. In contrast the sun bear is roughly 12–18 times smaller, weighing just 45–65 kilos. Bears live in a wide range of habitats, from the tropical forests of Asia to the Arctic tundra, and the Gobi Desert to the Andes Mountains. In parts of Europe and North America they may also venture close to human habitations, which can cause problems with damage to crops or livestock, the raiding of waste bins, or traffic accidents.

Although the brown bear is by far the most widespread, being found across much of the northern US and Canada, Europe and central and northern Asia, its estimated world population of 200,000 is dwarfed by that of the American black bear. Although that species only lives in three countries (US, Canada and Mexico) there are an estimated 900,000 individuals, making it more numerous than all the other seven bear species combined.

Bears are mainly diurnal in their habits, with an excellent sense of smell and the ability to run, swim and in some species climb. As the old joke goes: How do you tell a grizzly bear from a black bear, when you come across one? If it climbs a tree it's a black bear; if *you* climb a tree it's a grizzly. They live in dens, often in caves; and undergo a long period of dormancy in the winter, though this falls just short of true hibernation. They are usually the dominant wild creatures in their environment – apart of course from human beings – although tigers do predate brown, Asiatic black, sun and sloth bears.

Bears are generally solitary animals, and rarely come together apart from a very brief period of courtship and mating. The cubs – mostly born during the mother's dormant period in winter – are, like many baby mammals, blind and hairless, but soon grow strong on their mother's rich and fatty milk. Cubs remain with their mother for up to three years, though if they encounter a male bear during this period they may be killed and eaten to enable the male to breed with the female. Yet despite the fact that female bears are usually considerably smaller than males, they are able to drive away most intruders. Male bears can also be very aggressive towards one another, in fights over food or potential mates. But they will also gather together in large groups when food is plentiful, as when salmon are swimming upstream in the rivers of Canada, Alaska and the eastern Russian peninsula of Kamchatka.

People and bears have always had a healthy respect for one another, and for good reason: American black, brown and polar bears are easily big and strong enough to kill a defenceless human, while people armed with guns can shoot and kill bears. As with sharks, bear attacks are very rare, though hikers and visitors to national parks in North America are warned to be aware of the presence of bears, and especially not to keep food anywhere that the animals might find it. Fatal attacks from brown and black bears average about three per year, but because they usually gain widespread publicity the perception is that bears are far more dangerous than they actually are.

For centuries, human beings have made life difficult for bears. The Romans would kill up to a hundred bears in a single day at the Colosseum, while the 'sport' of bear-baiting was a popular pastime in Britain and the rest of Europe from medieval times until the nineteenth century. Specially constructed 'bear gardens', with a pit surrounded by seats for spectators, could be found in many cities. Once the bear had been chained to a post in the arena, its canines and claws removed, it would be set upon by trained dogs – often Old English bulldogs, known for their persistence and vicious nature. Both Henry VIII and his daughter Elizabeth I were fans of bear-baiting, with Elizabeth overruling Parliament when it tried to ban the pastime on Sundays. Ironically, given the cruelty shown towards them, the bears themselves became so famous that they were even given names, such as 'Blind Robin', 'George of Cambridge' and 'Kate of Kent'. Indeed according to a list compiled by John Taylor in 1638, of nineteen animals in one bear garden only one did not have a human name.

Bear-baiting was a major part of contemporary city life and there are many references to it in the plays and writings of the time. Shakespeare's theatre, the Globe, was very close to several bear gardens, and his audiences would have appreciated the first scene of *The Merry Wives of Windsor*, where Abraham Slender is trying to impress a young woman, Anne Page, by bragging about the time he saw a bear escape and attempted to catch it: 'I have seen [him] loose twenty times, and have taken him by the chain; / but, I warrant you, the women have so cried and shrieked at it, that it passed . . .'

Not to mention the most famous stage direction of all time, in Act III of Shakespeare's *The Winter's Tale*, when Antigonus is pursued – and killed offstage – by a huge, fierce creature: 'Exit, pursued by a bear'.

The seventeenth-century Dutch artist Abraham Hondius painted several pictures featuring bear-baiting, though by then the Puritans had tried to ban the sport (along with most other public entertainments) as ungodly. The popularity of bear-baiting was in any case waning, but it was not actually banned until the passing of the Cruelty to Animals Act in 1835.

Bear farming – the keeping of bears in captivity in order to harvest their bile, or digestive fluid – is a thriving industry in North Korea, Laos, Vietnam, Myanmar and especially China. Bear farming has its roots in traditional Chinese medicine, the practice dating back at least 1,300 years. Originally wild bears were killed and the gall bladder, where the bile is stored after being made in the liver, was removed. But like so many old Chinese customs it has now become big business – these poor bears are kept in cages so small that each animal cannot turn round or even stand up.

Bear bile – and its active ingredient ursodeoxycholic acid (UDCA) – is used to treat a wide range of common ailments including sore throats, fevers, epilepsy and liver disease. Whether efficacious or not, it sells for up to $24,000 a kilo, more than half the price of gold.

The Chinese argue that by farming bears the wild populations are safeguarded, as there is no need to hunt them. However, as the farms expand there is a constant need for more wild bears to replace those that have outlived their usefulness. With between 9,000 and 20,000 Asian black bears in captivity in China alone, and a wild population which may be as low as 25,000, the plight of this animal is getting more and more serious. And although the selling of bear products is subject to international legislation, this does not cover the illegal trade.

In the west, bears are at the centre of a revolutionary approach to maintaining and improving our natural heritage. 'Rewilding' is the twenty-first century's way of recreating large areas of habitat in order to allow a whole range of wild creatures to thrive. Instead of fencing off pockets of land as nature reserves, wild creatures are allowed to roam where they please; this takes place on a massive scale and finally – and perhaps most importantly – people who live in the area are integrated into the vision, so that they live alongside, rather than apart from, wildlife.

On mainland Europe, rewilding is making astonishing progress, even in populous countries such as the Netherlands. There has been perhaps understandable resistance to the idea of large carnivores such as the brown bear being brought back – and yet evidence shows that these apex predators can be reintroduced without causing any real harm to human populations.

The European approach is very different from that practised for many years in both developed counties such as the United States and Canada, and in the developing world in Africa, Asia and South America. There, conservationists favour the 'separation model', where humans and animals are largely kept apart. But in the European Union – whose population density is more than 100 people per square kilometre, three times as high as the United States, and far higher than most of Africa – this approach is simply unworkable. This has led to conservationists adopting what they call the 'coexistence model', integrating people and wildlife by modifying habitats on a highly ambitious scale.

It has worked. Today, Europe is home to twice as many wolves (more than 11,000) as the lower 48 United States, despite being only slightly larger in area. Thanks to this, even more surprisingly, the commonest large carnivore in Europe is now the brown bear.

The brown bear has experienced mixed fortunes since it recolonised much of Europe following the end of the last Ice Age about 12,000 years ago. For most of this time the population would have been fairly stable, although as humans settled down to an agricultural life, bears would have been persecuted because of the damage they did to livestock and crops. The decline accelerated further during the eighteenth and nineteenth centuries, when as the human population rose so the bears' forest habitat was lost, and hunting became more efficient. Their numbers and range began to drop rapidly, with populations retreating to mountainous areas with few human residents, where most bears live today.

But since reaching its low point in the 1950s, the numbers of bears in Europe have doubled, and they have begun gradually to recolonise some of their former range. Today, of a global population of about 200,000 brown bears, 17,000 – roughly 8.5 per cent – live in Europe. They do so, however, at very varied densities: ranging from just 0.5 bears per 1,000 square kilometres in Norway, to as many as 200 per 100 square kilometres in Romania – the equivalent of roughly 300 bears living in Surrey, or more than 15,000 bears in the whole of Scotland. Which brings us to the question, if bears can live alongside people in Sweden and Spain, Finland and Romania, why can't they be reintroduced into Britain?

Bears did live here, at least until Roman times, and survived in Scotland perhaps as late as the ninth or tenth centuries. They became extinct for the usual reasons: loss of their forest habitat and widespread persecution. But now that they are thriving on mainland Europe, shouldn't they also be brought back here?

Given, however, the hysterical headlines accompanying accidental or deliberate releases of beavers, and the continued opposition among many Scottish landowners to the reintroduction of the lynx, the restoration of bears to the British landscape seems unlikely, at least in the foreseeable future.

In the meantime, the world's largest and arguably best-known member of its family, the polar bear, is in big trouble. In the battle of the scientists, the polar bear has unwittingly found itself in a tug-of-war, with assertions, claims, propaganda and a bewildering range of statistics being brought out to claim either that polar bears are threatened with extinction or that there is nothing to worry about.

On one side, many environmentalists are rightly concerned about the rapid melting of the Arctic sea ice, especially in summer, which has accelerated at a rate not predicted by even the most pessimistic scientists. This, they argue, will mean that soon polar bears will not have anywhere to hunt their main prey of seals – an argument reinforced by emotive video footage and photographs of polar bears swimming long distances to get from one patch of ice to another.

But those who dispute this view – who include many well-respected scientists, not just those in the employ of the fossil-fuel lobby – point to the uneven loss of sea ice, which is far greater in some areas than others. They also raise the inconvenient fact that polar bear numbers, far from decreasing, are at their highest level for decades, with an estimated global population of at least 25,000, considerably higher than the estimated 5,000 individuals in the 1960s, largely because of better controls on hunting. As Dr Susan Crockford, one of the scientists arguing against the imminent extinction of polar bears, points out: 'On almost every measure, things are looking good for polar bears . . . It really is time for the doom and gloom to stop.'

Most of all, they argue that polar bears have been here before. Polar bears split from brown bears somewhere between 125,000 and 1.2 million years ago, which means they have experienced several periods of extreme warming, and survived. Admittedly, melting sea ice and warmer temperatures can create many problems for polar bears, causing their dens to collapse or making it harder for them to find food, or allowing the spread of disease. In a world where small differences can easily tip into population collapse, we may wonder if we want to take the risk of losing the polar bear.

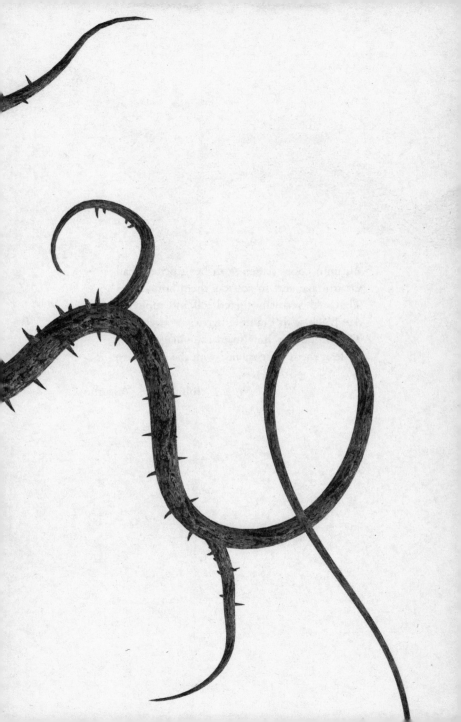

Autumn comes laden with her ripened load
Of fruitage and so scatters them abroad
That each fern smothered hill and molehill waste
Are black with bramble berries – where in haste
The chubby urchins from the village hie
To feast them there stained with the purple dye . . .

John Clare, 'Autumn'

16

Brambles

Reading the Landscape

One day in 1911, the body of a man was discovered buried in soft clay at Walton-on-the-Naze, along the coast of Essex. From clues found on (and in) the corpse, it was soon apparent that this was no modern crime scene. And on closer examination of his stomach, the last meal of this Neolithic man – who lived perhaps 5,000 years ago or more – was discovered to have been blackberries. As poet and countryside historian Geoffrey Grigson pointed out: '[This confirmed] what we would safely guess, that blackberries were eaten many thousands of years ago as they are today.'

Juicy, plump and tasty, blackberries are surely our most popular wild fruit. We forage for them on sunny days in late summer or early autumn, staining our hands and mouths with their juice as we greedily eat as many as we can, before gathering the rest to take home, to be made into jams, jellies, tarts and pies. For Richard Mabey, author of the food-forager's bible *Food for Free*, blackberrying provides a crucial link to our rural heritage:

Blackberrying is the one almost universal act of foraging to survive in our industrialised island and has a special role in the relationship between townspeople and the countryside. It's not just that blackberries are delicious, ubiquitous and unmistakeable. Blackberrying, I suspect, carries with it a little of the urban dweller's myth of country life: harvest, a sense of season, and just enough discomfort to quicken the senses.

As well as being a rich source of vitamin C, blackberries also contain a wide range of phytochemical compounds which have been used in research for cancer cures. Our knowledge of the blackberry's medicinal properties goes back to the ancient Greek physician Hippocrates who, in the fifth century BC, suggested using its leaves and stems in a poultice to treat gout. Pliny the Elder listed it as an astringent useful for the treatment of diarrhoea and commented that chewing the leaves soothes sore gums and tonsils. Later, medieval herbalists recommended placing the plant's leaves on to burns and swellings, in much the same way as children are taught to put dock leaves on nettle stings. Not all the uses were as effective: an old remedy for cholera was to boil blackberry juice with sugar, nutmeg, allspice, and then mix with copious amounts of brandy: the suggested dosage was two or three wine glassfuls two or three times daily – at least the patient would be well anaesthetised.

But before you imagine that this plant could offer a cure-all for all kinds of ailments, beware! There is a very definite season. Folklore from many parts of Britain warns us not to pick and eat black-berries after 11 October (Old Michaelmas Day), as the devil spits (or in some versions pisses) on them, making them unfit for human consumption. Like many folk beliefs, there is more than a grain of truth in this: towards the end of their growing season black-berries may be infected by moulds and mildews, brought on by wet autumnal weather. There's less truth behind another of the plant's nicknames, scaldhead, which comes from the old wives' tale that children who ate the fruit to excess became afflicted with a disease of the scalp called scald head – a threat obviously aimed at making them bring some home with them.

Blackberries are mentioned by the Greek playwright Aeschylus and the Roman poet Ovid; they also appear in Shakespeare where, in *Henry IV Part I*, Falstaff states: 'Give you a reason on compulsion? If reasons were as plentiful as blackberries, / I would give no man a reason on compulsion, I.'

There is even a handheld mobile device named after them: the BlackBerry smartphone, so called, it is said, because the inventors wanted a name from nature – something playful, in sharp contrast to the hi-tech world of e-mails and the rat race. The device has even entered street slang: according to the *Daily Mail*, for some urban gangs the phrase 'going blackberry picking' now means to go out to steal mobile phones.

With almost 400 different species – found both in the wild and as cultivated varieties throughout the temperate regions of the world – the blackberry is a well-known and popular fruit. But what of the plant that produces it: the bramble? What can this tangled mass of spikes, stems and leaves tell us about the natural world, and our often complicated relationship with it?

The bramble has stood as the symbol of untameable nature for thousands of years. Any film of the post-apocalyptic variety worth its salt shows nature rapidly reclaiming cityscapes, brambles and vines entwining around the remains of crumbling skyscrapers. Ever since mankind settled down to farm, having to clear woodland to do so, civilisation has been a constant struggle against the encroaches of nature. In the Book of Isaiah, a wrathful Old Testament God lays down his judgement on the nations of the world: 'And all her princes shall be nothing. And thorns shall come up in her palaces, nettles and brambles in the fortresses thereof: and it shall be an habitation of dragons, and a court for owls.'

Our earliest stories teach us that brambles should always be treated with respect. In the fairy tale, beautiful Rapunzel is hidden away in a tower surrounded by a dense thicket of brambles. When the wicked witch pushes the prince out of the tower window, the brambles he falls into scratch his eyes so badly that he is blinded. (Luckily for happy endings, Rapunzel's loving tears are enough to make him see again.) Generations of children have taken note that things might not necessarily end quite so well for them, if, overreaching for some particularly tempting fruit, they were to fall into the thorns.

The bramble *Rubus fruticosus* (along with other similar species and hybrid varieties) is a member of the rose family, with which it shares its thorny stems. These form highly effective defences against any wild creature that might be thinking of feeding on the plant. Brambles are widespread throughout Britain, apart from on very high ground and a few offshore islands, and are one of the most easily recognised of all wild plants. They are unusual among the British flora in that they provide us with succulent fruit, though they are also regarded by some as weeds. But the definition of a weed depends on who you ask. A gardener is likely to say that it's a plant in the wrong place. A botanist, on the other hand, will celebrate weeds as highly adaptable species that often employ a number of strategies to help them colonise habitats. Many weeds are annuals such as the corn poppy which produces thousands of seeds and can grow very quickly, within a single season. If conditions aren't right, the poppy's seeds can lie dormant for decades, waiting for the opportunity to germinate on freshly disturbed soil.

Brambles are perennials and more multi-skilled. Their seeds are spread by birds and other animals into suitable areas, but they can also spread by suckers and a single plant can romp through an entire woodland by this means. David Attenborough's groundbreaking BBC series *The Private Life of Plants* showed, using time-lapse sequences, how aggressively these long writhing ropes of bramble colonise new ground. Like vegetable octopuses, they clamber and arc over vegetation, producing rootlets where they touch the ground, often a metre or more from the parent plant. The resulting suckers soon form an impenetrable thicket of dense, arching stems almost impossible to get through without suffering pricks and scratches. Anyone who's strayed off a woodland path and stumbled through the undergrowth cursing as bramble stems trip them up, won't hesitate to regard the delicious blackberry as an annoying weed. But brambles break the usual weedy rules by being delicious as well as pernicious and maybe that's why we can admire and loathe them simultaneously.

Botanists often lump the British bramble as *Rubus fruticosus* agg. The 'agg' is an abbreviation for aggregate, meaning that microspecies have been grouped together under a single umbrella heading. The ability of brambles to cross-fertilise and to self-fertilise has allowed them to evolve into a vast number of microspecies; more than 320 are currently recognised in the UK alone. While some botanists flee in horror from the identification implications of this, others have become bramble specialists – known as batologists, from the Greek word for bramble, *batos*. These microspecies differ from each other in the amount and size of prickles, leaf shape and hairiness, flower colour and growth form, along with several other characteristics. Some grow in just a handful of places in the British Isles and so are as much a part of the landscape as rocks or architectural styles. Take a blindfolded batologist to any part of the United Kingdom and they may well be able to identify the location from the combination of different brambles that grow there.

Brambles adapt well to different soils and habitats, growing happily in woods, on hillsides, on brownfield sites and in gardens. As a result, they are often considered a pest, because they can spread very rapidly, especially on newly cleared ground. Not everyone considered these plants a pest, though: in the Middle Ages the arch formed when a bramble stem takes root was thought to cure hernias and ruptures in children: the unfortunate victim was passed back and forth through the arch, no doubt suffering cuts and scratches in the process.

There are other superstitions linked with brambles, too, many long forgotten. Graves covered with brambles were thought to prevent the dead from emerging by night and walking among the living; while another folk tale, retold by Geoffrey Grigson, refers to the way brambles tend to remove chunks of wool from passing sheep, and features three rather unlikely co-conspirators:

The cormorant was once a merchant dealing in wool. He went shares with the bat and the bramble in a boat, to carry his wool overseas. The boat was wrecked, so the cormorant is always diving after the lost cargo, the bat owes money and hides from its creditors till dark, and the bramble makes up its losses by stealing wool from the sheep.

Brambles produce their familiar white or pale pink flowers in late spring and early summer. Soon afterwards the fruits begin to form – though technically blackberries are not actually fruits or berries, being composed of many small segments known as 'drupelets'.

The flowers are an important source of nectar for bees and butterflies, and a host of other insects, while several species of butterflies, including the green hairstreak, grizzled skipper and holly blue, lay their eggs on the plant's leaves, which then become their caterpillars' food plant. As the berries ripen, they don't just provide a tasty source of vitamins for us; mammals and birds – especially migratory species such as warblers – feed voraciously on them in early autumn to get enough energy for their epic journeys across the globe.

Brambles are a useful reminder that nature is not all about us. Their fruit may be desirable, but their tangled confusion of spikes and stems, and long, sinuous creepers, make no concessions to human welfare. Yet inside this thorny, impenetrable mass the small, soft and vulnerable shelter, safe from the larger predators who dare not take on this feisty plant to seize their intended prey.

Brambles also form an important natural aid to the hedgerows that traditionally have edged fields and patches of woodland. Early farmers cleared woodland to create open spaces where they could plant their crops and raise livestock – the first fields. So they needed some kind of barrier to prevent animals escaping, and the hedge was born. Later, hedgerows were planted as boundaries between fields and properties. But the biggest change came when, in the late eighteenth and early nineteenth centuries, the Enclosure Acts transformed Britain's countryside by creating the 'patchwork quilt' of fields we know today. Some were specially planted, but others are far more ancient, as they are the remains of strips of ancient woodland.

But like so many features of the countryside that are good for wildlife, hedgerows are under threat. From the end of the Second World War until the early 1960s, roughly 150,000 kilometres of hedgerows were destroyed in Britain, and although some have now been restored, the total amount of hedges lost since the war is estimated to be close to half a million kilometres. This has contributed hugely to the decline in farmland species such as birds, bumblebees and butterflies.

One approximate method of estimating the age of hedgerows is by following 'Hooper's rule'. It works by counting the number of different species of woody plants along a 27-metre stretch of hedge; multiply this by 100, and the answer is roughly equal to the age of the hedge. So five different species could mean the hedge is approximately 500 years old.

The bramble is rarely, if ever, planted deliberately in hedges, but insinuates itself there, brought in by perching or roosting birds and small mammals. Hedges are an ideal habitat for brambles, often well-lit, regularly trimmed to avoid shading of the flowers and sheltered by surrounding shrubs from extremes of wind and weather. While the stems can be savagely prickly, the plant obligingly holds its flowers aloof from the tangle to allow insects to pollinate and birds – and us – to pluck the fruit. Although hedges are under threat in places from industrialised farming, they are still a magnet for jam-makers. Those of us who have gardens can't always spare the space needed to nurture a really productive bramble patch and so the hedgerow is a must for seasoned blackberry pickers.

In *Tales from Brambly Hedge*, a series of illustrated children's books written from 1980 onwards by Jill Barklem, homely families of mice create a world in a bramble hedgerow safe from the dangers outside. The idea for the books came to Jill when she was travelling back and forth to art college on the Central Line of the London Underground: 'I came to hate this journey, the carriages were crammed full of people, everything seemed so filthy. It was like a glimpse of hell.'

In an attempt to ignore her surroundings, Jill would close her eyes and escape into an imaginary world, daydreaming of a hedge bank populated by mice.

In Aesop's fable 'The Trees and the Bramble', dating back at least 2,500 years, and probably originating long before in a tale from western Asia, a pomegranate shrub and an apple tree hold a debate as to which is the more beautiful. As the argument reaches its height, a bramble bush intervenes. The rather snide moral of the tale is that when two sophisticated people argue, a vulgar person cannot help but join in, firmly putting the bramble in its place as the commoner of the woodland. An alternative interpretation might be that the bramble has more common sense than to waste its time on trivial disputes.

A poem written by the former favourite of Elizabeth I, Robert Devereux, Earl of Essex (1565–1601) recasts this. To him the bramble is a symbol of a simpler life. Caught up in wars and court intrigues, Essex had ample reason to long for a safer, better life:

> Happy were he could finish forth his fate
>   In some unhaunted desert, most obscure
> From all societies, from love and hate
>   Of worldly folk; then might he sleep secure;
> Then wake again, and give God ever praise,
>   Content with hips and haws and bramble-berry;
> In contemplation spending all his days,
>   And change of holy thoughts to make him merry;
> Where, when he dies, his tomb may be a bush,
> Where harmless robin dwells with gentle thrush.

Here country living and a diet of 'hips and haws and bramble-berry' offer a tempting alternative to the 'worldly' complexities and dangers of modern life. Sadly it was one that Essex was unable to take and he was beheaded on 25 February 1601 for his involvement in a plot against the queen.

But back in the real world, these tangled masses of brambles are becoming enmeshed in a much darker reality: a world of murder and detective work. For a small and highly specialised group of people known as forensic botanists, the bramble is a godsend: because it grows so well on ground that has been dug or disturbed, it can provide valuable clues as to suspicious goings-on, such as the burial or temporary location of a human body.

It all comes down to the plant's growing pattern. When the ground is disturbed, brambles will rapidly recolonise from adjacent areas, using the suckers on the end of their stalks to take root and spread. An expert can easily tell whether a colony of brambles on a particular piece of ground is long established, or has moved in recently; this enables them to rapidly check a wide area of habitat to look for places where a body might have been buried – even for a short time.

Brambles – or rather the blackberries themselves – may also help us track the progress of climate change. According to the UK Phenology Network, which tracks the timing of natural events in spring and autumn, the date when the first ripe blackberries appear is moving significantly earlier in the calendar.

During the period from 2003 to 2007, the average date for ripe blackberries to appear across the UK shifted forward by more than a week: from 14 and 15 August in 2003 and 2004, to 6 August in 2005 and 2006, to 4 August in 2007. Back in the late twentieth century the average date was towards the end of August, rather than as it is now, close to the beginning. Of course this does mask major geographical variations: in southern Britain blackberries ripen much earlier, with sightings normally around the time of the Wimbledon tennis championships in early July (or even late

June). In Scotland, where they ripen much later, they appear towards the end of August.

As always, we must be careful in ascribing seasonal changes from year to year to a long-term pattern. For example, the particularly early date for ripe blackberries in 2007 was the result of a very warm April followed by a damp late spring, allowing the plants to come into flower early and the berries to swell and ripen. Six years later, in 2013, a very cold and late spring meant that the average date for ripe blackberries was a full two weeks later, around 18 August. But the trend does appear to be shifting towards earlier ripening.

The jury may still be out on whether the appearance of blackberries earlier in the season is a genuine indicator of global climate change. What we do know, however, is that this succulent and desirable fruit, and the tangled, spiky plant on which it grows, offers a huge range of natural and cultural references, which would take as long to explore fully as it takes to wade through a bramble thicket.

Our parrot, winged mimic of the human voice, from farthest Ind, is dead . . .
O hapless one, thou wast the glory of birds, and now thou art no more!
With thy wondrous plumage, thou outshone the green fire of the emerald,
And the hue of thy beak was of the richest red.
No bird on earth could speak so well as thou, so great thy skill
In imitating, with thy nasal tones, the sounds that thou hadst heard . . .
Thou didst ask for very little; and since you loved so much to gossip,
Your beak had very little time for food. A nut was all thy dinner,
A poppy-seed or two would bring thee sleep,
And with a sip of water thou wouldst quench thy thirst . . .
In Elysium our parrot speaks and calls around him all birds of gentle soul.
His bones a mound doth cover, a little mound as doth befit his size,
And on it is a little stone that bears this little legend:

From this memorial, you may see
What love my mistress bore to me.
Whene'er to her I spake, my words
Meant more than any other bird's.

Ovid, *Amores*, Book 1, Elegy VI

17

Parrots

Colourful Characters

When most of us think of pets, a dog or cat is usually the first animal to come to mind. But to many medieval Europeans, cats were the agents of Satan, while dogs were working animals, bred for specific jobs such as herding, guarding, vermin control and hunting. Until about 300 years ago cagebirds were the animal companion of choice. Poorer households kept sparrows, canaries and finches; but the most sought after were parrots (called 'popinjays' before 1500). Kept as pets for over 4,000 years, they have been listed (as prized possessions) in Egyptian papyri and celebrated in many ancient artworks. The Roman poet Ovid's elegy for his mistress's dead parrot that opens the chapter uses the extreme language and imagery of epic poetry to deliberately comic effect, but what comes across is a noisily real bird with a nasal voice, loyal and affectionate, too busy gossiping to eat much. The poet's affection for it is palpable.

Kings and popes kept parrots as status symbols, perhaps also because they enjoyed the company of an avian equivalent of a court jester, which could say what it liked to the all-powerful ruler. For similar reasons parrots have formed a popular subject for writers ever since. The poet John Skelton, Henry VIII's court poet, wrote a long satire called *Speke Parrot* (Speak Parrot) in which a mad parrot rants about the excesses of Cardinal Wolsey, warning the king emphatically: 'His wolf's head, wan, blue as lead, gapeth over the crown.' Henry had a parrot rare in Tudor England, an African grey parrot from Congo, a highly social and intelligent species whose high level of cognition allows them to assign meanings to different sounds, and their wide range of vocalisation allows them to do this for a lot of objects. They are also known to employ cause-and-effect thinking. For instance, if an African grey observes someone running towards a ringing telephone, they are highly likely to imitate the sound later, just to catch your attention. By using a parrot as a mouthpiece, Skelton could get away with expressing dangerously extreme opinions. It wouldn't have been much of a leap for his readers to see his implication that if Henry's parrot could really talk he'd be warning the king about Wolsey.

And as the years passed, it wasn't just the great and the good who kept parrots any more. Robinson Crusoe caught one to keep him company in his long exile on his desert island: 'I did, after some painstaking, catch a young parrot . . . but it was some years before I could make him speak; however, at last I taught him to call me by name very familiarly.' Long John Silver, antihero of Robert Louis Stevenson's *Treasure Island* (1883) had one, named Captain Flint in mockery of his former captain – despite, or perhaps because, it was a female.

> 'Now that bird,' Silver would say, 'is, may be, two hundred years old, Hawkins – they lives for ever mostly, and if anybody's seen more wickedness it must be the devil himself. She's sailed with England – the great Cap'n England, the pirate. She's been at Madagascar, and at Malabar, and Surinam, and Providence, and Portobello . . . She was at the boarding of the Viceroy of the Indies out of Goa, she was, and to look at her you would think she was a babby.'

But as he points out, the problem for poor Captain Flint is that she's been tainted by her association with humanity, and that while she swears a blue streak, she is completely innocent of its meaning. No image of a pirate has been complete ever since without a parrot, shouting, 'Pieces of Eight, Pieces of Eight,' from its perch on their shoulder.

When it comes to the images of parrots themselves and how we see them, they found a champion in an unlikely Victorian artist.

The twentieth of twenty-one children (and youngest to survive), Edward Lear had a childhood marked by a series of epileptic seizures, asthma, bronchitis and depression. The Lear family were so poverty-stricken that when Edward was just four, he and his eldest sister Anne (who was twenty-one years older than him) had to move out of the family home in north London and fend for themselves. During these early years he developed a love of – some might say obsession with – the natural world, especially birds.

His artistic talent soon became apparent. By sixteen he was making a living as a serious 'ornithological draughtsman' employed by the Zoological Society, publishing his first book, *Illustrations of the Family of Psittacidae, or Parrots*, when he was just twenty. Should you have a cool $275,000 to spare you can purchase, from an upmarket New York gallery, one of just a hundred or so surviving copies of the first edition, with its forty-two beautiful lithographs of some of the world's most colourful birds.

The reasons Lear chose parrots for his first book were a combination of the practical, the aesthetic and the commercial. Parrots were widely kept as cagebirds, and so the impecunious artist did not have to travel further than London Zoo to enjoy close-up views of his subjects. They were beautiful, brightly coloured and charismatic, ideal for an artist still trying out his technique. And they were popular: wealthy aristocrats and merchants delighted in owning these intelligent creatures, which were not only very striking in appearance, but could also imitate human speech and many other sounds.

Where Lear differed from previous wildlife artists was in his insistence on working from live birds rather than museum specimens. It is this – along with the vivid reds, yellows, blues and greens he used – that gives the portraits such dynamism and energy, especially compared with the rather stiff previous bird illustrations.

In *Parrot Culture*, cultural historian Bruce Thomas Boehrer praises Lear for his ability to capture the nature of the living bird, especially in his lithograph of the scarlet macaw:

> This is a classic instance of Lear's innovative postures; avoiding a standard side-on view, the macaw turns its back on the viewer as if oblivious to him . . . But the best touch of all is the bird's gaze, which slyly, unexpectedly strays back to the viewer it seems at first to be ignoring. This is the parrot's equivalent of a nudge and a wink – a humorous suggestion that . . . its neglect of the audience may be both spontaneous and studied at the same time.

Despite huge critical acclaim, *Illustrations of the Family of Psittacidae* was a commercial failure, but it did launch the young Lear's career as a bird artist. For the remainder of his long lifetime he pursued his passions for art and writing, becoming professor of drawing to the young Queen Victoria, illustrating several volumes of Alfred, Lord Tennyson's poetry, and travelling extensively in Europe, Egypt, Ceylon (now Sri Lanka) and India.

All this art, travel, ornithology and passion for nature runs as a serious undercurrent through his much better-known nonsense verse:

> There was an old man of Dunrose;
> A parrot seized hold of his nose.
> When he grew melancholy,
> They said, 'His name's Polly',
> Which soothed that old man of Dunrose.

In almost two centuries since Edward Lear first produced his celebrated work on parrots, these charismatic birds have remained highly popular – not just among ornithologists, but with the public at large.

Although the world's 360 or so different species of parrots and cockatoos are mostly confined to the tropical, subtropical and equatorial regions of Central and South America, sub-Saharan Africa, South East Asia and Australasia, their ubiquity as cagebirds (and the subsequent establishment of feral populations of some species) means that they are familiar to almost everyone.

Parrots fall into two main family groups: 'true parrots', with roughly 330 species; and cockatoos, distinctive birds found only in Australasia, with about 20 species. Some authorities also separate the four endemic species of New Zealand parrots such as the kea and kakapo, which are very different in both appearance and behaviour from other parrots.

In the wild, parrots are a highly adaptable group of birds, found in a range of habitats from tropical rainforests to oceanic islands, deserts to grasslands, and in the case of several species introduced to Europe and North America (and those that have become adapted to this new and productive habitat in their native range), parks and gardens.

They are thought to have evolved around 66 million years ago, about the time of the last great extinction that wiped out the dinosaurs. Recent evolutionary studies have revealed that their closest relatives are the songbirds (Passeriformes) and, more surprisingly, the falcons (Falconiformes), which have now been separated from other birds of prey such as vultures, hawks and eagles.

Parrots are also very variable in size, with a greater difference in length between the largest and smallest than any other order of birds. At one end of the scale is the minuscule buff-faced pygmy-parrot of northern New Guinea, which at just 8 centimetres long, and weighing 10–15 grams, is smaller (though slightly heavier) than a wren. At the other end of the scale is the massive hyacinth macaw of the Pantanal in South America, which weighs in at up to 1.7 kilos and measures 1 metre from beak to tail. Although shorter in length, the flightless kakapo is even heavier, weighing up to 3 kilos – about the same as a medium-sized goose.

With such a range of size and habitat, it's hardly surprising that parrots vary dramatically in appearance, differences reflected in their names. There are lovebirds and lorikeets, fig-parrots and parakeets, macaws and amazons, rosellas and racquet-tails – the latter named after their protruding tail-feathers.

Some parrots are common and widespread: the parakeets that fly noisily around the London skies like a green version of the Red Arrows can also be found in many cities around the world, as well as their native India and Africa, while budgerigars can be seen in flocks numbering tens of thousands at waterholes in the Australian outback.

Others are so rare they are almost mythical, such as the night parrot, a nocturnal Australian desert-dwelling species so elusive that there have only been a handful of sightings in the past few decades – mostly involving birds found dead.

Parrots don't just live in pristine natural habits: one species, the aptly named rainbow lorikeet, has become one of Australia's commonest and most familiar garden birds. These multicoloured small parrots – a little larger than a blackbird – look as if they have been painted by a child let loose with a colouring set, sporting a purplish-blue head and belly, reddish-orange breast, green wings and a bright red bill. They roam in pairs or small flocks around suburban Sydney, Melbourne and Brisbane (and have accidentally been introduced into Perth and Auckland), showing surprising aggression towards any other birds competing with them for food.

But large or small, common or rare, what all these very varied species of parrot have in common is their powerful, curved bills and upright posture. They also have 'zygodactyl' feet, with two toes pointing forward and two back, allowing them to grip objects and clamber along tree branches or through dense foliage (a feature they share with woodpeckers, cuckoos and some species of owl).

Parrots mostly feed on seeds, fruits, nuts and flower buds; though some also feed on invertebrates, and several species regularly eat clay, which helps them absorb any potentially dangerous toxins in the fruit or seeds they have eaten.

Despite their diversity, their breeding habits are surprisingly uniform. Apart from a handful of species, including the monk parakeet of South America (which builds a huge nest out of twigs), they mostly nest in holes or hollows – either in trees or, in the case of the burrowing parrot, also from South America, in the ground, in colonies that may number many thousands of birds. They are mostly monogamous, with strong pair bonds, and as with many species that nest in holes, where darkness means there is no need for camouflage, they lay white eggs.

Parrots rival crows as the world's most intelligent birds, being able to learn language, use tools, and learn from their mistakes – aspects that put them on a par with dolphins and primates. They are also among the world's longest-lived birds, especially in captivity: Cookie, a male Major Mitchell's cockatoo at a zoo near Chicago, USA, turned eighty in June 2013 and is still going strong; while Cocky, a sulphur-crested cockatoo from Sydney, died in 1916, allegedly in his 120th year. In the wild, parrots and cockatoos struggle to live so long, but nevertheless can reach forty or fifty years old.

Today the worldwide trade in parrots involves an estimated million or more birds every year, most transported in such poor conditions that they often die before they arrive at their destination. This trade is nothing new. Parrots have been kept in captivity since the time of the ancient Egyptians and early Chinese and Indian civilisations, and were popular pets among the ancient Greeks and Romans. In the fourth century BC Alexander the Great brought a parrot home from his travels to India; this was probably a ring-necked parakeet, though his name was later given to another similar but larger Asian species, the Alexandrine parakeet. Soon afterwards Aristotle noted in his *Historia Animalium* (the first proper published work on natural history) that parrots could speak in 'human tongue', especially, he noted, after they have drunk wine.

Parrots were liked because they were intelligent and mischievous, with the Romans teaching them to perform tricks: a painting found at Herculaneum (the city next to Pompeii destroyed in the famous eruption of Vesuvius in AD 79) shows a parakeet in a harness, drawing a tiny chariot whose passenger is a grasshopper. Perhaps, as the use of parrots as comedy material today (most notably by Monty Python) shows, we haven't changed our views of these birds a lot since then.

The Romans also ate parrots – especially their tongues – maybe assuming this would give them greater eloquence. In the third century BC the boy Emperor Elagabalus served the severed heads of parrots at gargantuan feasts, and also to his captive lions (just before releasing the beasts to attack his unsuspecting guests). Pliny the Elder gave instructions on how to teach parrots to talk, which bizarrely included hitting them over the head with an iron bar.

The age of exploration, from Marco Polo in the thirteenth century through to Vasco da Gama, Magellan and Columbus during the late fifteenth and early sixteenth centuries, brought many opportunities to collect parrots from around the world and bring them back to Europe, where they were the subject of both curiosity and commercial trade. Pope Martin V appointed a 'Keeper of the Parrots' to look after his collection of birds. In the early sixteenth century Pope Leo X paraded his South American parrots, a gift from Manuel I, King of Portugal, through the streets of Rome.

Parrots feature prominently in medieval and Renaissance art, especially depictions of the Garden of Eden, such as Albrecht Dürer's engraving *Adam and Eve*. More widely, they were used as shorthand images for Paradise, and indeed still are, in the Jehovah's Witnesses' publication the *Watchtower*. The Virgin Mary is often depicted with a parrot, as in Rubens's *The Holy Family with Parrot*, from 1614. Incidentally, the familiar name 'Polly', which we still associate with parrots (partly because of its alliterative qualities) is a familiar version of the name Mary.

During the Victorian era, the keeping of parrots went from being the preserve of the rich and powerful to within reach of

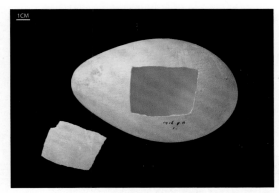

The infamous emperor penguin egg collected by polar explorer Apsley Cherry-Garrard, whose tale of his quest was told in the book *The Worst Journey in the World*

With almost one million individuals, the black bear is by far the commonest species of bear in the world even though it is only found in North America

MACROCERCUS ARACANGA.

Red and Yellow Macaw

The scarlet macaw, one of the world's largest and most colourful parrots,
painted by the Victorian artist and poet Edward Lear

Blackberry picking is one of the classic experiences of late summer and early autumn, though you need to avoid being scratched by the brambles

This basking Nile crocodile, one of the largest reptiles in the world, is ready to leap into action at surprising speed should it spot a potential victim within reach

Bunodes balli.

A precious example of
the famous Blaschka
anemones, glass replicas
of sea anemones showing
their elegance and beauty

The anemone *Calliactis
parasitica*: Philip Henry
Gosse's illustration from
his book *The Aquarium:
An Unveiling of the Wonders
of the Deep Sea*, 1854

PL. IV

P.H.Gosse, del.   Hanhart, Chromo lith.

THE PARASITIC ANEMONE &c.

An ornate carving on the 'casque'
of the helmeted hornbill, one of
the most spectacular members
of this diverse family of birds

Few groups of animals are as diverse in size and appearance as beetles, the largest group of wild creatures on the planet

Cockroaches may be repulsive to most people, yet they have inspired great works of art including Franz Kafka's *The Metamorphosis*

Tree, by Devon-based artist Tania Kovats, uses the branches of an oak to symbolise
Charles Darwin's tree of life, a representation of the theory of evolution

Pulgas vestidas, or dressed fleas, are a fine example of art in miniature, which reached its height in Mexico in the early years of the twentieth century

The famous Thames whale, a northern bottlenose whale that became stranded in London's river in early 2006 and sadly died

ordinary families, when a small species from Australia with the bizarre name 'budgerigar' (a corruption of a native Aboriginal word) was first brought to Europe.

In the wild, budgerigars are nomadic, following seasonal rains to find food and then breed. Their original shades are green and yellow, with black barring across the back, but selective breeding has produced a wide range of colours including blue, white and pink specimens. Easy to breed and keep, and excellent vocal mimics, budgies (as they were soon nicknamed) quickly became very popular cagebirds, and remain so today; they are said to be the third commonest pet in the world, after dogs and cats.

But birds kept in cages – especially those as intelligent and resourceful as parrots – tend to find their way out; and as a result of accidental escapes and deliberate releases of pet birds, several species of parrot are now firmly established in feral colonies in places where native parrots never lived.

In London, and other parts of south-east England (and sometimes beyond), feral flocks of ring-necked (also known as rose-ringed) parakeets are a familiar sight as they shoot across the evening sky. As they pass, they utter a call more familiar from the soundtracks of films such as *Slumdog Millionaire*, *Gandhi* and a host of lesser-known Bollywood movies, making a walk in Hyde Park on a sultry summer's evening feel like a stroll through the leafier streets of Mumbai.

They are not just in London: ring-necked parakeets have colonised Antwerp and Amsterdam, Tunis and Tokyo, Brussels and Barcelona, Los Angeles and even Hawaii. And they're not the only species to have done so: their close relative the monk parakeet, originally from South America, has also established free-flying colonies in various cities around the world, including around the set of the BBC's soap opera *EastEnders*, at Elstree Studios, north of London.

The origin of the UK's ring-necked parakeets is the subject of more urban myths than perhaps any other bird. One story claims that they escaped from the set of the 1951 Humphrey Bogart and Katherine Hepburn movie *The African Queen*; another that they were released by legendary rock guitarist Jimi Hendrix in 1969. Whatever their origin (and it is far more likely that they were simply set free by, or escaped from, pet owners or traders), they have not only survived but thrived. Coming from northern India, they are perfectly adapted to our cold winters, and a plentiful supply of food – both natural and that provided by us in the form of nuts and seeds – means that their numbers are booming.

The jury is still out as to whether they will displace native bird species, or prove destructive to commercial fruit growers. But for many Londoners, the sight of these flying green birds brings a welcome whiff of the exotic into their humdrum daily lives.

Ring-necked parakeets are just one of dozens of parrot species kept in captivity, ranging from the smaller budgies and lovebirds to enormous cockatoos and macaws. In some ways, this is rather odd, as many parrots – especially the larger ones – do not make good pets, being temperamental and easily bored, as well as noisy and destructive. And yet parrots have been kept in captivity longer than almost any other wild animal, and over the centuries tens of millions have been taken from the wild and brought to the western world to be kept in cages.

Perhaps the main reason why such potentially difficult birds are so adored and cherished is that, unlike dogs and cats, hamsters and white mice, they talk back. Language is often thought of as a uniquely human gift, and yet many parrot species are able to mimic human speech – including individual people's voices – so accurately that they can fool even their owners. But are they simply clever mimics, reproducing what they hear in what we might dismiss as 'parrot fashion', or are they intelligent enough to know what they are actually saying?

That's what US scientist Irene Pepperberg has spent her life trying to find out. Pepperberg closely studied an African grey parrot named Alex from 1977, when Alex was one year old, to 2007, when he died. The name 'Alex' was not chosen at random or on a whim; it is an acronym for 'Avian Language Experiment' (later changed to Avian Learning Experiment), a clue to Pepperberg's relentlessly practical approach.

She set out to prove that parrots do not simply repeat what they hear, but have the capability to learn language and then use it proactively to communicate their wishes and needs; even to ask abstract questions. Until her experiments began, it was widely believed that only advanced primates such as chimpanzees and gorillas (and of course humans) had the ability to use language.

Yet over time, Alex acquired a vocabulary of more than a hundred words; learned to identify fifty objects and recognise several different shapes and colours; and understand concepts such as 'bigger and smaller', 'over and under'. He even learned to say 'I'm sorry' when he sensed that a human being was annoyed. And every night, when Pepperberg left her laboratory to go home, Alex would call out: 'You be good. See you tomorrow. I love you.'

Not everyone in the scientific community agreed with Pepperberg that Alex's language skills were any more than subtle conditioning; that in effect she was helping him to get the answers to her questions right by subtle and perhaps subconscious gestures. However the majority of scientists have accepted that Alex did show genuine intelligence, learning and language skills, at about the level of a four- or five-year-old child.

Alex isn't the only example of a parrot acquiring an extensive vocabulary. During his brief eight-year lifespan from 1954 to 1962, a budgie named Sparkie learned 10 nursery rhymes, almost 400 sentences and over 500 different words. After winning the BBC International Cage Word Contest in 1958 he was disqualified the following year for being too good.

Sparkie had been trained by his owner, Mrs Mattie Williams. He featured in adverts for birdseed, appeared on the BBC *Tonight* programme, and even made a bestselling record. When he died he was stuffed and presented to the Hancock Museum, Newcastle upon Tyne, where he can still be seen today.

Inspiring though the stories of Alex and Sparkie may be, it must be admitted that the popularity of parrots as pets has not only brought them to the forefront of our consciousness, but has also led to the decline and disappearance of many species from the wild.

In his book *Extinct Birds*, Errol Fuller features the paradise parrot of Australia, the Cuban red macaw, the glaucous macaw of South America, and North America's only native parrot species, the Carolina parakeet, which was found in large numbers until the middle of the nineteenth century, and may even have survived until the mid-twentieth.

Fuller also notes – as do Julian P. Hume and Michael Walters in their book, also entitled *Extinct Birds* – the existence of dozens of 'hypothetical species' of parrots, now also extinct. Some of these may have been hybrids of two more familiar species, others inaccurate descriptions of escaped cagebirds or birds only glimpsed for a few moments, and mistakenly identified. But surely at least some were genuine species, which disappeared before scientists could even describe them properly.

These enigmatic creatures include the unicoloured lory, whose existence is solely based on the description of a now lost skin from a collection in Amsterdam; the crested Mexican parrot, dismissed by one ornithologist as 'an imaginary bird'; and David Livingstone's parrot from South Africa, 'known only from Livingstone's inadequate account'.

Most intriguing of all, perhaps, is a parrot that does not even have a name, and for which the only evidence that it ever existed at all is an enigmatic watercolour by eighteenth-century naturalist and bird artist George Edwards, known as 'the father of British ornithology'. The painting, which he completed in July 1764, is of a large, strikingly pinkish-red parrot with blue wings and white spotting and streaking. The title simply states: 'A very uncommon parrot from Jamaica. Drawn from Nature the size of life'.

The reverse of the picture gives more detail, with a description of how Edwards obtained the bird, which was lent to him by Dr Alexander Russell, having been 'Shot in Jamaica and brought Dryed to England'. Sadly the specimen itself has long vanished, so the only evidence this parrot ever existed is this single painting.

We know far more about the life, habits and eventual disappearance of two other species of parrot: the Carolina parakeet of North America, and Spix's macaw from Brazil. Indeed both species join the dodo, great auk and passenger pigeon as a select collection of species for which entire books have been devoted to their decline and fall.

Although it was never anything like as abundant and ubiquitous as the passenger pigeon, the Carolina parakeet was nevertheless a common, widespread and familiar species to the early settlers of North America. Its noisy and colourful flocks ranged across the south-eastern part of the continent from New England in the north to Florida in the south, and as far west as Colorado. It had the northernmost natural range of any of the world's parrots, though today other species such as the ring-necked parakeet have established feral populations further north.

The Carolina parakeet lived in large flocks of up to 300 individuals, nesting in holes in trees (as do most parakeets) and feeding on seeds and fruits, including those from trees planted by the settlers in orchards and backyards. Its grace and beauty can be seen in one of bird artist John James Audubon's most famous paintings, which depicts a flock of seven birds – six adults and a juvenile – feeding on cockleburs, a member of the daisy family with hard spiny fruits that not only stick to clothing but are also toxic to many animals; though not, evidently, to the parakeets.

Audubon's painting captures both the colours of the birds – pale green bodies, darker backs and wings and red and yellow heads – but also their acrobatic grace as they clamber around the plant. But even by Audubon's time, the species was in trouble, as he described in his *Journal* of 1831: 'Our Parakeets are very rapidly diminishing in number; and in some districts, where twenty-five years ago they were plentiful, scarcely any are now to be seen.'

Numbers continued to fall, records became fewer and further between, and following the last reported sighting of a flock of a dozen or so birds at a creek in Florida in 1904, the Carolina parakeet seemed to have vanished from the wild. A pair of parakeets called Incas and Lady Jane managed to hang on at Cincinnati Zoo (coincidentally the home of the last known passenger pigeon, Martha) until 1917 and 1918, and the species was formally declared extinct in 1939.

Its demise was explained by a number of reasons, all directly or indirectly caused by humans: shooting and trapping (the birds were considered a pest), disease, and possibly competition from introduced honeybees competing for nest sites. But as with so many stories of extinct birds, that may not be the end of the tale. Declaring a species extinct in the wild is not as simple as it sounds; after all, you cannot prove the total absence of one or two individuals, which might be hanging on undiscovered in a hard-to-reach location.

And as history shows, many species have been rediscovered long after they were supposed to be extinct: most famously, perhaps, a large, flightless species of rail from New Zealand's South Island known as the takahe (which looked like a giant moorhen), officially declared extinct after what were thought to be the last four specimens were taken in 1898, only for a population to be rediscovered half a century later in 1948.

Long after the Carolina parakeet had apparently vanished from the wild, sightings of this attractive (and you might think unmistakable) bird continued to surface. These included a flock of no fewer than thirty parakeets near Fort Drum Creek, Florida, in 1920, three nesting pairs in Okeechobee County (also Florida) in 1924, and two independent reports of birds flying overhead in the Santee River area of South Carolina as late as 1938. The problem with all these records, however, is that by this time several parakeet species were already at large in Florida, so there is a chance that the observers mistook feral birds for what they thought were Carolina parakeets.

More intriguingly, however, an ornithologist and park ranger named Oscar Baynard continued to report sightings of small flocks of Carolina parakeets in Florida well into the 1930s, and possibly even later; he was both an experienced observer and an 'unimpeachably honest' man, so it is highly unlikely that he was either mistaken or making up the sightings.

Ironically southern Florida – especially the city of Miami – is today home to more than twenty different species of non-native parrot, reviled by some but loved by many. Yet the Carolina parakeet – the one native species that, had it survived just a little longer, might have been saved by radical conservation measures – has gone for ever.

The fate of this beautiful and unique parrot has taught us the salutary lesson that no species – however common and widespread – is immune to the pressures that led to this bird's disappearance; and that parrots are even more at risk than others, with ninety species – roughly one-quarter of all the world's parrots – now considered vulnerable to extinction. So it is somewhat ironic that when the very last wild individual of another species of parrot, Spix's macaw, died in the year 2000, it did not disappear from the planet altogether; and that the trade in rare parrots that was its nemesis may yet prove to be its saviour.

One day in 1819 the German naturalist and collector Johann Baptist Ritter von Spix was out on the banks of the Rio Sao Francisco in a remote region of north-eastern Brazil, when he came across an unfamiliar bird – a medium-sized parrot with a cobalt-blue plumage and a greyish head.

He took aim and fired, and the bird fell dead to the ground. Many years later, it was found to be a new species of macaw, which although it had been sighted as early as the 1630s, had never been formally described or named. As is traditional, the species was eventually named (by the Emperor Napoleon's nephew, Charles Bonaparte) after its discoverer: Spix's macaw.

Spix's macaw was never very common or widespread; indeed after that first sighting it wasn't seen again for another eighty-four years. It was quite a fussy bird as parrots go, living in the very specialised habitat of dry tropical forest, and being entirely dependent on a single species of tree – the Caraibeira – for its food, nesting holes and roosting places. During the course of the nineteenth and twentieth centuries, this specialised habitat was destroyed by deforestation; compounded by the taking of wild birds to sell to wealthy private collectors – a trade that became more and more profitable as Spix's macaw became ever more rare.

The Brazilian government banned exports of this and other scarce parrot species in 1967, but the reality was that only a handful of legal traders were stopped; the much larger illegal trade in macaws and other parrots continued unabated.

By 1990 only a single male Spix's macaw could be found in the wild, close to where Spix had shot the original specimen more than 170 years earlier. Poignantly, in the absence of a female, it had paired with a different species, a blue-winged macaw. Ten years later, in October 2000, this lone bird vanished, and Spix's macaw was declared extinct in the wild.

But this did not mean that the species shared the fate of the dodo, passenger pigeon or Carolina parakeet, for one simple reason. Its popularity among cagebird enthusiasts meant that there were still a number of Spix's macaws alive in captivity. Yet with just fifteen known individuals, time was of the essence. Unless a breeding programme could be set up, the species was surely doomed to see out its last days behind bars.

Today, there are about a hundred Spix's macaws in captivity, eighty-three of which are involved in the captive breeding programme. But these descend from just seven wild birds taken from two nests, so there is a genetic bottleneck. Time will tell if the ultimate dream of the conservationists – to release these birds back into a newly restored habitat so that a wild population can be re-established – will ever bear fruit.

The story of Spix's macaw is an apt parable for our long and close relationship with parrots. During the 5,000 years or so since they have lived alongside us, we have taught them to speak and eaten their tongues; kept them in cages and accidentally released them back into the wild, thousands of miles from their original home; and most ironically of all, driven some species to the edge of extinction (and sometimes beyond), only to spend time, effort and millions of dollars trying to save them, using birds already held in captivity.

In January 1888, at the age of seventy-five, artist and poet Edward Lear died at his villa in San Remo, on the Mediterranean coast of Italy. Despite his fame, few travelled to attend his funeral, which was described by the wife of his physician as 'a sad, lonely affair'.

Yet his name lives on; and not simply through his verse and those extraordinary images of parrots he painted as a young man. For one particular species of South American parrot, *Anodorhynchus leari*, is named after him: Lear's macaw. Once considered to be a smaller and paler form of the world's largest parrot, the hyacinth macaw, and known only from museum specimens collected in the nineteenth century, Lear's macaw was finally given its rightful status when it was rediscovered in the heart of north-eastern Brazil in 1978. However, it was soon realised that the species was critically endangered. By 1983 there were thought to be just sixty Lear's macaws remaining in the wild, all in a tiny area of the province of Bahia, not far from where the last Spix's macaw was found. But in a rare success story among the world's endangered parrot species, by 2010 the population had risen to an estimated 1,100 birds, thanks to concerted efforts to prevent hunting and trapping, and the restoration of its forest habitat. Although Edward Lear never actually got the chance to see his macaw, he would surely celebrate the fact that at least one parrot species may have a bright future.

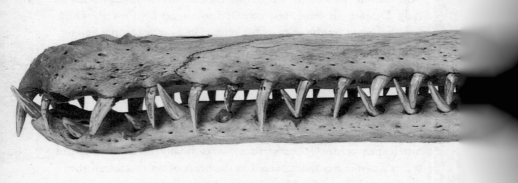

If you should meet a crocodile,
Don't take a stick and poke him;
Ignore the welcome in his smile,
Be careful not to stroke him.
For as he sleeps upon the Nile,
He thinner gets and thinner;
And whene'er you meet a crocodile
He's ready for his dinner.

Anonymous

18

Crocodiles

Admiration and Abhorrence

The ancient Greeks called it Crocodilopolis – the city of the crocodiles – after its inhabitants' object of obsession. Located in the
most fertile region in Egypt, Shedet (present-day Faiyum) was
renowned for its corn, vegetables, flowers and olives, and was also
the most important centre of the cult of Sobek, the crocodile god.
Although they no longer throng its banks, thousands of years ago
crocodiles dominated Egyptian history and culture. We know about
this today from many sources, such as archaeological finds, docu-
ments and hieroglyphics, but most vividly from Herodotus's
Histories. When he visited Crocodilopolis, the Greek historian wrote:
'The City of Crocodiles is more amazing than the Pyramids. It
has twelve covered courtyards surrounded by a huge wall. There
are three thousand rooms, half of which are underground. They
are built of fine stone and decorated with beautiful figures, and it
is hard to believe that men built them.'

Herodotus's readers were fascinated by his stories about the
strange animals they had never seen – in many ways his writings
were a precursor to today's natural history documentaries:

The following are the peculiarities of the crocodile: During the
four winter months they eat nothing; they are four-footed, and
live indifferently on land or in the water . . . It has the eyes of a
pig, teeth large and tusk-like; it cannot move its under-jaw

297

[Herodotus was wrong – it can], and in this respect too it is singular, being the only animal in the world which moves the upper-jaw but not the under. It has strong claws and a scaly skin, impenetrable upon the back. In the water it is blind, but on land it is very keen of sight . . . The crocodile is esteemed sacred by some Egyptians, by others he is treated as an enemy.

Sobek was the best-known Egyptian crocodile god. Usually depicted as a man with the head, jaws and teeth of a crocodile, he was closely linked with various creation myths, including the beliefs that he created order in the universe, fashioned the River Nile from his own sweat, and made the land on the banks of the river fertile.

The people of Shedet worshipped a living sacred crocodile, called Petsuchos. Crocodile eggs were incubated in mounds of sand in special nurseries, and the resulting small reptiles were carefully reared in temple ponds. Considered the living incarnation of the god, the crocodiles were decorated with gold and glass jewellery on their heads and bracelets on their forefeet, and fed roasted fish, beef, goose, cakes, milk and wine by the priests. Pilgrims flocked to Sobek's various temples across Egypt to help feed them and donate food. The behaviour of the animal towards visitors was taken as evidence of how the gods felt. Rank made no difference. The Roman historian Aelian told how when the pharaoh Ptolemy called 'to the tamest of the crocodiles, it paid him no attention and would not accept the food he offered. The priests realized that the crocodile knew that Ptolemy's end was approaching.' Like the pharaohs themselves, when one Petsuchos died, another replaced it.

But like the crocodile, Sobek had a darker side, as evinced in his various alternative names which included 'pointed of teeth' and 'he who loves robbery'. This ambivalence extended to the Egyptians' treatment of the earthly representatives of Sobek, the crocodiles themselves. Because while these crocodiles were worshipped in Sobek's temples, elsewhere and nearby they were being hunted down and killed.

The hieroglyph of a crocodile could mean greedy and aggressive, but it also signified command and control. The crocodile was at once admired for its speed, strength and hunting skills; and yet simultaneously reviled and feared. At the time protective crocodile amulets were highly popular. The crocodile's power to snatch and destroy its prey was thought to be symbolic of the might of the pharaoh – the strength of the reptile being a manifestation of the pharaoh's own power. The hieroglyphic for 'sovereign' was written with two crocodiles and a falcon. After their death, many Egyptian kings were buried along with mummified crocodiles, and sometimes also with crocodile eggs, enabling the dead king to gain Sobek's protection in the afterlife to come.

Because they were held as holy (along with other species such as cats, ibises and baboons), crocodiles were mummified and buried in special cemeteries when they died. Over 10,000 crocodiles have been found, one more than 5 metres long. One animal was surrounded by fifty tiny crocodiles that had just hatched, possibly its own brood. They were arranged in a little army, marching towards the head of the mummy. Baby crocodiles that had died were sometimes placed within a mummified adult's mouth, echoing the way mother crocodiles carry their young to the water.

According to Herodotus, even those killed by crocodiles enjoyed a special status:

> Whenever any one is found to have been carried off by a crocodile, the people of any city by which he may have been cast up on land must embalm him and lay him out in the fairest way they can and bury him in a sacred burial-place, nor may any of his relations or friends besides touch him, but the priests of the Nile themselves handle the corpse and bury it as that of one who was something more than man.

In Rudyard Kipling's much loved *Just So Stories*, the Elephant's Child – 'who was full of "satiable curtiosity", and that means he asked ever so many questions' – goes on a quest to find what the crocodile has for dinner. When he reaches the banks of the great grey-green, greasy Limpopo River, all set about with fever-trees, he discovers to his horror that he is the special on today's menu. Having enlisted the help of the Bi-Coloured-Python-Rock-Snake he manages to escape the crocodile's clutches; but not before his original short and stumpy nose has been tugged by the reptile into a proper trunk, which to his surprise the Elephant's Child finds remarkably useful.

Kipling's sly reptile, tricking the innocent pachyderm into coming close enough to allow him to grab his nose with those fearsome teeth, plays to the classic image we have of crocodiles: awesome (and, against our better judgement, admirable), yet at the same time absolutely terrifying. It is an image that is remarkably consistent. We see it in films such as the 1986 *Crocodile Dundee*, in which the sharp-witted rogue Mick 'Crocodile' Dundee, played by Paul Hogan, becomes famous for wrestling crocodiles, while his bushcraft skills prove even more useful in the urban jungle of New York. The same plot was later played out in real life, when another Australian daredevil, the late Steve Irwin, became 'The Crocodile Hunter', reaching a global TV audience of more than 500 million viewers.

Both these fictional and factual depictions portray crocodiles as monsters: cold-blooded killers whose techniques of killing their prey – grabbing the unfortunate victim in their huge jaws and wrestling with them until they drown or bleed to death – are especially horrific. There are numerous examples of unsuspecting bathers and swimmers being snatched and killed by crocodiles, often in shallow waters, close to the shore.

The expression 'crocodile tears' – meaning a false display of grief – comes from the ancient belief that crocodiles wept while luring or devouring their prey. Interestingly, recent scientific research has shown that this may have some basis in natural observation. Tears clean and lubricate the eyes and the crocodiles observed 'crying' may well have been out of water for quite some time. The image of an apparently remorseless creature such as a crocodile weeping over its victims has caught the imagination of many writers from Plutarch to Churchill. When Shakespeare's Othello convinces himself that his wife has been unfaithful he declares: 'If that the earth could teem with woman's tears, / Each drop she falls would prove a crocodile.'

Yet we admire crocodiles, too. The crocodile is used as the logo for a luxury brand of sports goods (named after the French tennis player René Lacoste, nicknamed 'the Crocodile' because of his tenacious playing style). And we admire their longevity: 66 million years ago, when a catastrophic meteor strike wiped out the rest of the earth's giants, including the dinosaurs, crocodiles somehow survived and, in the absence of competition, went on to flourish. So what exactly are crocodiles, and do they really live up to their perennial image as ruthless, cold-blooded killers?

The sixteen currently recognised species of true crocodile, in the subfamily Crocodylinae, are (mostly) large, semi-aquatic animals found in both freshwater and marine habitats throughout the tropics: from North and South America, through Africa and Asia, to Australasia. Although they look remarkably similar to other crocodilians such as alligators and gharials, they are subtly different, with a more V-shaped snout and a notch in the upper jaw that allows a large tooth to show through when the animal's mouth is shut. Crocodiles are also generally much more aggressive than their cousins.

Crocodilians are reptiles. Despite this they are more closely related to (and descended from a common ancestor of) birds and dinosaurs than they are to other reptilian groups such as snakes and lizards. Crocodiles share some physical traits with birds, and build nests in which they lay eggs. Their distant ancestors evolved more than 200 million years ago, originally as terrestrial animals, but later adopting a more aquatic lifestyle.

Some of these early crocodilians were fearsome beasts: *Deinosuchus*, which lived in the rivers of North America some 80 million years ago, grew to 10 metres long, weighed up to 10 tonnes, and may even have preyed on huge dinosaurs such as tyrannosaurs. This compares to the largest extant species – the Australian saltwater crocodile – that can reach a length of over 6 metres and weigh well over a tonne, making it the heaviest living reptile on the planet.

Crocodiles have changed remarkably little over the millennia. For the crocodile is not far short of the perfect predator: it has a long, streamlined body shape, enabling it to swim rapidly, but also to run very fast on land albeit in short bursts only. The Australian freshwater crocodile has been recorded at a speed of 17 kilometres per hour, easily quick enough to catch a panicking human being who strays close to the water's edge. Their webbed feet allow them to turn speedily in the water to pursue their prey, while like sharks they are able to replace their rows of teeth constantly throughout their lives, to maximise their biting and gripping efficiency.

Although often territorial, they can also be highly social (unlike most reptiles) and – again, unlike other reptiles – very vocal. They do share one characteristic with other reptiles such as tortoises however: crocodiles are generally very long-lived, with some species reaching 60–70 years old, and a few individuals possibly living for a century or more.

Crocodiles have excellent sensory abilities, with very good night vision (they mostly hunt by night), vertical slit-like pupils (like cats), which help to protect their eyes from bright sunshine during daylight hours, and a clear membrane that covers the eye when they are underwater. They have an acute sense of smell, which allows them to locate (or relocate) carcasses of animals in murky water, and good hearing. Their ears, eyes and nostrils are all located at the top of their head, so they can remain almost entirely submerged without compromising their ability to attack. This is a great advantage for these 'ambush predators', as they can conserve their energy while floating unseen beneath the surface, before dashing out to grab their unsuspecting victim. This may be a mammal as large as a wildebeest or zebra, or something less substantial such as a bird, fish or amphibian. Crocodiles have catholic tastes, depending mostly on their size.

Once the prey is caught, crocodiles usually kill it by a war of attrition, turning and twisting their victim around in the water (in an action grimly known as the 'death roll') until it gives up its fight for life. Then they take their booty down beneath the water and store it until it rots and becomes easier to dismember and eat. Crocodiles' stomachs are more acidic than that of any other animal, and they are able to digest the hooves, horns and bones of their prey.

Like their distant relatives the birds and dinosaurs, crocodiles reproduce by laying eggs in a nest, which are then guarded by one or both parents until they hatch. The temperature at which the female maintains the eggs is crucial: those incubated at temperatures of 30 degrees Celsius or below mostly hatch into females; between 31 and 32 degrees both males and females are produced, and from 32 to 33 degrees they are mostly males; though at even higher temperatures this reverts to females.

The ancient Egyptians may have been the best-known civilisation to worship crocodiles, but they certainly weren't the only one. Crocodilians – including alligators – have long been at the centre of many people's beliefs. The Australian aborigines hunted the enormous freshwater and saltwater crocodiles for food, but also revered them, singing ritual songs and performing dances in their honour, believing that their dead relatives are reincarnated as crocodiles.

Crocodiles have also been worshipped in the West African state of Mauritania, where they are linked with the preservation of precious water resources; while in Papua New Guinea, young men go through a painful initiation ceremony during which a series of shallow cuts are made on their back which, when they heal, resemble the skin of a crocodile. Without going through this ordeal, no boy can be recognised as a man.

Further west, the independence of the new nation of East Timor in 2002 was marked by a renewal of interest in the myth of the island's creation. The story goes that a small boy rescued a stranded crocodile and returned it to the sea, thus saving its life. The crocodile promised to serve him any time he needed help. Many years later, when the boy grew up, he decided he wanted to see the world, and called on the crocodile to carry him on his back to far-flung places. When it was time for the crocodile to die it turned itself into a beautiful island, where the man and his descendants could live.

Take a look at a map of the island of Timor, and it is easy to see how this myth arose, for its shape is uncannily like that of a crocodile. Unfortunately the story has had one very negative effect: the people of Timor still revere crocodiles, and believe that they will not be harmed by them; as a result, several people are killed each year as they swim in the seas around the island. In more recent years this reverence has lessened, as the presence of crocodiles discourages lucrative tourism.

In the New World, the crocodile's relatives the alligators and caimans are also at the centre of many ancient beliefs and rituals. The Aztecs of what is now Mexico regarded the caiman as a symbol of the earth as it floated in the waters of the early universe, and they incorporated the creature – known as 'Cipactli' – into their complex calendar. The gods Quetzalcoatl and Tezcatlipoca were supposed to have created the earth out of the caiman's body, after it had bitten off Tezcatlipoca's foot, which he had used to lure the animal into captivity.

Today, long after most of these ancient beliefs have died out or been forgotten, we still have an ambivalent relationship with these mighty beasts. The stories of crocodile attacks are as feverishly followed as those of sharks. They remain one of the world's most dangerous animals: although most human deaths go unreported, it is thought that crocodiles in Africa and South East Asia kill hundreds of people each year.

A battle in the Second World War is the unlikely holder of the Guinness World Record for most deaths in a crocodile attack. On 19 February 1945, 900 Japanese soldiers crossed 16 kilometres of

Burmese mangrove swamps full of saltwater crocodiles in an abortive attempt to rejoin a larger battalion. Twenty were captured by the British, and almost 500 are known to have escaped; the exact number of deaths is disputed but many of the remainder were probably eaten by the crocodiles. A naturalist with the British troops, Bruce Stanley Wright later wrote a vivid account of it in his 1962 book *Wildlife Sketches Near and Far*:

> That night [of 19 February 1945] was the most horrible that any member of the M.L. [motor launch] crews ever experienced. The scattered rifle shots in the pitch black swamp punctured by the screams of wounded men crushed in the jaws of huge reptiles, and the blurred worrying sound of spinning crocodiles made a cacophony of hell that has rarely been duplicated on earth. At dawn the vultures arrived to clean up what the crocodiles had left.

Being attacked by a crocodile remains one of the most primal human fears to this day. Given that the stories we have come to expect are in the crocodile-wrestling vein of *Crocodile Dundee* makes this following account all the more interesting. In 1985 the eco-philosopher Val Plumwood was canoeing along a remote lagoon when she encountered a saltwater crocodile. She tried to reach the shore to escape, but the beast was too quick for her, and she was grabbed:

> Few of those who have experienced the crocodile's death roll have lived to describe it. It is, essentially, an experience beyond words of total terror. The crocodile's breathing and heart metabolism are not suited to prolonged struggle, so the roll is an intense burst of power designed to overcome the victim's resistance quickly. The crocodile then holds the feebly struggling prey underwater until it drowns. The roll was a centrifuge of boiling blackness that lasted for an eternity, beyond endurance, but when I seemed all but finished, the rolling suddenly stopped. My feet touched bottom, my head broke the surface, and, coughing, I sucked at air, amazed

to be alive. The crocodile still had me in its pincer grip between the legs. I had just begun to weep for the prospects of my mangled body when the crocodile pitched me suddenly into a second death roll.

Eventually managing to escape but so badly injured that she had to spend months in intensive care, Plumwood later wrote a fascinating essay about the encounter, called 'Being Prey'. The rangers who eventually find her assume that the crocodile that attacked her should be destroyed but she is adamant that he should be spared: 'The story of the crocodile encounter now has, for me, a significance quite the opposite of that conveyed in the master/ monster narrative. It is a humbling and cautionary tale about our relationship with the earth, about the need to acknowledge our own animality and ecological vulnerability.'

Even in ancient Egypt where they were seen as semi-divine, crocodiles were hunted for food and for their tough and beautiful hides. But in recent years crocodile farming has become big business. Latest estimates suggest that well over 1 million crocodilians are farmed and killed for their skins each year, the most popular species being the American alligator and Nile crocodile. In the state of Louisiana alone, alligator farming is worth at least $60 million a year.

But maybe when it comes to exploiting crocodiles and alligators we're missing a trick. Scientists have often been puzzled about one aspect of crocodilian biology: when these animals fight one another in violent and prolonged territorial battles, and often suffer terrible injuries as a result, why do these wounds so rarely become infected?

The answer appears to be in the reptiles' blood. When tested, the blood of the American alligator has been found to destroy more than twenty different strains of bacteria, including some normally resistant to antibiotics. Even when tested on HIV – the virus that causes AIDS – it depleted the virus by a significant amount. The reason appears to be that the proteins in the blood

– known as peptides – help the animals fight off any potentially fatal infections. Now, scientists are hoping to isolate these and create anti-bacterial and anti-viral drugs from them.

So although we may regard crocodiles as some kind of 'living fossil', that does them a great injustice. As zoologist and crocodile expert Adam Britton notes, a modern crocodile is closer to a Ferrari than a Model T Ford: both have four wheels, an engine and seats, but one does the job a whole lot better.

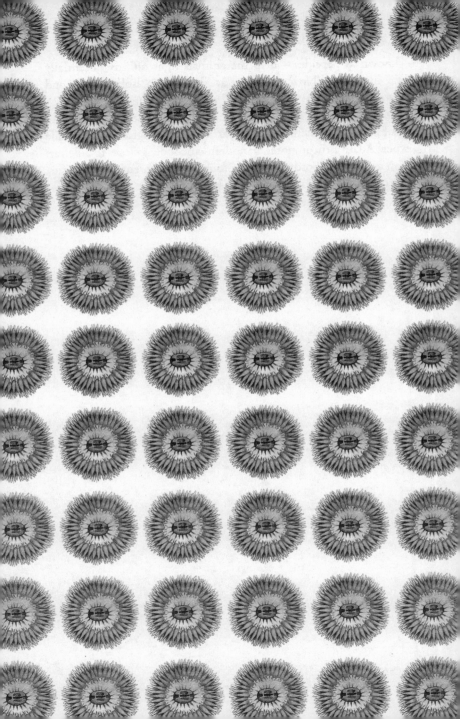

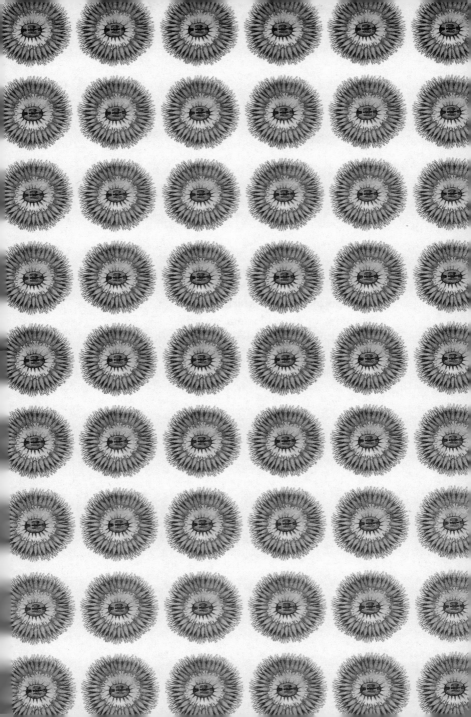

Here too were living flowers
Which like a bud compacted
Their purple cups contracted
And now, in open blossom spread
Stretch'd like green anthers many a seeking head

Robert Southey, 'The Ancient Sepulchres'

Sea Anemones

Victorian Aquariumania

Visit almost any rocky shore around the British Isles at low tide and you'll see what look like well-sucked wine-gums glued to the stones. Touch them and they are soft and yielding, almost too vulnerable, you might think, to survive a twice-daily battering from the waves. But with the return of the tide, they blossom like hothouse flowers, extending sticky tentacles to trap small sea creatures. They are sea anemones, creatures that subvert our view of animal life and which, as we'll find out, may hold the elixir of life itself.

Sea anemones are related to the corals and jellyfish. They have a simple structure, a ring of tentacles that feed small invertebrates or tiny fish into the soft hollow column that acts as a stomach. Food goes in and waste products come out of the same oral disc. Anemones can produce eggs that hatch into free-swimming larvae which, depending on the species, soon settle down on rocks or in mud. They can also reproduce asexually by budding, producing small identical replicas of themselves much as plant bulbs do.

The most conspicuous British species is the beadlet anemone. It anchors itself to rocks, but is also surprisingly mobile and can float or crawl slowly to a better location. They even fight each other in extreme slow motion, using their electric-blue beadlets (acrorhagi) which are just below the rings of their tentacles. These beadlets harbour stinging cells. Each anemone lashes at the other with mini-harpoons which adhere to its opponent's surface, creating damaging weals. Not to be messed with, these 'flowers'. They are tough too and can survive exposure to summer heat, drying winds and winter cold as well as varying levels of salinity in their rock pools.

Anemone means 'wind-flower' and to our ancestors these strange creatures with their tentacles waving in the ocean currents must have resembled something botanical rather than zoological. For a long time the sea anemone was thought to be a missing link between the world of plants and animals. We've endowed some of our common species with two flower names. The dahlia anemone is a thick-tentacled sunburst of a creature which could easily win Best in Show at a country fête, while the daisy anemone is a burrower in mud and sand.

But not all look floral. One of the most spectacular species is the snakelocks anemone which sports long green tresses of violet-tipped tentacles which it is unable to retract fully and so remains open, hence its alternative name, 'opelet'. Its Medusa-like appearance is very striking as it sways among kelp fronds in rocky gullies. As wide as 20 centimetres across, its bright green colour is the result of algae living symbiotically within its body tissues. Their chlorophyll fixes sunlight filtering through the water and distributes the organic compounds produced by photosynthesis to the anemone. Its tentacles are sticky to touch and loaded with stinging cells with which it catches a variety of small swimming creatures, though one species of crab, Leach's spider crab, is happy to live alongside or even inside the deadly snakelocks.

Plumose anemones are creatures of the sea-bed and often decorate wrecks and reefs in hundreds or thousands. Their long columns are crowned with a feathery mass of delicate tentacles which both capture plankton and secrete the enzymes needed to dissolve their tiny shells.

Other sea anemones live in mud, or on rocks. One, *Calliactis parasitica*, rides on top of the shells chosen as homes by hermit crabs. It deters predators that might attack the crab, and happily sweeps up morsels of food that the crab leaves behind: hermit crabs can be messy eaters.

The lives of sea anemones are fascinating enough, but it was their bright colours and ornate appearance that enchanted early naturalists. In the early nineteenth century they became very desirable aquarium animals. The challenge was that it was impossible to keep them alive in glass tanks. Without aeration and the correct amounts of salt and other minerals, the water soon became fetid and the anemones and other marine creatures died.

It was the desire to observe and understand strange underwater life that drove the popularity of aquaria. The idea of keeping plants and aquatic life in glass cases was pioneered by surgeon Dr Nathaniel Bagshaw Ward in the 1830s. He noticed that ferns and other plants thrived in the humidity created by a glass container and that the addition of plants to water allowed its inhabitants to survive for longer. Before this, zoologists such as Anna Thynne had observed that adding weed to water and movement of the water prolonged the life of creatures there, but without realising why. Until Ward's revolution in understanding how plants could oxygenate aquaria, anyone who wanted to keep fish or marine creatures in still water was forced to change the water daily to prevent it becoming stagnant. This was a tedious and time-consuming process unless, like the marine biologist Sir John Dalyell, you had servants to bring a fresh supply of seawater daily to your house. This combination of wealth and willing servitude, according to one account, allowed him to keep a beadlet sea anemone (affectionately known as 'Granny') alive for twenty-eight years: the animal outlived him by decades and was at least sixty-six years old when it finally perished in 1887.

Dr Ward's invention, known widely as the Wardian case, transformed the study of natural history and sparked a mid-Victorian obsession with collecting aquatic creatures and especially ferns which thrived well in the limited light of gloomy Victorian parlours. Pteridomania, the craze for collecting ferns, swept through the country and fern-sellers could be found at London street-corners, hawking roots ripped from far-flung rural spots. So extensive were their depredations that many fern populations have since failed to recover and some counties lost particularly sought-after species such as the Royal Fern.

Using the expanding steam railway network, Victorian naturalists ventured further afield and were to be seen in favoured places such as Tenby and Torquay swarming over coastal rocks to harvest their bounty. Seaweeds, anemones, starfish and shrimps, all were fair game and it was considered a seemly pastime for women who waded in while their husbands looked on. Some of the collecting was on a commercial scale. Aquaria had become so popular – thanks to the removal in 1845 of excise duties on plate glass which brought its price within the range of the middle classes – that a huge aquarium warehouse was set up near Regent's Park for the sale of what Rebecca Stott, Professor of English Literature at the University of East Anglia, calls 'theatres of glass'. One journalist wrote in 1856: 'In London itself the collecting seems to be at fever point. In West End squares, in trim suburban villas, in crowded city thoroughfares, in the demure houses of little frequented backstreets and in the wretched streets of Spitalfields and Bethnal Green, everywhere you see the aquarium in one form or another.'

As this craze gathered momentum, natural history writers were producing guides to collecting and identification. Sea anemones were championed by Philip Henry Gosse, a reluctant schoolteacher who willingly forsook a career in the classroom for that of an author and illustrator. He was a devoutly religious man, a member of the Plymouth Brethren, and firmly believed that Christ would return to earth in his lifetime. Gosse had been inspired by the nature he'd seen living in North America. When he returned to London in 1839, he hankered for the coast and quickly moved to Devon where he spent most of his time collecting specimens, painting and writing. We can gauge some measure of his absorption in natural history by his diary entry on the birth of his only child: 'Received green swallow from Jamaica. E. delivered of a son.'

This child, Edmund, grew up to be a poet and critic who

chronicled his charged relationship with his father in a vivid memoir, *Father and Son* (now the only one of the two Gosses' many books remaining in print), describing 'the hush' around stern father and lonely son 'in which you could hear a sea anemone sigh'. But at the time it was Philip's books that had the most impact. He was responsible for the widespread use of the word 'aquarium'. His 1854 book *The Aquarium*, the last word on the subject, became so popular that it was sold at railway stations and, along with five other works, earned him over £4,000, a sum that equates to around £250,000 in today's money. He experimented with different minerals to provide the right conditions for his tanks of creatures and spent many hours observing the inhabitants. This fascination raised many questions in his mind. For instance, observing the anemone *Calliactis*, he wondered who was influencing who. Was it the hermit crab transporting the anemone around, or the anemone that controlled the crab in some way? He even drew human analogies between warring anemones and crabs, likening the activities of the 'male' crab and 'female' anemone to a married relationship.

His greatest achievement was *Actinologia Britannica*, a study of the British sea anemones and corals, published between 1858 and 1860. Gosse's precise and accurate depictions of these creatures in this highly coloured work are some of the finest ever produced. Bizarre tentacled 'flowers' surmount stubby gelatinous columns in the limpid waters of secluded pools or cling to romantic rocky shorelines, awaiting the return of the tides. Outstanding in their use of colour and design, the illustrations are supported by a sweeping breadth of knowledge. These dazzling images combined with lucid descriptions and enthusiastic science brought sea anemones to a wider audience.

The height of the aquarium boom was between 1850 and 1865. These aquaria were not just decorative items, rock pools in the parlour, but also opened a window on a previously inaccessible world. The journalist George Henry Lewes was asked to write about the aquarium craze and went with his lover Mary Ann Evans (who wrote under the pseudonym George Eliot) to study marine life over two summers in Devon and South Wales. The pair brought their daily trophies back to local guesthouses where they improvised aquaria from pie-dishes. According to Rebecca Stott, George Eliot was transfixed by the marine melodramas played out in these makeshift rock pools and, maybe inspired by them, shortly afterwards wrote her first novel, *Scenes of Clerical Life*: 'I think it's extraordinary that Mary-Ann Evans had not published a novel and woke up one morning with stories spilling out of her head full of comedy and witty observations of village life.'

For George Henry Lewes, observing marine life at close quarters provoked all kinds of philosophical questions:

> We must always remember the great drama which is incessantly acted out in every drop of water in every inch of Earth. Then and only then do we realise the mighty complexity, the infinite splendour of nature. Then and only then do we feel how full of life, varied, intricate, marvellous, world within world, yet nowhere without space to move is this single planet on the crust of which we stand and look out onto shoreless space peopled by myriads of other planets larger if not more wonderful than ours.

There was a larger fascination behind the aquarium craze. It coincided at its peak with the publication of Charles Darwin's *On the Origin of Species* in 1859. Many Victorians were questioning the use of different creatures to humanity, and the purpose of other life on earth. Faced with the variety of bizarre species that could be brought into the sitting room, it became clear that these animals existed completely independently of us. Rebecca Stott sees this as another stage in a growing perception of a challenge to the human place at the centre of the world, what H.G. Wells would later call the 'dethronement of man'.

It's ironic that they should have been championed by a man who had been largely rejected by the scientific establishment for quite the reverse, his valiant attempt to explain the latest scientific discoveries as part and parcel of God's plan. Calling his theory

Omphalos, Greek for 'navel', Philip Gosse took as his starting point that while Adam, because he had been made not born, wouldn't have needed a navel, nevertheless he must have had one; and following the same logic he proposed that fossils were instantly formed by God at the moment of creation. The book came out two years before Darwin but the reaction was still very negative. Even Gosse's close friend, the novelist Charles Kingsley, wrote that he had read 'no other book which so staggered and puzzled' him, that he could not believe that God had 'written on the rocks one enormous and superfluous lie for all mankind'.

The aquarium craze offered owners a new vision of themselves as one animal among millions of others. The big question was what man's place in nature should be. The number of recognised species was multiplying so rapidly as a result of empire and sea exploration that it was fundamentally changing perceptions of functions such as reproduction. Slowly it became apparent that how humanity reproduced was not the dominant way that organisms on the planet did. Anemones that could either lay eggs or produce buds came as a revelation.

For all this fascination, aquaria were a short-lived fad and by the mid-1860s the craze began to wane. The tanks and their inhabitants were never easy to manage, even with an army of servants, and so they were thrown out or turned into display cases.

The real creatures proved rather less permanent, losing their shimmering colours when preserved as specimens in formaldehyde and alcohol. One way to catch the transient beauty of anemones and jellyfish was suggested by a curator of Dresden Museum in the 1860s. He commissioned father and son glassmakers, Leopold and Rudolf Blaschka, to create models of anemones and jellyfish to display their elegant features and subtle colours. Both men were skilled in lampwork, the drawing out of molten glass over a hot flame, a technique that was perfect for creating fine tentacles: any particularly tricky appendages were attached using fine copper wire. A fine speckling of paint on the glass gave the impression of translucent hues and a work of art was born. How they coloured and assembled the models is still being investigated by the Natural History Museum. Originally it was thought that they might have made each model individually to order, but it seems they made the parts separately in batches and assembled the components as orders came in.

The superb Blaschka sea creatures and flowers were originally intended as instructional models, but were soon in demand by museums and teaching colleges around the world. Miranda Lowe is curator of the Invertebrate Collection at the Natural History Museum, which commissioned over sixty-eight sea anemones in 1866 to show to the public. She is particularly fond of a specimen of *Bunodes ballii*, mounted on a plaster base painted with flecks of green and yellow to interpret the sandy or rocky shore on which the anemone lived. The anemone's body has touches of pale yellow and red and its central part comprises an array of glass tentacles made from glass-coated copper wire. The Blaschkas were inspired to create anemones in glass by Philip Gosse's illustrations and his scientific descriptions. Less reliably perhaps, they also received live specimens from a 'Mr Smith' in Weymouth, though it took three days for them to reach Dresden by post. Although Leopold and Rudolf supplied organisations around the world, they were driven more by a desire to teach and create than to make money. Towards the end of their career, they were commissioned by Harvard University to make 4,500 glass flowers for their botanical collection. But because they didn't pass on their techniques, the secret of their extraordinary art died with them.

There are 185 Blaschka models in the London Natural History Museum's collection including jellyfish, a Portuguese man-o'-war and several complex radiolarians, minute single-celled aquatic creatures with a complex shell or testa, made of silica, the same material that forms the basic ingredient of glass. These complex, bristling orbs, barbed and interwoven with copper wire and held together with resins, are astonishingly fragile and are now on display as one of the museum's 'Treasures'. Computerised tomography (CT) scanning of jellyfish in the museum's collection, which provides screen images built up from several X-rays of the sculptures, is revealing their complex internal structure and, importantly, how they were made.

Although we understand sea anemones better now, they continue to spring surprises. Daniel Rokhsar at University College, Berkeley has studied the genome sequence of the starlet anemone *Nematostella vectensis* and discovered that these strange sea creatures are more closely allied to vertebrates, including fish and amphibians, than to insects or worms. For animals without brains, they also have genes that can create specialised nerve cells, though Rokhsar is not yet sure what these do.

As Sir John Dalyell's sexagenarian anemone proved, these animals can live for a very long time. Their power of regeneration allows them to grow new tentacles. Rokhsar's particularly tantalising discovery is that, even in old age, they don't seem to develop cell aberrations or cancers, something that is very unusual. It could be that they slough off their skin cells so fast that they are continually replenishing themselves, but they may also contain some inhibitor to tumour growth. An even more exciting discovery is that *Turritopsis dohrnii*, a species of small jellyfish found in temperate to tropical regions, are biologically immortal. This means that when sick, old or in a state of stress they promptly revert to the polyp stage. They do this by altering the state of their cells, thereby transforming into new types. Since the species is immortal, its numbers could be rising fast. 'We are looking at a worldwide silent invasion,' said Dr Maria Miglietta, scientist at the Smithsonian Tropical Marine Institute. So, if jellyfish and anemones really are more closely related to us than we think, could studying them help us understand how we grow old? Far from being mere gumdrops on a rocky shore, anemones could offer the key to living longer.

The voice of these birds is very harsh and grating. It is heard occasionally when they are flying, and also when they are alarmed. When, however, a bird is wounded or captured alive, the horrible noise it makes is perhaps not surpassed in the animal world. It is something between a bray and the shriek of a locomotive, and is kept up continuously, so as to be absolutely unbearable.

Alfred Russel Wallace,
The Malay Archipelago, 1869

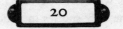
Hornbills

Myths and Ornaments

At first glance Tring seems an unlikely place to find hidden treasure. But the former private museum of Walter, Baron Rothschild, in this small Hertfordshire town, is full of surprises. Along with one of the finest collections of stuffed mammals, reptiles and insects in the UK, it is also home to the bird collection of the Natural History Museum, its darkened rooms full of avian treasures. Skins and specimens of now extinct species such as the great auk and dodo are stored next to those of the familiar birds we take for granted, along with tray after tray of eggs, collected from all over the world. But of all these remarkable specimens, one stands out: an object so unusual it takes a moment to realise what it is.

It is the skull of a helmeted hornbill, a bird native to the Malay Peninsula, Sumatra and Borneo in South East Asia. But this is no ordinary skull, for its rich, buffy-orange front is covered with intricate and beautiful carvings, done in such detail you need a magnifying glass to appreciate their beauty. It depicts a band of Chinese warriors in a town alongside a river, with a man holding a flag showing a Chinese character that means 'literature' or 'culture'. As Jo Cooper, Senior Curator of the avian anatomical collections, notes, there is also a tiny kingfisher caught at the very moment when it dives into the waters.

Technically speaking, the carving is not actually on the skull itself, but on the 'casque': a large plate on the bird's forehead, which it uses in fights with rivals. Other hornbills sport casques, but the helmeted is the only species in which the front few centimetres of the casque is completely solid, making it suitable for carving.

The skull was donated to the museum collection by Philip Burton, former Principal Scientific Officer at the ornithology department, who had been given it by the eminent ornithologist Phyllis Barclay-Smith shortly before she died. The story this object tells is a complex one, combining ancient tribal beliefs, commerce, art, natural history and conservation. It takes us from this bird collection in the heart of the Home Counties, all the way to Asia and Africa, and back again. And it reveals some astonishing facts about one of the most fascinating groups of all the world's birds: the hornbills.

Few of the world's 230 or so bird families are quite as distinctive as hornbills. Even though most people will never have seen one in the wild, hornbills are familiar from zoos and bird collections, while their fame has spread in the last two decades or so thanks to the Disney film *The Lion King*. This features a hornbill named Zazu, who serves both the original lion king Mufasa and his son Simba, flying around frantically and commenting sardonically on what is going on.

As their name suggests, each of the sixty or more recognised hornbill species sports a distinctively huge bill, with that unique horny casque – sometimes huge, sometimes little more than a narrow ridge – on the top of the beak. The pioneer of evolutionary biology Alfred Russel Wallace tried to describe them for Victorian England in 1863:

> The hornbills are large and clumsy birds, seldom adorned with bright-coloured plumage, but in many cases bearing a really prodigious bill . . . The form varies in every species, varies often in the sexes of both species, varies even in the same bird from youth to

age, yet . . . it is always considerably curved . . . generally forming a sharp keel along the top.

The bill is so heavy that the hornbills' first and second neck vertebrae (known as the atlas and axis) have fused together to allow the body to carry this heavy weight – a feature not found in any other group of birds. These unique qualities, along with molecular evidence, have recently contributed to hornbills being allocated their very own order of birds, the Bucerotiformes (a name that derives from the Greek for 'ox horn').

Hornbills come in many different sizes: from the red-billed dwarf hornbill of equatorial West Africa, which at 30 centimetres long and weighing between 84 and 122 grams is about the same size as a mistle thrush; to the massive southern ground-hornbill found across much of sub-Saharan Africa, which can reach a length of 1 metre and tips the scales at 4.5 kilos – equivalent to a Canada goose. Some larger individuals have been estimated to weigh 6 kilos.

They are not generally very colourful, being mainly black and white, grey or brown; but their size, shape and appearance, together with splashes of colour (usually yellow or red) on their heads and bills, make them just as striking as gaudier tropical species such as bee-eaters, kingfishers and rollers, to which they were, until recently, thought to be closely related. Some also sport large, rather attractive eyelashes – described by one scientist as the avian equivalent of sunglasses – to shade their eyes from the glare of the sun.

Hornbills are found across a broad swathe of the Old World, through the tropical and subtropical regions of Africa, Asia and Melanesia (the western Pacific). The greatest variety of species is found in west, central and east Africa, the Malay Peninsula, India, Borneo, Sumatra and the Philippines. However, fossil remains of hornbills dating from the late Miocene period (roughly 5 million years ago) have been found as far away as Morocco in north-west Africa and Bulgaria in south-east Europe.

The hornbills found in Africa and Asia display strikingly different lifestyles. All but one of the Asian hornbills live in forests, while about half of the African species are birds of the open savannah, some living in very dry, virtually desert environments. Some hornbills, such as the African grey, are widespread, while others, including the five species of tarictic hornbills of the Philippines, are confined to individual islands, and are perilously close to extinction. Incidentally the unusual name 'tarictic' is an onomatopoeic representation of the birds' calls, which have a staccato quality that carries well through their forest habitat.

Hornbills are fairly catholic in their choice of food, though their diet does vary between species. Some, especially those that live in forests, eat mainly fruit, which they pluck carefully from the trees in a surprisingly delicate manner. Others, especially those on the African savannah, hunt a wide range of small animals including insects, molluscs, birds and rodents; and in the case of the two ground-hornbills, prey as large as hares, mongooses and even cobras.

They have a very distinctive feeding action: because their tongue is too short to swallow items of food held by the tip of their bill, they jerk their head back to toss them down their throat. Unlike most birds, they have binocular vision, which enables them to focus more precisely when feeding. Perhaps surprisingly, however, most never drink water, obtaining hydration directly from their food.

When hunting, several species of African hornbills will follow other creatures to find things to eat, including army ants. Two species, Von der Decken's and eastern yellow-billed hornbills, have evolved a mutually beneficial relationship with dwarf mongooses, in which the birds act as sentries, warning of any danger from predators, while the mongooses find the food. One scientist even observed hornbills waking up the mongooses from their sleeping quarters inside termite mounds, chivvying them by calling loudly when they had overslept.

But of all the extraordinary behaviours, by far the most bizarre – and widely known – is the strange custom in which the nesting female hornbill is walled up into her nest for the whole of her incubation period. During this time she lays her eggs, incubates them, feeds the chicks, and takes advantage of being safe from predators by undergoing a full moult of her feathers. It is a common, though mistaken, belief that the male walls up the female; in fact the female usually does the work herself, using a combination of mud and her own droppings. At the last moment she enters, and the male seals the entrance shut, leaving just enough space for her to stick her beak through to be fed.

Some commentators have used this behaviour to comment on human relationships, but this apparently odd conduct is in fact perfectly sensible. Hornbills are not agile at the best of times and this keeps the nesting female and fragile offspring safe from predators such as snakes and arboreal mammals. And the male hornbill is too busy to stray, as he must constantly bring food to his mate; hence making a compelling if unromantic case why hornbills are mostly monogamous.

After hatching, the chicks grow inside the nest, defecating through the tiny entrance, so that by the time they are ready to leave, the conditions around and beneath the nest-hole can be somewhat insanitary. Finally the mother breaks through the hard mud seal – a process that can take several hours from start to finish – and they can all leave the nest.

Of all the world's species of hornbill, perhaps the most striking is the helmeted – the bird whose skull resides in the collection at Tring. As it calls from the depths of its native home, the rainforests of Borneo and Sumatra, it sounds more like a monkey than a bird: a trumpeting sound followed by a peal of ringing laughter, which hangs as an echo in the air before fading away. Despite its large size – males can be more than 1.2 metres in length, including their long and impressive tail – this is a difficult bird to see, as it forages high in the canopy of the tallest trees, hunting for snakes, squirrels and birds, and sometimes even preying on smaller species of hornbills.

If you do catch a glimpse, be prepared for a bird that appears bizarre even by hornbill standards. The plumage is mainly dark brown, with an enormously long white tail marked with a band of black towards the tip. But it is the head and neck that are most striking: apart from the front of the casque and the tip of the bill, which are yellow, the head is bright red; and the neck is not covered with feathers, but consists of rough bare skin – red in the male and pale blue in the female.

The helmeted hornbill's casque does indeed look rather like a helmet. It uses its weight like a hammer to dig into rotten wood or pull back pieces of tree bark to obtain food, and also as a weapon in aerial jousts between rival males (and occasionally females), usually in competition for food or nesting resources. In their authoritative *The Ecology and Conservation of Asian Hornbills* (2007), Margaret F. Kinnaird and Timothy G. O'Brien describe this extraordinary display: 'When collisions occur the resulting sound – a loud CLACK! – can be heard in the forest understory at least 500 metres away. Most collisions occur while gliding, and the impact can be so powerful that one or both birds are thrown backward, performing dramatic, acrobatic flips before righting themselves and flying level.'

Despite this unusual behaviour, the casque itself is smaller than that of its relatives the great and rhinoceros hornbills. Yet it has a quality unique even among this unusual family: unlike all other hornbill casques, which are hollow and spongy, that of the helmeted hornbill is heavy and partially solid. It is this peculiar departure from the norm that may ultimately lead to the species' downfall.

For the helmeted hornbill's casques have long been valued in various western and Asian cultures as hornbill ivory. Also sometimes known as 'golden jade', the casque is neither jade nor ivory, but keratin – the same substance that makes hair, horns, hoofs and teeth in mammals. It was probably carved into ornaments by the indigenous peoples living in the species' range – the Malay Peninsula, Sumatra and Borneo – for thousands of years. But it was only when the area was discovered by Chinese, and later European, explorers that the trade in hornbill ivory really took off.

The anthropologist and ornithologist Tom Harrisson – also the founder of the Mass-Observation social research movement in the 1930s – devoted much of his later life to the study of the birds and indigenous cultures of South East Asia. In his contribution to the landmark 1960 book *Birds of Borneo* he wrote:

> It is likely that the casques were mainly exported raw, and worked with a heat treatment and pressing . . . to preserve and heighten the lovely deep golden and surface red patina of the fresh ivory . . . The uses of hornbill casques in Borneo are various and frequently effective; [but] while the Borneo usages persist to this day, all trace of the art of the Chinese carver seems to have vanished. Very little has survived of a remarkable craft which undoubtedly paid for many of the old jars, plates, and beads still decorating the long-houses or wives of better-off Bornean pagans many generations later.

During the Ming dynasty, which ran from the mid-fourteenth to the mid-seventeenth centuries, it is said that hornbill ivory was valued even more highly than elephant ivory. The Japanese, too, wanted this unusual product: from the seventeenth century onwards they used it as the raw material for those delicate miniature sculptures known as 'netsuke'. The fad for collecting these exquisitely beautiful carvings soon spread to the west, and netsuke made from hornbill ivory became a much sought-after addition to the display cabinets of rich Victorian households. Those coloured red – from ivory stained by the bird's preen gland – were especially highly prized.

Later on, live hornbills imported into Britain from Asia and Africa caused amazement among those who saw them, as their almost human-like gait, strange calls and bizarre bills were unlike any bird Europeans had ever encountered. Curiosity only increased when people learned of the birds' strange breeding behaviour. London Zoo held a number of captive hornbills, which were always among the most popular attractions, and were regularly depicted in publications such as the *Illustrated London News*. Not everyone was impressed, though: Edward Stanley, the Bishop of Norwich and author of some of the most inaccurate and sentimental works on birds ever written, dismissed their 'seemingly deformed and monstrous bills'.

But by the end of Queen Victoria's long reign in 1901, the constant demand for hornbill ivory had led to the birds' rapid decline. Sadly that decline has accelerated in recent years. Today hornbill ivory can reach as much as £4,000 per kilo – more than three times that for true elephant ivory – making the trade a lucrative one for organised crime syndicates. In one region alone helmeted hornbills are being killed at an estimated rate of 6,000 every year.

There is one possible piece of good news: in Indonesia, the native peoples regard the helmeted hornbill as a very special creature which guards the thin veil between life and death, ferrying souls between earth and heaven. Conservationists are now trying to enlist this ancient and sacred belief to help protect the species as it disappears at an alarming rate, by enlisting these rainforest tribes to protect both the bird and its special habitat.

Although all hornbills share the same unmistakable characteristics, together with a number of internal, morphological traits such as the fused vertebrae in their neck, two African species are considered to stand apart from the others, and have been placed in their own sub-family, *Bucorvinae* (the others are in the sub-family *Bucerotinae*). These are the northern (or Abyssinian) and the southern ground-hornbills, and they too display an intriguing combination of bizarre behaviours and cultural significance.

Whereas the other hornbills of the African savannah mostly perch on high vantage points in trees and bushes, occasionally dropping down to grab an item of prey, the two ground-hornbills mainly stay, as their name suggests, on the deck. Huge – about a metre tall – and black, with colourful wattles on the throat and around the eye (blue and red for the northern, red for the southern), and white on the wings, they walk in a slow, shuffling gait, rather like elderly gentlemen out for a stroll.

But as soon as they see potential prey, their demeanour changes. They stop in their tracks, and move slowly and carefully forward like a stalking lion, before jabbing at the ground like a pickaxe with that huge, fearsome bill, and grabbing their victim. The unfortunate animal is then despatched in the classic hornbill manner, with a jerk of the head and a rapid swallow. Their more or less exclusively carnivorous diet means that, unlike most other hornbills, they do not have a pouch beneath the bill in which to store fruit.

Ground-hornbills hunt in pairs or small packs, taking insects and other invertebrates such as snails and scorpions, or frogs and toads, for their hors d'oeuvres, and then moving on to a more substantial meal: anything from snakes and lizards to squirrels, hares and even the occasional tortoise. When feeding on snakes, including the highly venomous puff adder, the bird must use a combination of speed and its huge bill to despatch the reptile before it has the chance to bite.

The southern ground-hornbill, found across a wide swathe of southern and eastern Africa from Kenya to Botswana, has another claim to fame in the bird world. It breeds less frequently than any other species – sometimes only every three years – and is also among the longest lived of all the world's birds, reaching up to sixty years old. Even when they do breed, only the largest male and female in the social group actually do so; the others (probably close relatives of the breeding pair) act as helpers, in a co-operative breeding strategy.

Like some birds of prey such as the larger eagles, their eggs hatch asynchronously, so that the first chick is larger and heavier than its sibling; as a result, the younger chick usually dies before it gets the chance to fledge and leave the nest. Because southern ground-hornbills are such slow breeders – sometimes rearing only one chick to adulthood every nine years – they are very vulnerable to changes in their environment; so although the species is not yet seriously threatened, it is currently in decline.

The southern ground-hornbill has a central place in African folklore and culture, which has helped protect the bird – at least until recently. Like many birds with loud calls elsewhere in the world, it is associated with the coming of the rainy season; more unusually, groups of the birds (whose sexes are very similar, though not identical) are negatively associated with homosexuality, while a Zulu word for the species, 'Ingududu', is used as an insult, suggesting that the recipient is not particularly intelligent. In Kenya, ground-hornbills used to be a problem on golf courses, as they would mistake stray balls for eggs and steal them. Some clubs even formulated rules to cover how to continue play when hornbills had stolen a ball.

One detailed South African study, published in the *Journal of Ethnobiology and Ethnomedicine* in 2014, showed that the southern ground-hornbill is also closely associated with death or some other impeding calamity; but also paradoxically seen as a protective influence against evil spirits and witchcraft. The bird is also thought to be able to use its powers to alter people's perceptions of the world, and to be a good and accurate timekeeper (for example being able to predict changes in the seasons or the start and end of the working day).

The authors point out that some of these characteristics are helpful to the protection and survival of the species, while others may lead to its harm. They conclude that the more we know about such cultural practices and beliefs, the easier it will be to conserve the southern ground-hornbill, by encouraging positive beliefs and discouraging negative ones. Whether or not this will ultimately lead to a stabilisation in the southern ground-hornbill population and range is too early to say, but it is a good example of how to use traditional beliefs in modern conservation, by working sensitively with different cultures instead of – as has happened all too often in the past – simply dismissing these ancient beliefs as superstitious nonsense.

As we've seen, as well as helping to protect these unique birds, traditional beliefs can threaten them too. The rhinoceros hornbill, a huge and conspicuous black and white bird with a massive bill and casque, was described thus by Alfred Russel Wallace:

> In the great rhinoceros hornbill the bill attains perhaps its greatest size and beauty, the rich hues of orange crimson and ivory white with which it is adorned in the living bird being scarcely capable of imitation . . . It is this bird which excited the wonder of the early voyagers to Ceylon (where a variety of it exists) who believed it to have two heads – a statement which was long credited in Europe and which may serve to teach us that the wildest and most improbable fictions of early ages had probably a foundation in some curious natural phenomenon.

Yet it is not the bill that has led the rhinoceros hornbill into trouble, but its long tail feathers, which are pure white with a black band towards the tip. For centuries the indigenous peoples of northern Borneo have coveted these striking feathers, which they use in their traditional costumes and in displays of dancing. They also make an effigy of the bird and hoist it high on the end of a pole, to summon their god of war to seek out and kill members of enemy tribes.

But this reverence comes at a price. Each group of dancers uses about 400 tail feathers, so they need to kill roughly forty birds. Because the species is so long-lived it breeds very slowly, which means that traditional hunting – especially when combined with habitat loss through logging activities – is putting too much pressure on an already rapidly dwindling population. Although hunting is illegal, it is very hard to enforce the law in such remote regions.

Ironically, the rhinoceros hornbill is the state bird of Sarawak, a part of Malaysia on the north-west of the island of Borneo, which promotes itself to tourists as 'Sarawak – Land of the Hornbills'. Sadly this does not appear to be doing the birds much good.

Elsewhere in South East Asia, in the Philippines, a tribe living in hill country about 145 kilometres north-east of the capital Manila have long regarded rufous hornbills as deeply significant. A 1968 study calculated that more than 90 per cent of Ilongot men over twenty years old had taken at least one human head. Headhunting and hornbills are closely related in their mythology. The hornbills were understood to act as spirit birds, guiding and protecting the hunters. The bird's shrill cry was likened to the screams of victims receiving their deathblows. The night before a raid, hunters sang in high-pitched tones to persuade the life-force of their victims to fly to them.

Skilled hunters often also wore elaborate headdresses featuring the entire beak and crest of a rufous hornbill. But it was the acquisition of hornbill earrings with dangling shell pendants (called *batling*) that represented the pinnacle of achievement in the life of an Ilongot boy. A man only earned the right to wear *batling* – or even to marry – once he had taken a head. According to the ethnographer Dr Renato Rosaldo, who spent several years doing fieldwork with the Ilongot: '[These] earrings announced to enemies, to allies, to family, to friends, that the person they saw before them was a formidable headhunter. Hunters wore their batling for the rest of their lives. Upon their death, the earrings were buried with them, thrown away, or given to an initiated relative.'

In north-east India, hornbills are not just part of an ancient tribal culture, but are also the centrepiece of a very modern event, the annual Hornbill Festival. Held in the state of Nagaland – known as the 'Land of Festivals' – during the first week of December, the event was first organised by the state government in 2000, to bring several disparate festivals under a single larger banner.

The name of the festival is a tribute to the largest species of hornbill in the country: the great (also known as the great pied or great Indian) hornbill. Found in western and north-eastern India, this large and impressive species is much admired by the Naga people for its appearance and behaviour, and has inspired some of the ornate dances and songs performed at the festival. But not all the hornbill-related events are quite so traditional: there is also a hornbill rock contest, international motor rally and photo competition, while the opening ceremony features a 100-strong choir performing a specially composed 'Hornbill theme song'.

So what is the future for the world's sixty-plus species of hornbills? Despite efforts to use deep-seated tribal beliefs to conserve them and their habitat, we might consider it fairly bleak. As the authors of the monumental *Handbook of the Birds of the World* concluded in 2001, it is reasonable to assume that despite their wide global range across much of Africa and Asia, hornbills are in decline, 'since the habitat changes wrought by man are rarely beneficial to the members of this intriguing family'.

That destruction began thousands of years ago, with the coming of agriculture, and the widespread use of fire and axes to clear forested areas, but it has accelerated rapidly in recent decades, thanks especially to widespread logging. This particularly affects hornbills as – especially in the larger forest-dwelling species found in South East Asia – they tend to nest in the oldest trees, which are in turn the most attractive to loggers.

But we can ill afford to lose such unique and splendid birds. Nigel Collar of BirdLife International sums up both the cultural and ecological importance of all hornbills:

Hornbills hold a special attraction for all of us – one of the few kinds of bird that everyone knows, revered by tribal peoples, sought after by birdwatchers, gasped at by visitors to zoos, used by several Asian states as symbols. Yet their vital ecological function, as seed-dispersers particularly of fig-trees (which are themselves crucial components of tropical forests), is barely appreciated and poorly understood.

Back in the Natural History Museum Bird Collection at Tring, the carved skull of the helmeted hornbill serves as a timely reminder of the fragility of not just hornbills but of all tropical bird species, which are increasingly threatened by habitat loss and collecting for profit. Only by understanding their scientific and cultural significance, and working with local peoples for whom birds such as hornbills are so important to their way of life, will we stand any chance of saving these extraordinary birds.

As when, upon a tranced summer-night,
Those green-rob'd senators of mighty woods,
Tall oaks, branch-charmed by the earnest stars,
Dream, and so dream all night without a stir,
Save from one gradual solitary gust
Which comes upon the silence, and dies off,
As if the ebbing air had but one wave.

John Keats, 'Hyperion'

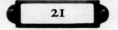

21

Oaks

Quiet Endurance, Longevity and Strength

Monolithic is the word that first comes to mind. The second is cavernous, the third, hydra. A broken ring of grasping tentacles sprouts above a woody cave, its exterior bossed with warts and knots, twisted in places as if it had been given a Chinese burn by a giant hand. In places, yawning gashes in the saurian skin have opened up allowing rainwater to create rock pools several feet above the ground. This vast squat entity is so old that it was probably well grown when the Domesday Book was compiled in 1089 – a veteran English oak.

English oaks are famously long-lived. An old saying goes that an oak takes 300 years to become adult, 300 to mature and another 300 years to die. The tree described above is the Old Man of Calke, which takes pride of place among a host of ancient trees at the National Trust's Calke Abbey, growing in parkland where their branches are able to spread, free of close competition. Mature oaks look their best when given space.

At Moccas Park in Herefordshire there is an extraordinary collection of trees in an ancient park that was formerly wood pasture, mature woodland undergrazed by livestock. Its oaks were immortalised by the Reverend Francis Kilvert, vicar of the nearby church at Bredwardine who wrote in April 1876 of a visit to Moccas:

As we came down the lower slopes of the wooded hillside . . . we came upon . . . what seemed at first in the dusk to be a great ruined grey tower, but which proved to be the vast ruin of the king oak of Moccas Park, hollow and broken, but still alive and vigorous in parts and actually pushing out new shoots and branches . . . I fear those grey old men of Moccas, those grey, gnarled, low-browed, knock-kneed, bowed, bent, huge, strange, long-armed, deformed, hunch-backed, misshapen oak men that stand waiting and watching century after century . . . No human hand set those oaks. They are 'the trees which the Lord hath planted'. They look as if they had been at the beginning and making of the world, and they will probably see its end.

This apparent immortality and ability to transform as it ages make the English oak magnetic, both for us and for wildlife. Oak supports hundreds of invertebrates, more than any other British tree, and as it grows in girth, fungus creates weaknesses, crannies and fissures appear in its trunk, providing a home for owls, bats and many other animals. There are two native species of oak, both with distinctive roundly lobed leaves. The English or pedunculate oak has stalked acorns and very short leaf-stalks and tends to be commoner in the lowlands; sessile oak has unstalked acorns which sit on the twigs and longer leaf-stalks and is more frequent in the north-western and western parts of the British Isles. To make life more interesting, the two species hybridise freely and in many places the hybrid can be the most common oak. Providing shelter for our wildlife and, as we'll see, for our navy and even for a king, the oak is a remarkable tree.

But it can be easy to overlook. Visitors to the Natural History Museum's Treasures Gallery could be forgiven for keeping their eyes focused on the collection of twenty-two exhibits gathered together, chosen to showcase the range and variety of the museum's collection. These include: the skeleton of a dodo; one of three precious emperor penguin eggs collected by the polar explorer Apsley Cherry-Garrard; a Barbary lion skull unearthed from the royal menagerie at the Tower of London; and a piece of moon rock brought back to earth by the Apollo astronauts. But glancing upwards, they will come face to face with an extraordinary work of art.

Tree, by Devon-based artist Tania Kovats, is a 17-metre longitudinal section of an entire, 200-year-old oak tree. The branches, trunks and roots have been cut into wafer-thin pieces and inlaid into the gallery's ceiling. Against the white background, the pale buffish-yellow of the tree's interior, its grain etched across the surface as if delicately drawn, stands out. Looking up, the effect is to place you, the viewer, at the very heart of a huge oak tree.

She was inspired by leafing through one of Darwin's early notebooks:

> The words 'I think' are written at the top of the page, and the spindly lines become a branching form resembling a tree. Seeing the original is like standing over Darwin's shoulder as the thought emerges. To me it actually looks like thought, given how significant the tree form is in representing our thought processes. The tree is a model of connectivity, ancestry and genealogy, and each branch traces change or chance.

When it came to choosing a particular species of tree to represent Darwin's thoughts and ideas, there was only one contender:

> I wanted to express scale, to create something big, and an oak is like the blue whale in the woods . . . I wanted something old, something that has been here a long time. We think in tree shapes. The idea of ancestry, for example, is expressed in trees, the family tree. Trees are an image of connectivity, thoughts branching out but connected to where they came from.

———•·•———

We have rested beneath the shade of oaks in summer, sheltered beneath them from rain in winter, climbed them as children, collected their acorns, and over centuries used their bark and wood for everything from building great vessels such as the Tudor flagship the *Mary Rose*, Captain Cook's *Endeavour* and Nelson's *Victory*, to buildings, including the ceiling of the House of Commons.

The oak tree is at the heart of both ancient and modern cultures across Europe, Asia and North America. It was sacred to the Greeks, where it was closely associated with the god Zeus; to the Romans, whose emperors were often presented with crowns made of oak leaves; and to the Druids, who would worship in oak clearings. Druids worshipped the spirit of the oak and the parasitical mistletoe that grew on it. Roman history and natural history is full of speculation about the Druids' dark secrets. Here is Tacitus's vivid description from the *Annals* of the decisive battle between Suetonius's army and the British Druids in AD 60:

> On the opposite shore stood the Britons, prepared for action. Women were seen running through the ranks in wild disorder; their apparel funereal; their hair loose to the wind, in their hands flaming torches, and their whole appearance resembling the frantic rage of the Furies. The Druids were ranged in order, with hands uplifted, invoking the gods, and pouring forth horrible imprecations. The novelty of the fight struck the Romans with awe and terror. They stood in stupid amazement, as if their limbs were benumbed, riveted to one spot, a mark for the enemy. The exhortations of the general diffused new vigour through the ranks, and the men felt the disgrace of yielding to a troop of women, and a band of fanatic priests; they advanced their standards, and rushed on to the attack with impetuous fury. And the Britons perished in the flames, which they themselves had kindled . . . The religious groves, dedicated to superstition and barbarous rites, were levelled to the ground. In those recesses, the natives had stained their altars with the blood of their prisoners, and in the entrails of men explored the will of the gods.

The thoroughness of the Roman destruction of the sacred groves and suppression of the Druids meant there are many gaps in our knowledge of ancient religious beliefs and practice but recent archaeological breakthroughs, particularly in the area of dendrology (the science and study of wooded plants) have shifted the way we see the ancient world's relationship with nature.

The most telling evidence of the oak's ancient importance was discovered in 1998 in the beach at Holme-next-the-Sea, Norfolk. Four-thousand-year-old Seahenge was constructed of a circle of oak timbers with a huge, upturned oak boss at its centre. It was the oaken altar used in Bronze Age funeral rites. At low tide, Seahenge's snaggle-toothed circle of stumps loomed out of the mud, casting ancient shadows across the ooze. Dr Francis Pryor, archaeologist and author of *Seahenge*, believes the symbolism of this upside-down oak is key to understanding the Bronze Age mind.

> We often find everyday objects deliberately turned upside down at Bronze Age sites. The inverted oak is a very complex statement. It is the world turned upside down, just as death is an inversion of life. From a ritual point of view it symbolises taking objects out of this world and placing them in the next.

We have focused on the stone circles and monuments left starring our countryside because they're the ones that remain but Seahenge shows there were probably many more less permanent wooden ones crucial to Bronze Age beliefs. Oaks also appear throughout myths and legends, in the Bible and fairy tales. The Norse god Thor – god of thunder – is also associated with oaks, possibly because the oak is more likely to be struck by lightning than other trees, growing as it does so commonly and often in the open. In their *Compendium of Symbolic and Ritual Plants in Europe*, Marcel de Cleene and Marie Claire Lejeune compare the status of the oak with that of two other unchallenged natural symbols: 'Thus, the biggest, strongest and most useful tree became the king of the plant kingdom in Europe, just as the lion is the king of land animals and the eagle rules the skies.'

Oak has remained an important symbol throughout our more recent history too. Royal Oak Day was for two centuries an official public holiday, marked out with bonfires, peals of bells and special church services. When Charles II rode into London on his birthday, 29 May, in 1660 and restored the monarchy to Britain, the day was officially declared one of national celebration. Royal Oak Day celebrated the new king's chosen trademark. After losing the Battle of Worcester in 1651, and on the run from Cromwell's forces, Charles had hidden in an oak tree as his enemies searched the surrounding Shropshire woodland. Charles later told Samuel Pepys that while he was hiding in the tree, a Parliamentarian soldier had passed directly below it. The exhausted prince had fallen asleep, and his worried companion was 'constrained . . . to pinch His Majesty to the end he might awaken him to prevent his present danger'. A vivid symbol of his lowest moment, the choice of the oak leaf showed an appealing sense of the humility his father had lacked. This story is still commemorated on the signs of more than 500 pubs across the country, making 'The Royal Oak' the third commonest pub name in Britain even today. (Incidentally the tree standing on the site today is not the original but a 200- or 300-year-old descendant known as 'Son of Royal Oak'. The original Royal Oak was destroyed during the seventeenth and eighteenth centuries by over-enthusiastic tourists who cut off branches and chunks as souvenirs.) Chelsea Pensioners still wear oak leaves in memory of Charles's escape from capture.

Royal Oak Day managed to combine the celebration of recent history with many of the most popular features of pagan spring celebrations, including maypoles. The dominant custom of the day was the wearing of sprays of oak leaves (preferably with an oak apple attached), which were worn by 'almost everybody, high or low, male or female, adult or child, throughout the eighteenth and nineteenth centuries'. Representing a return to the spirit of 'merry England' so harshly suppressed by the Puritan revolution that they had even banned Christmas, it was wildly popular. A spirit of misrule reigned. Any child who did not wear their oak leaves was 'attacked unmercifully by their school-fellows and could be pinched, stung with nettles, kicked or pelted with birds eggs (sometimes rotten ones)', according to folklore historian Steve Roud in *The English Year*. The day was officially Royal Oak Day but all the local terms for it rapidly dropped the historical element in favour of the natural and it was known as Shick-Shack (dialect for oak apple), Arbour Tree or Oak and Nettle Day.

The Green Man, a motif showing a human face made of leaves (often those of the oak), is found in many ancient cultures, and appears to be a pagan spirit related to fertility and rebirth. Another man in green, the legendary outlaw Robin Hood, is said to have made his hideout in an ancient oak tree known as the Major Oak, in the heart of Sherwood Forest. All over England places have been immortalised by their famous trees: Bowthorpe Oak in Lincolnshire, is thought to be 1,000 years old, while Marton Oak in Cheshire is even older; and the Crouch Oak on the borders of Windsor Great Park in Addlestone, Surrey, is said to be the tree under whose shade Queen Elizabeth I, on one of her lengthy summer progresses around the kingdom, stopped for a picnic.

Britain is also full of place names that refer to oaks, from Accrington (acorn farm) to Sevenoaks (which should perhaps have been renamed when six of its seven original ancient oaks were destroyed in the Great Storm of 1989). The north London district of Gospel Oak – marking the parish boundary between Hampstead and St Pancras – is a survivor of an ancient tradition of gospel oaks, once widespread through the country, that were once taken as convenient, enduring marks of the exact boundary line. Before the Reformation, crosses were carried and traced on the ground, and the gospels were said or sung to the corn under the Gospel Oak. Geoffrey Grigson suggests that that could have been 'some survival of tree worship in this respect for the oak tree'. After the Reformation the ceremonies weakened, and were gradually abandoned.

Behind all these symbolic, cultural and practical examples, there is a real, living tree. So what exactly is an oak, and why does it hold such an important place in our lives, and in the lives of so many other plants and animals?

Just as there is no simple, self-contained definition of a 'tree' – either in botany or popular culture – so there is no easy way to define an 'oak'. This is partly because there are so many different kinds – at least 600 extant species – but also because people around the world have named various trees 'oaks', even though they belong to other tree families. Most oaks, however, belong to the genus *Quercus*, and are native to the northern hemisphere continents of North America, Europe and Asia, with the greatest variety of species occurring in the United States and Mexico, and also in China. Oaks can be either deciduous – losing their leaves in autumn in order to conserve water – or evergreen, keeping their leaves all year round.

But when we speak of 'oaks', we usually mean the English oak *Quercus robur*. Also known, because its leaves grow on a long stem, or peduncle, as the pedunculate oak, this is the commonest tree species in Britain, with its main strongholds in the southern and western parts of the country, on wet, clay soils. Some ancient specimens have reached a height of 40 metres, though most are closer to 20 metres. Strangely, the tallest trees are not, as you might expect, the oldest: oaks stop growing after about 300 years, and may even shrink as they get older to prolong their life. They also grow hollow as they age.

English oaks are easily identified by their distinctive leaves, arranged spirally around the twig, with four or five individual 'fingers' or lobes on each side, creating the classic shape with which we are so familiar, and which are produced in bunches from May onwards. In spring oaks also produce both male and female flowers – the male flowers being long and easily visible catkins, while the female flowers are much smaller. Pollen from the male catkins is blown by the wind to fertilise the female flowers.

Over the summer these gradually mature into fruit known colloquially as an acorn. The name comes from the Old English word *aecern*, and not, as is sometimes suggested, a corruption of 'oak' and 'corn'. In fact the word simply means 'fruit' or 'nut', and although this originally applied to any species, during the medieval period it gradually attached itself to the particular fruit of the oak tree, which was an important foodstuff for swine. Green at first, as they ripen acorns turn a pleasing shade of brown, and when mature they loosen in their cups and eventually fall from the tree. The vast majority of these will never germinate, as they are swiftly collected and eaten by a wide range of woodland creatures including deer, mice, red and grey squirrels and jays. But not all the acorns they collect are eaten straight away; in autumn, both jays and squirrels regularly store them as an insurance against food shortages later in the year. Unable to remember where they bury every one, they inadvertently help spread the seeds; indeed oak woods have spread to higher altitudes through jays carrying the acorns uphill.

Oak apples, by the way, only look like fruit: they are galls created by a small wasp which induces by chemical means abnormal growths in the oak tissues to create a safe home for their grubs. Oak apples are just one of many species of oak galls that can grow on the leaves, the catkins, the acorns, the twigs or the bark.

As an oak tree matures, it forms a characteristic shape, with a broad, spreading crown and thicker, sturdier branches beneath, at right angles to the main trunk. Because unlike beech trees their canopy is relatively open, it allows plenty of sunlight through to the forest floor, which gives oak woods their varied flora, notably primroses and bluebells.

Oak trees – and oak woods – provide excellent habitats for wildlife, supporting a far greater variety of species than any other native tree. Almost 300 different kinds of insects, from moths to beetles and weevils to wasps, depend on oaks, as do many species of birds and mammals. These include hole-nesting birds such as tits, woodpeckers and nuthatches, and treecreepers, which nest in crevices beneath the bark.

Three long-distance migrants from Africa, the wood warbler, redstart and pied flycatcher, arrive back in our western sessile oak woods each spring to breed; while other wildlife supported by oaks includes bats, which roost beneath the bark or in old woodpecker holes, several hundred species of lichen, and a wealth of fungi, which thrive in the leaf mould created as the fallen leaves decay in autumn. So many caterpillars feast on oak leaves it is amazing that the trees survive. Species whose common name contains the word 'oak' include the oak bush-cricket, oak jewel beetle, oak woodwasp, oak mining bee, oak leaf-roller weevil, and a whole range of moths, such as the oak eggar, oak lutestring, oak hook-tip and the evocatively named oak beauty.

However, not all moths enjoy such a benevolent relationship with this mighty tree. In recent years, naturalists and conservationists have become increasingly alarmed by a non-native moth, the oak processionary, which first appeared in Britain from its home in southern Europe in 2005. Its caterpillars seriously damage the tree's foliage, eventually even leading to its death. And it's not just the oaks that are under threat. It's us too: the caterpillars' toxic hairs present a real danger to the health of nearby humans.

The oak tree – and its leaves – has often been used as a kind of symbolic shorthand because of its perceived values of endurance and longevity. Oaks feature on the coat of arms of Estonia, as the logo of Britain's Conservative Party, and on coins in both Germany and the UK. Oak leaves are also the symbol of both the Woodland Trust and the National Trust. And the oak is Britain's national tree, though fifteen other countries or provinces, including Estonia, Germany and the United States, also claim it as their own; as too, unfortunately, did the Nazi regime, in which the Knight's Cross with Oak Leaves was the highest honour a soldier could win.

The tree's products, including its bark, acorns and galls, were widely used in herbalism and ancient medicine, as a cure for a range of ailments from snake bites and mouth sores to diarrhoea and kidney stones; while until the cultivation of wheat began, about 10,000 years ago, acorns were ground up for flour. Today, we still use oak to make barrels in which the finest wines and malt whiskies are left to mature for years or even decades, the oak imparting its subtle flavour to the liquid within.

One of the main reasons the oak is so dear to our hearts is not, however, symbolic, but practical. The linguistic root for oak is 'dur' and among its meanings are 'door' and 'durable' (it has been suggested that the word Druid also derives from it). Our place names remember it: Derwent, Darent and Dart all mean 'river abounding in oak'. Oak timber is one of the densest, hardest and most durable of all woods – indeed the second part of the English oak's scientific name, *robur*, derives from the Latin meaning 'strength and power'. Oak timbers have been used for centuries to make beams for houses and also ships; hence the naval association. The timber is just as long-lasting as the tree itself; perhaps even longer: the tomb of Edward the Confessor in Westminster Abbey is as strong today as when it was carved, almost 1,000 years ago.

Peter Ackroyd wrote: 'Oaks mean something to us and somehow the old oak stands for England.' And the sense that the oak is at the heart of what it means to be both English and British (whatever exactly that means) has found an outlet again and again in patriotic song and poetry. We'll leave you with 'Heart of Oak' – originally composed more than 250 years ago – which is the official march of the Royal Navy. Its words, by the eighteenth-century actor and playwright David Garrick, were written as a rallying cry to sailors:

Heart of oak are our ships.
Heart of oak are our men;
We always are ready;
Steady, boys, steady;
We'll fight and we'll conquer again and again.

In a purely technical sense, each species of higher organism – beetle, moss, and so forth – is richer in information than a Caravaggio painting, Mozart symphony, or any other great work of art.

Edward O. Wilson

22

Beetles

Technology From Nature

If the words 'Porsche' and 'beetle' occur in the same sentence, it is usually because a motoring journalist is snidely comparing the shape of two of Germany's best-known cars. But more recently, the luxury-car manufacturer has used the appearance of a particular species of beetle to develop a revolutionary new paint for their latest model. The car designers got the idea from fossilised beetles, whose bright gold and silver shades had survived for millions of years, their colour undimmed. Porsche's scientists were fascinated to discover that it was because their colour is not produced by a pigment, but instead formed by the crystal structure of the animal's carapace, and so remains constant and strong.

The first beetle-like organisms found in the fossil record date back roughly 270 million years, while true beetles – the ancestors of our modern-day species – followed soon afterwards. So beetles were already in existence long before the supercontinent Pangaea began to break up to form the landmasses we know today, and like birds and mammals they managed to survive the cataclysmic events of 66 million years ago, when a meteorite hit the earth and wiped out not just the dinosaurs but three-quarters of all species on the planet.

As a group, beetles are tough, adaptable and pretty good at coping with change in their environment; indeed the more challenging life gets, the more beetles seem to be able to step up to the plate and perform. Take, for example, a beetle that lives in one of the driest places in the world – the Namib Desert in south-west Africa, where the average rainfall is only 1.4 centimetres a year – and yet it does not die of thirst. The fogstand beetle *Stenocara gracilipes* (the second part of its name meaning 'slender-footed'), takes advantage of a particular climatic event. Each morning, huge banks of fog move inland from the coast of the Atlantic Ocean to the west, blanketing the desert. As soon as the sun begins to heat the land, the fog dissipates. But in the brief window of opportunity around dawn, the fogstand beetle climbs to the top of the highest sand dune, raises the back end of its body at an angle of 45 degrees towards the early morning breeze, and captures the precious moisture it needs to survive.

It does so by catching tiny water droplets, each measuring just 15–20 microns across – between 1/67th and 1/50th of a millimetre – on its hardened outer wings. Those wings have evolved an uneven surface, in which the bumps are hydrophilic, meaning that water sticks to them, while the troughs between are hydrophobic, so that the water stays on the bumps.

As the water droplets hit the surface of the beetle's wings, they flatten out, which stops the breeze blowing them off, and this creates a larger area on which more droplets can attach themselves. At the point at which the water droplet becomes too large and heavy to stay where it is – roughly 5 millimetres – it begins to roll slowly down towards the beetle's mouth, enabling it to drink. It has recently been discovered that on days too humid to form fog, the beetles can also collect water from early morning dew.

At the Massachusetts Institute of Technology (MIT) in the United States, researchers have mimicked the fogstand beetle to create a textured surface covered with alternating hydrophilic and hydrophobic materials, which could then be used to extract water from the atmosphere using the same principles that the beetle has been employing for millions of years. This technology, which is still in its infancy, also has exciting applications wherever water condensation can cause fogging – for example on the interior surface of car windscreens, or on bathroom mirrors – to make a surface that allows the water to disappear rapidly. Even more exciting is the possibility that the technology could be used to extract moisture from the air to provide a reliable supply of clean drinking water in some of the world's driest regions.

In 2011 a young Australian engineer, Edward Linacre, won the James Dyson Award (funded by the British technology pioneer) for a water pump he had developed by studying the fogstand beetle's water-gathering technique. The Airdrop works by pumping desert air through a system of underground pipes, which allow it to cool and produce water in the form of condensation. Although the amount of water collected is just a few millilitres per cubic metre of air, over time this could provide enough water to be able to irrigate crops.

The way that Linacre and other designers and technologists are taking inspiration from nature now has a name: 'biomimicry' – from the Greek words meaning 'life' and 'imitation'. Although it did not appear in the dictionary until the early 1980s, biomimicry has a long and distinguished pedigree.

Almost since civilisation began, human beings have wanted to fly, and for centuries they looked at birds in order to discover ways of doing so. Most famously, the Italian Renaissance artist, inventor and polymath Leonardo da Vinci sketched birds alongside rough diagrams for 'flying machines' in his notebooks, though he never actually attempted to build one. Four centuries later, pioneering aviators Orville and Wilbur Wright relied heavily on their observation of the flight of pigeons – particularly on their changing the angle of their wingtips to make their bodies roll right or left – when designing their first successful powered aircraft, which took to the air on 17 December 1903 at Kitty Hawk, North Carolina.

Another early pioneer was the American biophysicist Otto Schmitt, who during the 1950s developed the science of biomimetics, taking inspiration from everywhere in the natural world to revolutionise the way engineers and designers would work. For

Schmitt, this was not some arcane academic theory, but a way of seeing the world around us:

> Biophysics is not so much a subject matter as it is a point of view. It is an approach to problems of biological science utilizing the theory and technology of the physical sciences. Conversely, biophysics is also a biologist's approach to problems of physical science and engineering, although this aspect has largely been neglected.

For a short while, the way nature inspired science was known as 'bionics', but after various science-fiction writers had borrowed the term to refer to a 'bionic man' – one who gained advantage from artificial body parts – the term was ditched in favour of 'biomimetics' and later 'biomimicry'. In her 1997 work *Biomimicry: Innovation Inspired by Nature*, US science writer Janine Benyus defined it as a 'new science that studies nature's models and then imitates or takes inspiration from these designs and processes to solve human problems'.

As Sir James Dyson noted when he presented Linacre with his award:

> Biomimicry is a powerful weapon in an engineer's armoury. Airdrop shows how simple, natural principles like the condensation of water, can be applied to good effect through skilled design and robust engineering. Young designers and engineers like Edward will develop the simple, effective technology of the future – they will tackle the world's biggest problems and improve lives in the process.

More recently, rather than replicating elements of successful insect technology, scientific breakthroughs have added to it. In March 2015 scientists at Berkeley and Singapore's Nanyang Technological University (NTU) unveiled their research into how beetles and other flying insects' mastery of flight control – integrating as they do sensory feedback from their visual system and other senses to navigate and maintain stable flight, using minimal energy – could be controlled by electrical signals. The scientists strapped tiny computers and wireless radios on to the backs of giant flower beetles (which are around 6 centimetres long). Carefully positioned electrodes passed messages to the beetle about which direction to fly and which way to turn.

The results were impressive. 'Beetles are ideal study subjects because they can carry relatively heavy payloads,' said Hirotaka Sato, an assistant professor at NTU. 'We could easily add a small microphone and thermal sensors for applications in search-and-rescue missions. With this technology, we could safely explore areas not accessible before, such as the small nooks and crevices in a collapsed building.' The fact that this fascinating research has been funded by DARPA (Defense Advanced Research Projects Agency), the technology arm of the US Army, suggests, however, that there could be less benign uses for these insect cyborgs or living drones in the future.

When it comes to taking inspiration from nature – not just for science and technology but also in the fields of art and design – beetles have inspired us for far longer than we might imagine. The ancient Egyptians revered the scarab beetle *Scarabaeus sacer* as the giver of life, for a giant heavenly beetle was thought to roll the sun across the sky each day in the same way its terrestrial counterparts rolled a ball of dung across the ground. Egyptian soldiers wore live scarab beetles as jewellery – a kind of living brooch – as the insect was supposed to protect them from danger.

Inspired by this, during the 1980s, a fashion arose in Mexico of wearing living specimens of the Maquech beetle – a large but docile species from the genus *Zopherus* – encrusted with colourful semi-precious gemstones. Having been decorated, the unfortunate creature was then attached to the wearer's clothing using a safety pin and short leash, so that it could walk round a little. This custom goes back hundreds of years to the Mayan peoples, but its modern incarnation has attracted widespread condemnation from animal rights campaigners, who regard the practice as cruel and unnecessary.

Perhaps it's not surprising that beetles are at the forefront of the many different ways in which we take inspiration from nature. After all, when the great British biologist J.B.S. Haldane was asked what his lifelong study of the natural world had taught him about God, he reputedly replied: 'That the Creator, if He exists, has an inordinate fondness for beetles.'

Haldane's sardonic response is based on the fact that beetles – those insects in the order *Coleoptera*, which means 'sheathed wing' – make up roughly one-quarter of all known living species on the planet, and about 40 per cent of all the insects: up to 400,000 different species in all, with an incredible 1 to 4 million more species – up to 90 per cent of all beetle species – yet to be discovered.

Perhaps not surprisingly given the large number of species, beetles are one of the most varied of all insect groups, though they do mostly have two pairs of wings – the front pair being hard and shell-like in order to protect the softer body. Like all insects, their body is in three parts: head, thorax and abdomen; and like many other insects, including butterflies and moths, they undergo a complex process of metamorphosis from egg through larva to adult.

Beetles can be found in virtually every terrestrial habitat, apart from the two polar regions, where it is too cold for them to survive; and the sea, where like all insects they have not managed to adapt to the environment, and molluscs and crustaceans rule. Their diversity and geographical spread are a result of their versatility: beetles are able to feed on a huge range of plant and animal material, including living plants and their detritus, carrion, fungi and even dung. Some are predators, others vegetarian; some are specialists, others omnivores; some are even parasites, living off another animal.

As one might expect for such a widespread group, beetles are also an important prey for a whole range of (mainly) larger creatures, including birds, mammals, reptiles, fish and other insects.

So both as feeders and as food, they play a crucial part in maintaining the biodiversity of ecosystems throughout the world.

Some beetles have entered our culture and mythology more than others. And of all the British families, surely the most familiar and best loved are the group of small, colourful insects we call ladybirds. The *Coccinellidae*, as the family is known to scientists, include about 5,000 species worldwide, though only fifty or so are found in Britain, and can mostly be recognised by their small size (usually between 5 and 10 millimetres long), and bright colours, often featuring a number of black spots on the coloured background.

It is this pattern that gave these insects their popular name, a contraction of the phrase 'Our Lady's bird', referring to Jesus's mother Mary. Mary was often depicted in early medieval art wearing a bright red cloak, and the seven black spots of one of the commonest European species, the seven-spot ladybird, were supposed to represent her seven joys and seven sorrows.

There is something very pleasing about the shape and appearance of a ladybird: that rounded body and short legs do not usually repel people, in the way that so many longer-legged invertebrates such as spiders seem to do. Like butterflies, their bright colours help us to like them; even though they are actually warnings to predators that the insect's body is distasteful to eat. Our liking for ladybirds may also be linked to the idea that they are 'useful': as voracious predators of aphids and other agricultural and garden pests.

Ladybirds are associated, as one might expect from such a widespread and colourful insect, with a wealth of folk mythology and superstitions, most of which, as is often the case with the natural world, is total nonsense. Ladybirds are supposed to bring good luck in many European cultures, while Victorian folklorist James Napier reported that when girls caught a ladybird they would hold it in their hands, and repeat the following couplet:

Fly away east or fly away west,
And show me where lives the one I like best.

Perhaps the best-known example of all ladybird folklore is the rather grim children's rhyme, which has a number of variations, all of which end in tragedy:

Ladybird, ladybird fly away home,
Your house is on fire and your children are gone . . .

The widely held belief that ladybirds can in some way foretell the future led to them being used as weather forecasters, such as the Welsh rhyme that suggests that if you hold out a ladybird and it falls from your hand, rain is on the way; whereas if it takes to the wing, there will be fine weather. Other beetles are also linked with forecasting the weather: in his *Handbook of Weather Folk-Lore*, published in 1873, the Revd C. Swainson claimed that: 'The clock beetle, which flies about in the summer evenings in a circular direction, with a loud buzzing noise, is said to foretell a fine day.'

Swainson also claimed that this kind of beetle was the species that was consecrated by the ancient Egyptians to the sun, though as we have seen this was in fact the scarab, a much larger species. However, his remark about scarabs is not so far-fetched as these beetles do belong to the scarab group.

German folklore suggests that if ladybirds with more than seven spots are particularly prevalent, there will be a good harvest; but if most have fewer than seven spots, there will be a poor one. Other myths connected with the ladybird's spots claim that the number of spots indicates the insect's age, whereas of course it varies depending on the species in question: as entomologist Peter Marren has observed, in Britain alone there are ladybirds with 2, 4, 5, 7, 11, 13, 14, 16, 18, 19, 22 and 24 spots.

Elsewhere in the world, beetles are being used in many new, different and not always benign ways, including as pets, for food, and especially in Asia to fight each other for entertainment and gambling. In the latter, the larger members of the scarab beetle family – including rhinoceros beetles, which may be 11 centimetres long and weigh 50 grams – are pitted against one another in small arenas. Males are used, and the mating call of the female is sometimes replicated to encourage them to do battle. The winner is the creature that has either driven its rival over the perimeter of the ring, or flipped it over in the manner of a judo or wrestling practitioner.

Of course the fighting is merely an excuse to gamble vast sums of money on the outcome, much like other widespread animal encounters such as dog- and cock-fighting. Insect fights have a long pedigree in China and other parts of South East Asia, going back as far as the Tang dynasty of the seventh to the tenth centuries.

A more sustainable use of these huge beetles currently gaining popularity in parts of Africa and Asia is to use them – or more usually their larvae – as food. Although we in the west may baulk at the idea, eating insects is already regularly practised by approximately 30 per cent of the world's population, or roughly 2 billion people. Agronomist Séverin Tchibozo, based in the West African state of Benin, suggests that insects – including the larvae of some of the world's largest beetles – could help solve the growing problem of food shortages in the developing world. He points out that the larva of the rhinoceros beetle contains about 40 per cent protein: twice as much as chicken and beef. But if we were to rely on beetles for food in the future they would have to be farmed on a massive scale:

Deforestation and global changes mean that there are fewer and fewer to harvest from the wild. Some species are becoming rare and others are threatened with extinction. So it's vital to continue to carry out inventories of edible species, establish through biochemical analysis their nutritional quality, and to start trying to rear them commercially as foodstuffs.

It could be worthwhile: studies have shown that farmed insects require less land, and use far less water and energy in their rearing process, produce less waste – including a fraction of the greenhouse gases such as methane produced by other livestock such as cattle – and can be fed on animal waste without causing harm to human consumers. We may find the idea of eating a nice plump beetle larva unpalatable, but these humble creatures might just end up saving our world.

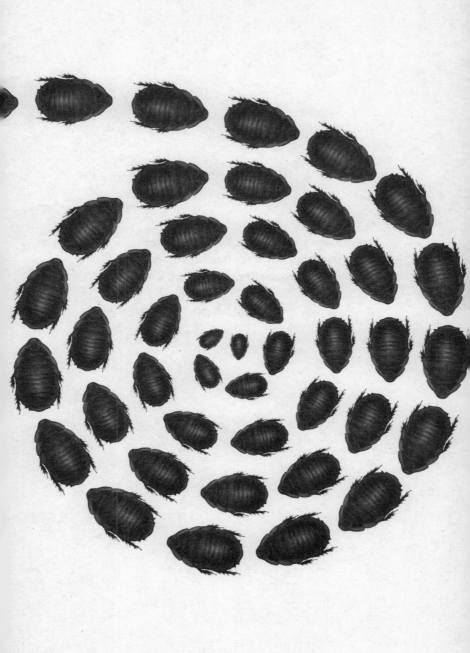

A cockroach likely has no less brainpower than a butterfly, but we're quicker to deny it consciousness because it's a species we dislike.

Jeffrey Kluger, *Time* magazine

23

Cockroaches

Indestructible Survivors

As opening lines go, it's up there with *Pride and Prejudice*: 'As Gregor Samsa awoke one morning from uneasy dreams he found himself transformed in his bed into a gigantic insect.'

In Franz Kafka's novella *The Metamorphosis*, first published in 1915, the unfortunate travelling salesman then has to deal with the consequences of his sudden and bizarre transformation. Kafka himself (and most translators) refrained from assigning the insect to a specific type, beyond the idea that it might be some kind of beetle. The original German term was *ungeheures Ungeziefer*, literally 'monstrous vermin'; in Kafka's letter to his publisher of 25 October 1915 he uses the term *Insekt*, saying: 'The insect itself is not to be drawn. It is not even to be seen from a distance.' And yet in the minds of most subsequent readers and commentators, the insect has been firmly fixed as a cockroach. And unlike the beetles in the previous chapter, cockroaches have few admirers.

Myths and truths about cockroaches tend to blur together. We are told that they are the only creatures left alive after a nuclear explosion (not necessarily true, though cockroaches can withstand at least ten times as much radiation as we can). It's said that they avoid light (generally true, but not for all species), and that they can survive without their heads – true, at least for a few weeks until they need to drink. They can also live for at least a month without eating, survive underwater for up to half an hour, and despite their usual preference for warmth, survive below-freezing temperatures for a short while.

It is this reputation for toughness that has led to a wealth of horror stories about cockroaches laying their eggs beneath people's skin, which then hatch out into grubs. Except of course they don't – it's another urban myth. But why do cockroaches feature so prominently in these modern morality tales? And do we understand them yet?

Cockroaches are generally fairly large insects, ranging in size from less than 3 millimetres to the massive rhinoceros cockroach of Australia, which can reach a length of 8.5 centimetres and weigh over 30 grams. They are mostly silent, apart from the occasional species which hisses to scare away potential predators, but a few species use sound in courtship.

Cockroach-like insects have been around for as long as 300 million years. This means they were scuttling around the earth several tens of millions of years before the dinosaurs turned up. There are roughly 4,600 different species of cockroach, all in the order Blattodea, which now also includes the 3,000 known species of termites.

The earliest English mention of cockroaches is found in the writings of Captain John Smith, the English adventurer who helped found the British colony of Virginia in 1607. In a work first published in 1624, Smith describes the insects on the islands of Bermuda: 'Musketas and Flies are also too busie, with a certaine India Bug, called by the Spaniards a Cacarootch, the which creeping into Chests they eat and defile with their ill-sented dung.' The name 'cockroach' is a distortion of the original Mexican Spanish word *cucaracha*, which merges two words meaning 'fast bug'.

Some cockroaches are social creatures, while others lead a solitary existence, apart from when they pair up and mate. In general they prefer warm rather than cold environments, but those that have learned to live alongside us and become pests are nothing if not adaptable when it comes to diet and habitat. A peculiarly modern problem is their growing liking for laptops, in which, as one contributor to an online gaming forum warned, they might be getting an inadvertent helping hand from the machine's owner:

> Roaches are attracted to heat, moisture and food . . . [So imagine] the living conditions of a typical early 20s gamer, who uses their laptop at home and doesn't move it around much. Their play area may even have bits of food (chips, pizza, etc.). The gamer will never see the roaches while he is awake because roaches like to move around in the dark. Once the lights are out the roaches come out, scrounge for food, and then go to where they detect heat . . . most likely from the still warm laptop. And all it takes is 1–2 to start a colony . . .

Despite their reputation, of all the thousands of different cockroach species just thirty (less than 1 per cent) live alongside humans, and of these only four are serious pests: the American, German, Asian and Oriental cockroaches. However, this quartet can cause huge problems both to individuals and communities, and also to businesses – particularly the restaurant and hotel industries. Cockroaches transmit diseases by contaminating food with their faeces, and they also act as vectors for disease by carrying pathogens from place to place on their legs. In the US alone it has been estimated that between 25 and 30 million people may be allergic to cockroaches. Allergy to cockroaches was first confirmed in 1943, when participants in experiments reported rashes on their skin after contact with a cockroach. They can also cause or aggravate allergies, possibly including asthma, especially in children.

As a result human beings have developed many ingenious ways to try to eradicate or at least control cockroaches, including biological warfare using predatory wasps or centipedes, and a bizarre range of traps, including the legendary 'Roach Motel', marketed under the slogan 'They can check in – but they won't check out!' Home-made traps use a range of products to attract their quarry, including stale beer and coffee grounds, with Vaseline smeared around the edge of the container to stop the insect escaping.

But perhaps the most ingenious way developed to control cockroaches – without resorting to poisons or squashing – is to use compounds known as Insect Growth Regulators (IGRs), chemical copies of natural hormones that effectively stop the cockroach from developing into an adult insect. The cockroach stays alive, but is never able to reproduce, in what Roger Meola from Texas A&M University described as 'Peter Pan Syndrome'. This approach is clearly far more environmentally friendly than the indiscriminate use of poisons, which can kill more benevolent insects and also be dangerous to humans.

To call someone a cockroach is a very loaded insult. The fear of 'the other' is not confined to alien invaders; as we know from recent conflicts in the Balkans, Africa and the Middle East, the greatest level of hatred is often directed at people's nearest neighbours, simply because they have a different ethnic background, tribal culture or religion. There was international outrage when Colonel Gaddafi compared the rebels in Libya to cockroaches. The suggestion is plain: they are lesser, expendable and should be eradicated. As US author Richard Schweid wrote in his 1999 book *The Cockroach Papers*: 'If you want to say something nasty about someone, call him a cockroach: that lowest of the low, vilest of the vile, most easily eliminated without a pang of remorse, the cheapest of all lives . . .'

One of the triggers for the 1994 genocide in Rwanda – in which a million people were massacred – was Hutu radio show hosts referring to their Tutsi neighbours as *inyenzi*: cockroaches. When President Habyarimana's plane was shot down, the radio called for a 'final war' to 'exterminate the cockroaches'. During the genocide that followed, they broadcast lists of people to be killed and advised killers where to find them. A United Nations tribunal later convicted three media executives who had worked for the private radio station, of incitement to murder.

*

It's not all death and destruction however. There are some positive depictions of cockroaches: in the Pixar movie *Wall-E* the eponymous robot's sidekick is a cockroach who has managed to survive in a world so overwhelmed by rubbish that humans had to leave centuries before.

The Mexican dance La Cucaracha is likewise double-edged: it can simply be seen as a celebration of the insect's survival skills – its spinning, stamping steps, the dancer's attempts to crush a cockroach scuttling across the floor. But during the Mexican Revolution of the early twentieth century, its words were rewritten and used as a satirical weapon against political opponents, by both the government and the rebel forces, the latter led by the legendary Emiliano Zapata.

And while Gregor Samsa's insect trapped in his old bedroom has to be the best-known fictional character, another anthropomorphic cockroach (also created amid the destruction of the First World War) is almost his complete antithesis, being sympathetic and also quite cute. Archy, along with his partner-in-crime, the alley cat Mehitabel, first appeared in a newspaper column in the New York *Evening Sun* in 1916, when the writer Don Marquis claimed to have discovered the eponymous insect composing verse on the office typewriter, leaping about to press the keys for each letter. But because Archy could not type while simultaneously holding down the shift key, all his poems were in lower case.

This cockroach was a reincarnated poet and as such had a highly unusual and entertaining worldview: 'The human race may be doing the best it can, boss, but that's an explanation, not an excuse.' Don Marquis's columns were a bizarre mixture of social comment and free verse and became hugely popular.

But cultural historian Marion Copeland, author of the fascinating *Cockroach*, argues that there was much more to Marquis's stories than simply entertaining his readers. She believes that he was consciously following in the tradition of African-American folklore, in which cockroaches frequently feature as underdogs and survivors, something that resonated powerfully with an audience whose recent ancestors had been slaves, and who were still fighting prejudice and discrimination every day:

> [This explains] why the cockroach continues to figure in contemporary folk tradition as the survivor who sees life from the underside and 'tells it like it is'. It also, in the modern context, makes Archy a champion of both human and nonhuman underdogs and, indeed, the predominant tone in his voice is irony and satire, comedy but comedy with dark undertones.

Archy's column continued to appear for many years. He also featured in a number of stage musicals, TV programmes and animated films. In 1943 the US Navy named a ship after him, while in 2011 the magnificent new door of Brooklyn Public Library's building in New York featured Archy and Mehitabel cast in bronze and coated in gold, along with Tom Sawyer, Moby Dick and Edgar Allen Poe's raven. As one journalist observed, 'Archy, who always dreamed of public acclaim yet endured a life in lowercase letters, must indeed be proud.'

So, with all the hysteria surrounding cockroaches, are we missing a trick? Could we turn the unavoidable presence of cockroaches to our advantage? And if so, would that change the way we view these fascinating insects?

Previous civilisations were less squeamish. The Greeks and Arabs boiled or ground them up and used them to cure various ailments, the people of nineteenth-century New Orleans used to swear by boiled cockroach tea as a remedy for several complaints, and the Chinese have used cockroaches to treat wounds and illnesses for several hundreds of years.

Analysis has revealed a number of active ingredients in the cockroach, which is now being hailed in China as a 'miracle drug' to cure heart disease and help the healing of burns. And this isn't on the fringes of medicine: one farmer in Shandong province has more than 22 million cockroaches living in concrete bunkers, and sells his entire output – more than 100 tonnes a year – to leading pharmaceutical companies. Elsewhere in China cockroaches are regularly sold as food: usually grilled, fried or boiled (once their heads and legs have been removed) and served in a variety of sauces.

In the west, cockroaches are even kept as pets. However, these are not the species we call exterminators, but the splendidly named Madagascar hissing cockroach, a large (up to about 8 centimetres long), wingless creature with a mahogany-coloured carapace, which produces its famous sound by forcing air through the respiratory openings in its abdomen. In Australia, cockroaches are used for racing, while one New York amusement park holds an annual cockroach-eating competition – the record number consumed being thirty-six.

On 14 September 2007, a cockroach named Nadezhda – meaning 'hope' – was sent into space by the Russians. Rather less celebrated than Laika the dog (and much more expendable), she turned out to be a truly versatile astronaut. Several days after the launch it was announced that Nadezhda had successfully produced thirty-three baby cockroaches, making her the first – and so far, only – living creature to give birth in space. However, there is some doubt as to whether the babies actually hatched in space, or appeared after she had returned to earth. The Russian scientists behind the mission were reportedly delighted, though they did have some concerns that the weightless environment might have some effects on the baby insects' colour. Cockroaches are born with a transparent carapace, which then gradually darkens, as they get older, whereas these ones turned dark soon after birth.

But the scientists' fears proved groundless, and the following May Nadezhda became a proud grandmother when her offspring spawned a whole new generation of cockroaches. Rumours that NASA is scouring Florida's fast-food restaurants for the US space program's very own astronaut cockroaches have – so far at least – proved unfounded.

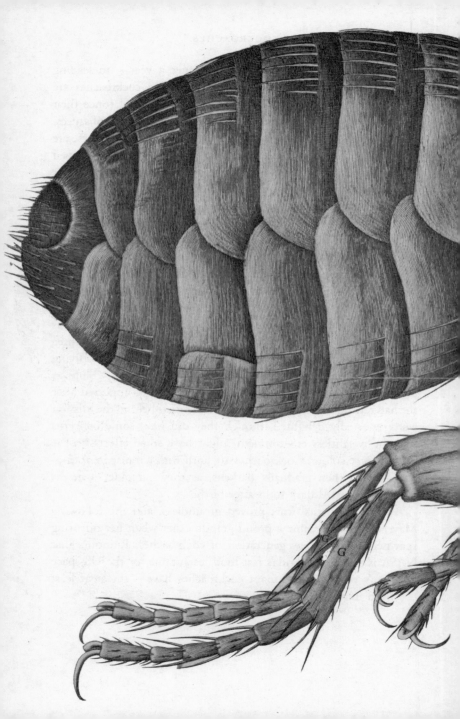

So, naturalists observe, a flea
Has smaller fleas that on him prey;
And these have smaller still to bite 'em,
And so proceed ad infinitum.
Thus every poet, in his kind,
Is bit by him that comes behind.

Jonathan Swift, *On Poetry, a Rhapsody*, 1733

Fleas

Miniature Marvels

They stand next to one another, hand in hand, as happy and proud as any newly married couple. He is dressed in a smart black morning-suit, she in a long white gown, with accompanying veil and train. Take a closer look, and you can see the intricate detail of these beautifully made costumes.

But to do so, you'll need a very powerful magnifying glass. For this is the smallest representation of the marriage ceremony you are ever likely to see. They stand in a tiny frame, about 3 by 6 millimetres in size; so small that even when using a magnifier you have to squint to see the detail. For these intricately detailed costumes are being worn not by human models, but by fleas.

Dressed fleas, or *pulgas vestidas* as they are known in Spanish, were a traditional form of folk art practised by women in Mexico – including, reportedly, nuns – from the late nineteenth century onwards. They didn't just make married couples – although these were perhaps the most popular examples and may have been given as wedding gifts – but all sorts of tableaux. For a short period, these bizarre examples of folk art were much in demand, but nowadays the practice appears to have died out, at least in Mexico – although one Yorkshire-based zoologist, Tim Cockerill, has recently revived the art.

Today, we can see some fascinating examples of *pulgas vestidas* in the Rothschild Collection of Siphonaptera in the Natural History

Museum. They really are astonishing examples of dedication to their craft, though they are in fact an illusion: the bodies, arms and legs of each minuscule figure are crafted out of tiny fragments of paper and cloth, with the body of a flea placed on top to form the figure's head. The overall impression – and that clearly intended by the maker – is that the flea's body is much longer than it actually is.

The dressed fleas make up only a tiny part of this vast collection, which contains an estimated 200,000 different specimens, representing roughly three-quarters of the more than 2,500 different species of fleas discovered and described so far. Most are mounted on microscope slides and stored in wooden cabinets to protect them from the damaging effects of light; others are suspended in preserving fluid. They include the world's largest species, the mountain beaver flea of North America, which parasitises the rodent of the same name and can reach a length of 8 millimetres; and one of the smallest, the cat flea, which despite being only 1 to 3 millimetres long has virtually conquered the earth, thanks to its association with one of our most popular domestic pets.

The immensely rich Rothschild family and one of the world's largest collection of fleas seem on the face of things an unlikely partnership. Charles Rothschild, a noted naturalist and scientist who named and described hundreds of fleas new to science including the plague flea, passed his love of the natural world and science on to his daughter. When Charles Rothschild committed suicide in October 1923, fifteen-year-old Miriam took over her father's enthusiasm for fleas and turned it into a scientific passion. She catalogued his vast collection in six huge and immensely detailed volumes (a task that took her thirty years), and made several crucial discoveries about their complex life cycles.

Fleas are parasites, living on the bodies of birds or mammals (including, of course, human beings), which means they have had to evolve ways of synchronising their own life cycles with those of their hosts. Miriam Rothschild discovered that the rabbit flea was able to control the timing of its own fertility to coincide with that of its host, so that when baby rabbits were born, so were the baby fleas. When the disease myxomatosis devastated Britain's rabbit population in the early 1950s, it was she who discovered that the vector for the disease – the species helping to transmit it from one rabbit to another – was not, as had been originally thought, the mosquito, but the humble flea.

She also spent countless hours studying the morphology of these minuscule creatures, trying to discover how they could jump so high and so fast – equivalent to a human being taking off at the speed of a space-rocket and reaching a height of 180 metres – again and again, without any noticeable loss of energy. It turned out that there is a pad of a special protein called resilin inside the flea's hip joint which, when squeezed and released, propels it to such incredible heights, at such rapid speeds. By this means it can easily jump from host to host, an especially useful skill when one animal dies and the flea needs to find another one to live on.

In her 1952 book *Fleas, Flukes and Cuckoos*, a study of bird parasites packed with extraordinary facts and stories, Rothschild includes a worm that feeds off a hippo's tears, a feather louse that travels to Africa and back in the feathers of a swift – equivalent, as Rothschild memorably put it, to 'a man with a couple of large shore crabs scuttling about in his underclothes' – and a fluke that 'ends up living happily ever after under the tongue of a frog'.

But it is the fleas that are the most captivating. For example, Rothschild revealed that the fleas that parasitise the sand martin, which spends half the year in Africa, lie dormant in the nest-burrow during its six-month-long absence, only to greet the bird when it returns from Africa in the spring: 'It is sad to think that when the sand martin reaches its breeding haunts in April, having successfully endured the hardships and hazards of migration, it is met by a reception committee in the form of thousands of ravenous fleas which can be seen waiting around the entrance to the nests.' Rothschild once said, 'I must say, I find everything interesting,' and this was nowhere more apparent than in her obsession with fleas. So what was it about these tiny creatures that so captured her imagination?

Fleas are insects belonging to the order Siphonaptera, a name that derives from the Greek for 'wingless pipe' – referring to the fact that fleas are wingless and have powerful sucking mouthparts.

Fleas have the same basic body structure as all insects – with six legs and a body in three parts, the head, thorax and abdomen – though, as with other insects, this has been modified by natural selection over millions of years to create the specialised forms and functions we see today. Fleas' hind legs are much longer and more powerful than the other two pairs, to enable those prodigious feats of jumping, though most of us never get a close enough look to appreciate this. As the seventeenth-century natural philosopher Robert Hooke – clearly a fan – memorably wrote: 'Though this little Creature is almost universally known to be a small brown skipping Animal, very few are acquainted with its real Shape and Figure, with the Structure, Strength, Beauty of its Limbs and Parts, or with the manner of its Generation and Increase.'

Fleas are one of the most successful groups of insects on the planet. Having been around in more or less the same form for at least 200 million years, today they can be found in virtually every habitat, from inside the Arctic Circle, via the temperate regions, to tropical rainforests and hot, arid deserts: wherever their hosts can live, so can fleas.

They even used to parasitise dinosaurs, which had giant fleas about 2.5 centimetres long. Fossils of these prehistoric insects – dating back between 125 and 165 million years – have recently been unearthed at several sites in China. Examination revealed that these massive fleas had the same siphon-like mouthparts as modern fleas, with serrated edges, enabling them to pierce the thick skin of their hosts. The males also had large, exposed genitalia. But they had not yet developed the jumping abilities of modern fleas, according to André Nel, a palaeontologist at the Museum of Natural History in Paris: 'They were not jumping insects . . . [Instead] probably creeping between the feathers or the fur of animals they came across.'

When the dinosaurs died out, and mammals and birds began to dominate, it appears that these early fleas adapted to their new hosts, becoming smaller in size and learning to jump from one animal to another, an adaptation that has made fleas so successful today.

Today's fleas are nowhere near as large – a typical individual is between 1.5 and 3.3 millimetres long, wingless and usually light red-brown to almost black in colour, with long hind legs and tube-shaped mouthparts to enable the insect to suck the blood of their hosts. Their bodies are hard and smooth, and laterally compressed (flattened from side to side), making it easier for them to move around on the hair, fur or feathers of their host's body. Their tough outer casing also makes them very resistant to being squashed.

Like insects such as butterflies and moths, fleas go through a complex metamorphosis in four distinct stages: egg, larva, pupa and adult. The females can lay about 25 eggs a day in the host's nest, burrow or regular sleeping place. The eggs hatch in about five days and the non-parasitic, legless and completely blind larvae scavenge on any organic material they can find, including the adult fleas' faeces, which contain undigested blood, an essential ingredient to larval development. After two to three weeks they spin a silk cocoon. The white pupa darkens steadily and is often camouflaged by the dust and debris of the nest or burrow which sticks to the pupa. In a couple of weeks, if the conditions are right, they emerge as adults, which then feed solely on their host's blood. If the conditions are not right, for example if the host is absent for long periods, the adult fleas will lie dormant in the pupal case and emerge when the host returns. Adult fleas can live for several months without feeding, and may survive for more than a year and a half.

About 95 per cent of fleas around the world are parasites on mammals and 5 per cent on birds, but in Britain the situation is rather different: about 25 per cent of Britain's sixty or so flea species use birds as their hosts. Most are adapted to living on a few species – notably domestic animals such as dogs or cats – though cat fleas will also bite humans, as we know to our cost.

When our prehistoric ancestors first domesticated wild animals such as dogs to help them with their hunting – somewhere between 16,000 and 32,000 years ago – they little realised that they were unwittingly inviting a much smaller creature into their lives: fleas. In fact fleas may well have annoyed humans for much longer than this; they would have lived on many of the animals hunted by these early hominids, and could easily have jumped from the hides, worn by hunters to keep warm, on to their skin. When we switched from being nomadic hunter-gatherers to a more settled, agricultural existence fleas thrived, which explains why we are the only primates to suffer habitually from fleas. Indeed we have our very own species, the human flea *Pulex irritans*.

Ever since we first noticed them, fleas have – perhaps not surprisingly – gained a certain notoriety and unpopularity due to the itching which is our bodies' response to the anti-coagulant in their saliva which stops the blood clotting when they are feeding; and more seriously because of the diseases they carry.

Of all these, without doubt the most notorious is the bubonic plague. This is a bacterial infection, *Yersinia pestis*, carried by the oriental (also known as tropical) rat flea *Xenopsylla cheopis*, and spread when the bacteria block the blood meal from entering the flea's stomach, and so the starving flea frantically feeds on anything warm-blooded, like humans, and bites multiple times, pumping in bacteria-laden saliva with each bite. Having entered the body through the skin, the infection then rapidly spreads via the lymphatic system, producing swellings (buboes) on the body – usually in the armpits and groin area. Death generally follows within hours, or at the most days, while fewer than half of those infected recover.

The first known epidemic broke out in Constantinople (now

Istanbul) in AD 541. Named the Plague of Justinian after the emperor at the time, within a year it had spread throughout the eastern half of the Roman Empire, killing an estimated 25 million people. It continued to recur for the next 200 years, and was responsible for as many as 50 million deaths in all. Among the lucky survivors of the disease was the Emperor Justinian himself.

One observer, the historian Procopius, noted both the devastation wrought by the plague and the suffering and hardship that followed, pinning much of the blame for this on the emperor:

> When pestilence swept through the whole known world and notably the Roman Empire, wiping out most of the farming community and of necessity leaving a trail of desolation in its wake, Justinian showed no mercy towards the ruined freeholders. Even then, he did not refrain from demanding the annual tax, not only the amount at which he assessed each individual, but also the amount for which his deceased neighbours were liable.

The next major outbreak – and by far the best known – struck Europe in the middle of the fourteenth century, and is commonly known as the Black Death. Again, the numbers of people killed by the plague can only be estimated, but most historians agree that it was about 25 million, or between 30 and 60 per cent of the population of Europe at the time.

The first outbreak occurred in 1347, having spread westwards via black rats in trading ships from central Asia. Further events would regularly recur during the next few hundred years, most notably from a British point of view the Great Plague of London, from 1665 to 1666. The last major outbreak in Europe was in southern France in 1720, but major pandemics continued to kill millions of people in Asia and Australia right into the early decades of the twentieth century, while even as late as 1994 a minor outbreak in India resulted in more than fifty deaths.

Rats were usually held to blame, but then, in the late nineteenth century, the French physician and bacteriologist Alexandre Yersin discovered that the true culprit was a tiny bacterium, named *Yersinia pestis* in his honour. His colleague Paul-Louis Simond, based in the city of Karachi in what is now Pakistan, then conducted a series of experiments which led him to claim that the bacterium was transmitted not by the rats themselves, but by the fleas that lived on them which, when rats came into contact with humans, could transfer on to people. At first, his fellow scientists were sceptical, but within a decade he had been widely recognised for this ground-breaking discovery.

By then bubonic plague had largely – and thankfully – been brought under control. But its legacy was huge: in the same way that the demise of dinosaurs made room for smaller mammals like us to thrive, so these outbreaks of plague had major social and economic effects. The Black Death led directly to the Peasants' Revolt: supply and demand meant ordinary working people could now demand higher wages, better working conditions and didn't have to stay in the place they were born all their lives. The ruling classes could see their serfs as insects no longer.

Fleas have generally been associated with negative things. A disreputable place is a fleapit; a mangy donkey is flea-bitten. If you're telling someone off, you're putting a flea in their ear. There is even a colour named after the flea but it is the ugliest in the spectrum: puce (the French word for flea). Puce's purplish brown is that of a bruise or a bloodstain, and the argument goes that it is rather the colour of squashed fleas, full of the blood of their human victims.

Latin and Renaissance poets often used the image of the flea as a metaphor for sex and sexual desire. A flea was tiny, agile (and bloodthirsty enough) to get under the clothes of their beloved. In 1582 a cycle of ponderous poems *La Puce de Madame Des Roches* was written by a French literary circle inspired by the sight of a flea on the breast of the poetess Catherine Des Roches. In Marlowe's play *Dr Faustus*, all the vices become characters; thus Pride announces: 'I am like to Ovid's flea. I can creep into every corner of a wench; sometimes like a periwig I sit upon her brow; next like a necklace I hang about her neck; then like a fan of feathers I kiss her; and then . . . do what I list.'

This speech may well have inspired the writing of the most famous poem about the flea by the poet John Donne, later the Dean of St Paul's Cathedral. Probably written some time around 1610, 'The Flea' opens in blunt style, with a direct address to the narrator's reluctant partner, trying to persuade her to have sex with him:

> Mark but this flea, and mark in this,
> How little that which thou deniest me is;
> It sucked me first, and now sucks thee,
> And in this flea our two bloods mingled be;

Contemporary readers would have appreciated the intended pun in the repeated use of the word 'suck', which would have appeared on the page with an initial letter resembling an 'f' rather than an 's'. Donne was a Metaphysical poet, which means his poems tend focus on a neat or apt point or story, which he often inverts or twists. His flea is no exception, as the tiny insect grows dramatically in size and importance:

> This flea is you and I, and this
> Our marriage bed, and marriage temple is;
> Though parents grudge, and you, we are met,
> And cloistered in these living walls of jet.

The poem's tone is colloquial. The woman is silent, but her answer to the poet is eloquent and emphatic – she kills the flea, and with it the poet's hopes:

> Cruel and sudden, hast thou since
> Purpled thy nail, in blood of innocence?
> Wherein could this flea guilty be,
> Except in that drop which it sucked from thee?

In the poem's final twist, the irrepressible narrator then uses the flea's death as another last-ditch attempt to change her mind:

> Yet thou triumph'st, and say'st that thou
> Find'st not thy self, nor me the weaker now;
>   'Tis true; then learn how false, fears be:
> Just so much honour, when thou yield'st to me,
> Will waste, as this flea's death took life from thee.

Like so many of Donne's poems, the blend of bizarre imagery, complex and ingenious argument, bravura wit and direct, colloquial language make 'The Flea' unforgettable. More than 400 years after it was written, it remains one of the most unusual love poems in the English language.

Of all our cultural and social interactions with fleas, which as well as poems include numerous songs or pieces of (usually very fast and frantic) music, surely the most bizarre must be the flea circus. These are a peculiar form of entertainment in which fleas apparently pull loads on carts, or perform other feats of strength. Some of these are genuine, but many are tricks performed using electrical, mechanical or magnetic energy. Some 'flea circuses' are in fact completely illusory, with no fleas involved at all, such as one regularly featured on television during the 1960s starring comedian and former Goon Michael Bentine.

The use of performing fleas dates back to the sixteenth century, when watchmakers used the insects to show their ability to work in miniature. In 1578 the clockmaker Mark Scaliot attached a flea to a chain with a tiny lock and key made of iron and brass, in order to demonstrate his skills. This evidently became widely known, and was even celebrated in verse by Thomas Muffet (father of 'Little Miss Muffet' of nursery rhyme fame).

The first true flea circuses emerged during the early years of Queen Victoria's reign. They continued for another century or so, into the inter-war era in Britain (where they were especially popular in seaside resorts), and slightly later in the US, although one in Manchester was still going as late as 1970. Many had wonderfully elaborate names, including Professor Hype's Dinky Di Aussie Flea Circus, Captain Franko's Fantabulous Flea Circus, Phydeaux's Flying Flea Circus of Fate and Professor Payne's Phantasmagorical Flea Circus. But the doyen of flea circus ringmasters was Louis Bertolotto, whose Extraordinary Exhibition of the Industrious Fleas was watched by HRH Princess Augusta of Cambridge, granddaughter of King George III, who witnessed a host of flea-based acts including 'A first rate Man of War, of 120 guns . . . drawn by a single flea; two fleas, deciding an affair of honour, sword in hand; and a gig drawn by a flea, containing a lady and gentleman'. Sadly we do not know whether the princess enjoyed this miniature spectacle.

Flea circuses have now gone the way of other once-popular entertainments such as the music hall, and died out. In the meantime, as linguist and psychologist Steven Pinker has pointed out, human beings are 'warm, dry, we're not hungry, we don't have fleas and ticks and infections. So why are we so miserable?' Maybe we preferred a world where we did all have fleas – little creatures living on our bodies that reminded us we are part of a wider animal kingdom.

After all, fleas are wonderfully egalitarian – they bite king and pauper alike – and will always be with us. Love them or hate them – or simply, like Miriam Rothschild, find them fascinating – fleas will be here long after we have gone. And like so many creatures, they also serve as useful metaphors, as in this wry observation from the twentieth-century Polish poet and aphorist Stanisław Jerzy Lec: 'Thoughts, like fleas, jump from man to man, but they don't bite everybody.'

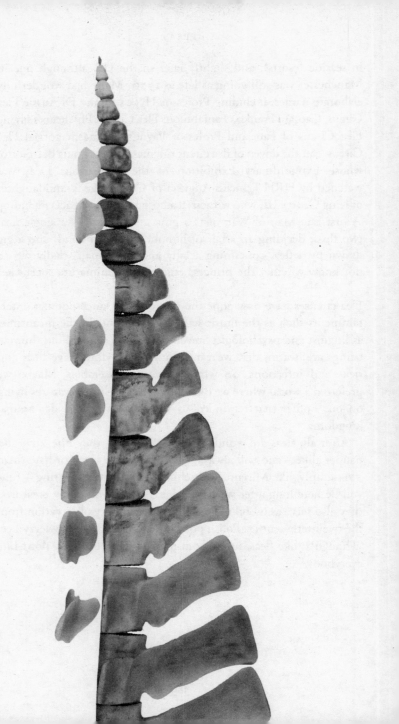

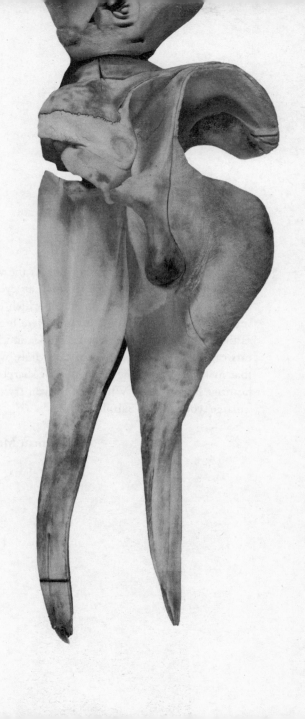

Is it not curious, that so vast a being as the whale
should see the world through so small an eye,
and hear the thunder through an ear which is
smaller than a hare's? But if his eyes were broad
as the lens of Herschel's great telescope; and his
ears capacious as the porches of cathedrals; would
that make him any longer of sight, or sharper of
hearing? Not at all. – Why then do you try to
'enlarge' your mind? Subtilize it.

Herman Melville

Whales

Massive Media Stars

If there's one book that sums up man's fascination with the natural world, it's *Moby-Dick*. And it's not just because it's the only nineteenth-century novel that devotes a full chapter to cetology – or the study of whales. The novel was inspired by the true story of the sinking of the *Essex* in 1820. Owen Chase, the first mate, later wrote a vivid account of the angry wounded sperm whale's attack that caught the attention of nineteenth-century schoolboys everywhere, including Herman Melville:

> I turned around and saw him directly ahead of us, coming down with twice his ordinary speed, and with tenfold fury and vengeance in his aspect. The surf flew in all directions about him with the continual violent thrashing of his tail. His head about half out of the water, and in that way he came upon us, and again struck the ship.

For Chase and the handful of survivors, the sinking of the *Essex* was only the start of an ordeal that was to take in extreme privation, starvation and eventually cannibalism. A chequered career followed and years later, after being discovered compulsively hiding food away in his attic, Chase was institutionalised. In *Moby-Dick* Melville explored what might have happened if he had decided to seek revenge instead. The novel's story follows Captain Ahab's quest for a white whale named Moby Dick, which had destroyed his ship and caused him to lose part of his leg: 'He piled upon the whale's white hump the sum of all the general rage and hate felt by his whole race from Adam down; and then, as if his chest had been a mortar, he burst his hot heart's shell upon it.'

Whalers hunted their prey through the world's deepest oceans and most remote places and at the mercy of the elements. This far away from land (when the *Essex* sank it was thousands of miles away from land) the balance was firmly in nature's favour. Herman Melville had been a whaler himself and his pressing need to detail the science, mythology and poetry of whales rings through every line of the book but, despite all this effort, Moby Dick refuses to be pinned down and escapes, sinking the ship in the process. Melville's whale remains an enigma.

There are roughly thirty-eight species of whale, across seven different families. The smallest is the dwarf sperm whale, which at 200–270 centimetres long, and weighing 136–280 kilos, is still considerably larger and heavier than a newborn baby elephant. At the other end of the scale the blue whale is the largest and heaviest creature ever found on earth – even bigger than the mightiest of the dinosaurs. Whales are able to reach such vast sizes simply because their aquatic existence allows the ocean's waters to support the weight of their enormous bodies.

A typical blue whale is about 30 metres long – almost as long as three London buses – and at roughly 150 tonnes weighs about the same as over 2,000 adult human beings or about twenty African elephants. Indeed a blue whale's tongue alone weighs as much as an elephant, while its heart weighs about the same as a small family car. The blue whale also has the largest penis of any living creature, measuring roughly 2.4–3 metres long and with a girth of about 30–36 centimetres.

The blue whale's feeding habits are pretty extraordinary, too. Although you might expect them to take large marine mammals as their prey, they actually feed on shrimplike creatures known as krill, most of which are less than 2 centimetres long. This prey is so tiny that blue whales must eat them in industrial quantities, taking up to 40 million krill (weighing almost 4 tonnes) in a single day. They catch them by diving to depths of over 100 metres, and staying underwater for up to twenty minutes at a time, before – as being mammals, they must – returning to the surface to breathe.

It's hardly surprising that whales have become the stuff of legend, since only in the last century have we been able to approach or even begin to understand them. But where giant squid translated directly into terrible sea monsters, these even vaster creatures have become something stranger and more interesting. Leviathan, the Old Testament monster that dominates the Book of Job, has all kinds of whalelike characteristics and in fact the modern Hebrew word for whale is 'leviathan':

> Canst thou draw out Leviathan with an hook? or his tongue with a cord which thou lettest down? . . . Canst thou fill his skin with barbed irons? or his head with fish spears? . . . He maketh the deep to boil like a pot: he maketh the sea like a pot of ointment. He maketh a path to shine after him; one would think the deep to be hoary [frozen]. Upon earth there is not his like, who is made without fear.

Where sailors' tall tales about giant squid twisted them into creatures from nightmares, whales were seen as something terrible but awe-inspiring, as God's monster. This happened most memorably in the story of Jonah.

There is evidence that Jonah was a real man: a famously curmudgeonly prophet living in what is now the northern part of Israel, near Nazareth in Galilee, some time around the eighth century BC. Coming in at forty-eight verses and just over 1,300 words, the Old Testament Book of Jonah is one of the shortest books in the Bible. Yet what it lacks in length, it makes up for in fame and impact.

God calls on a reluctant Jonah to go to the city of Nineveh, and preach against its heathen inhabitants, but he runs away, boarding a ship heading in the opposite direction. When a huge storm arises, the sailors cast lots and, when Jonah loses, reluctantly throw him overboard. The sea promptly calms. Jonah is swallowed by a large fish in which he spends the next three days and nights, praying and repenting. When he is spat out on the shore, God commands Jonah to go to Nineveh. This time he goes and enters the city, crying, 'In forty days Nineveh shall be overthrown.' He is so much in earnest that the people of Nineveh begin to believe him. The king of Nineveh puts on sackcloth and sits in ashes, decreeing fasting, sackcloth, prayer and repentance. God sees their repentant hearts and spares the city. Jonah, who finds it hard to believe that so many sinners should get off so lightly when he had suffered such an ordeal, goes out into the desert to wait in vain for God to change his mind and destroy the city.

The unfortunate prophet also features strongly in nautical superstition: sailors refer to someone on board a ship who is thought to bring bad luck as 'a Jonah'; and this phrase has entered the language to refer to anyone who brings bad luck, in any sphere of life.

There is just one problem. Although we usually refer to 'Jonah and the Whale', the original Hebrew text simply means 'big fish', suggesting perhaps a shark or mythical sea serpent. At some point this was translated into the Greek *ketos mega*, and then in the early sixteenth century the translator of the first English Bible, William Tyndale, rendered it both as 'greate fyshe' and later 'whale', compounding the confusion.

Since then, scholars and zoologists have attempted to work out which species of fish or cetacean would be most likely to be able to swallow a human being. Rejected candidates include the world's largest fish, the aptly named whale shark, which although it can reach a length of over 12.5 metres, and weigh over 21.5 tonnes, is a filter feeder with a throat just 10 centimetres wide, so could not possibly ingest a human.

Likewise the biggest whales – known as baleen whales, and including the blue, fin and humpback varieties – are also filter feeders, unable to eat anything larger than krill. The great white shark is more likely, but no one swallowed by one of these huge predators is likely to come out alive.

Debating which particular sea creature might have consumed and then regurgitated Jonah is missing the point, however. Like many Old Testament stories, the tale is clearly an allegory, in this case about disobedience, punishment and ultimate repentance. What is perhaps more interesting is that despite linguistic evidence to the contrary, we continue to assume that the species involved is not a fish, but a whale.

In almost 3,000 years since the tale of Jonah there have been regular reports of people being swallowed and then regurgitated by whales. One typical story appeared on the website Rock City Times in July 2013. A man visiting Chicago's Shedd Aquarium, the largest indoor aquarium in the world, was apparently seized by a beluga whale, which then swallowed him whole, before regurgitating him three days later. During his ordeal, the man is said to have 'remained relaxed', and communicated with friends and family by text messages from his mobile phone.

If you are already sceptical, two things may confirm your doubts. First, the man's name is Jonah; second, the final paragraph states that he 'hopes to return to Arkansas to visit his cousin Daniel who is in a critical condition following a fall into the lion exhibit at Little Rock Zoo'.

A potentially more credible claim is that of James Bartley, who in August 1891 appeared in an anonymous article in the *Yarmouth Mercury* newspaper with the arresting headline 'Man in a Whale's Stomach – Rescue of a Modern Jonah'.

The story said that while Bartley's boat was pursuing a sperm whale off the Falkland Islands in the South Atlantic Ocean, he accidentally fell inside its mouth and was swallowed. When the whale was eventually caught and killed, some hours later, the crew cut it open and rescued the unfortunate sailor, whose skin had been turned white by the whale's stomach acid. He had also gone permanently blind. Bartley apparently survived for another eighteen years, and his tombstone in a Gloucester churchyard reads 'James Bartley – a modern-day Jonah'.

The prevalence and persistence of the Jonah myth may say more about us than it does about whales, giant fish or Christianity. Whereas creatures such as the lion feature hugely in myths and legends, even in parts of the world where they are either absent or have not lived for many thousands of years, whales are not very prominent. There is one exception: the peoples who have lived around the edge of the Arctic, and for whom whales are very much part of their daily lives, a tradition dating back hundreds, and probably thousands, of years.

The Alaskan city of Kaktovik is one of the remotest settlements in the whole of North America. Situated in the north-eastern corner of Alaska, on the edge of the Arctic Ocean, the town lies at just over 70 degrees north, well within the Arctic Circle, and is a five-hour flight from the state's main city, Anchorage. The average temperature varies from a high of 7.4 degrees Celsius in July to a bitterly cold minus 25.5 degrees in February, made even worse by the icy wind that blows from the north, right across the frozen ocean.

The area around Kaktovik, Barter Island, was originally a trading post between the Canadian Inuit and the Alaskan Inupiat peoples in the nineteenth century – hence the name. In the 1950s, during the height of the Cold War, a military early warning station and runway were installed, and the settlement of Kaktovik gradually grew up nearby. Today, fewer than 300 people – mostly Inupiat or mixed race – live in Kaktovik. Although they are full US citizens, and in many ways live their lives just like other small town Americans, they still pursue the ancient tradition of subsistence whaling.

Each year, as summer comes to an end and the temperature begins to drop, the people of Kaktovik take to the sea in pursuit of bowhead whales. They are allowed to take up to three whales each autumn, a quota worked out per head of population, to allow them to have enough whale meat to survive the winter.

As soon as the whale is brought ashore, there is no time to lose. With expertise honed from years of custom and practice, the people of Kaktovik take the whale apart: first making deep incisions in the skin with their ultra-sharp tools; then slicing the skin, blubber and flesh in a criss-cross pattern before cutting off huge chunks the size of a man's head.

Within two or three hours, the whale has been reduced to a bloody carcass. And not a moment too soon – if the dead whale is left for even a few hours its body heat will render the meat inside spoiled and inedible. The meat and blubber – a delicacy known as 'muktuk' – are cut up and shared out. Parties are held to celebrate nature's benevolence, during which visitors are invited – even impelled – to try different cuts of the once mighty beast, now mostly reduced to oily chunks of fat and flesh.

But this is not simply a way of providing food. The Inupiat people revere the whale, and with good reason: it is likely that their ancestors would never have survived in this hostile environment had they not hunted, killed and eaten whales. Indeed some anthropologists believe that the discipline required for whaling helped these societies become more advanced, ironically leading to inter-tribal warfare.

Through whaling the Thule people, whose culture arose in Alaska around the time of the Vikings in northern Europe and lasted into the late Middle Ages, soon became dominant in an area reaching from the Bering Sea in the west to Greenland in the east. In doing so they displaced an earlier culture, the Dorset. Evidence also suggests that as well as eating whales the Thule also used their huge bones as supporting structures for their homes, and buried their dead in coffins made from whale carcasses.

Today the carcasses fulfil an entirely different function. After they have been stripped of meat and blubber, what remains is dumped a few miles out of town, where it attracts a large and spectacular gathering of polar bears. In turn, the bears attract tourists eager to see this unique spectacle, and to pay good money for the privilege. Thus the whale harvest continues to benefit the people of Kaktovik in a new and very novel way.

For most of human history, the small-scale killing of whales had absolutely no effect on whale populations. But as technology improved during the seventeenth and eighteenth centuries, bigger and faster boats, with more accurate and effective weapons, began to shift the balance in favour of the whalers. Where once these mighty marine mammals roamed the oceans in their tens and even hundreds of thousands, their populations gradually declined at the hands of this new and very profitable trade.

By the time Melville wrote *Moby-Dick*, in the middle of the nineteenth century, whaling had become a massive global industry. The whales provided not just meat but fat for heating and fuel, and also a host of other products, as Eric Jay Dolin noted in his 2007 work *Leviathan: The History of Whaling in America*: 'American whale oil lit the world.'

At a time when oil-based fossil fuels had yet to be discovered and exploited, whale oil was also used in the manufacture of a wide range of products from soap to paint, while 'whalebone' (actually the baleen through which the whale filtered its food) was used to make corsets and hooped skirts. A substance taken from sperm whales known as 'spermaceti' was made into candles, and ambergris – a substance from the digestive system of sperm whales also known as 'floating gold', or more prosaically, 'whale vomit' – was a very valuable ingredient in the making of perfumes.

But obtaining the whales to produce this array of products had its costs – notably among the men sent to sea to catch the whales, who had to endure great hardship and danger in order to fulfil their quest, as Dolin points out: 'They survived boredom, back-breaking work, tempestuous seas, floggings, pirates, putrid food, and unimaginable cold . . . Many whalemen died from violent encounters with whales and from terrible miscalculations about the unforgiving nature of nature itself.'

By the early twentieth century huge factory ships, which processed the entire animal as soon as it had been killed, meant that whale hunting had become even more efficient. By the time the Second World War broke out in 1939, at least 50,000 whales were being killed worldwide every year.

Like us, blue whales are very long-lived mammals: they usually live for between eighty and ninety years, with the oldest recorded specimen reaching roughly one hundred and ten. And like other long-lived mammals (including human beings), they reproduce slowly, with relatively few offspring during their lifetime. As a result, they were extremely vulnerable to intensive hunting.

In 1986 the International Whaling Commission (IWC) – an organisation that for most of its existence was considered to be defending the whalers – finally banned virtually all whaling. Well, almost all. There were two important exceptions: one generally accepted by the anti-whaling groups, the other definitely not.

Communities such as Kaktovik, where subsistence whaling was considered part of their culture and way of life, were permitted to take a quota of whales each year. Far more controversially, the IWC allowed some hunts – by whaling ships from Norway, Iceland and Japan – to continue under the label of 'scientific whaling', on the bizarre principle that this will help us learn more about whales and so protect them more effectively.

In the meantime, protection has both dramatically reduced the number of whales being killed, and also allowed populations to begin a slow but steady recovery. From a low point of perhaps 5,000–12,000 individuals, the global population of blue whales has now risen to an estimated 10,000–25,000, mostly in the North Pacific, Indian and Antarctic Oceans.

But the danger for blue whales, and the other vulnerable species, is not yet over. Other problems include collisions with ships or becoming entangled in the nets of fishing trawlers; becoming disoriented by commercial or military sonar, which may interfere with their vocal communications; the accumulation of chemicals in their bodies; and now global climate change, which is likely to reduce drastically the amount of krill in the world's oceans by causing a warming of sea temperatures.

While so much remains mysterious, one undisputable fact about whales is that they are sea creatures. So the sighting of one in the Thames on the morning of 20 January 2006 came as a surprise to everyone concerned.

Even more so when Richard Sabin of the Natural History Museum identified it as a member of the family known as 'beaked whales'. These species are among the least known of the world's marine mammals, because they prefer very deep offshore waters, so are rarely seen either by scientists or whale-watching enthusiasts. The northern bottlenose whale is one of the largest of the beaked whales, with large adult males reaching up to 10 metres in length and weighing as much as 10 tonnes. The Thames whale was a juvenile female, about 5 metres long and weighing roughly 7 tonnes. But this was still far too big to be comfortable in the narrow River Thames.

As the day went on, and the tide began to recede, the whale began to get into trouble, frequently beaching herself on the foreshore. Later on, it was reported that she was swimming towards the sea at Greenwich, causing a collective sigh of relief from both the media and the watching public. Sadly, though, their optimism was both premature and misplaced, and during the course of Friday night she headed back upstream to Battersea.

By Saturday morning the watching experts from the organisation British Divers Marine Life Rescue (BDMLR) realised the whale was in distress. By noon they had successfully stranded her, and a few hours later she was lifted by crane on to a waiting barge, her vast body cushioned by an inflatable raft, with water being constantly poured over her to avoid her becoming dehydrated. Meanwhile the rolling news channels covered the unfolding series of events, as anxious crowds gathered along the river's embankments and bridges.

Out of the water, the whale's own body weight was no longer supported, and she was slowly but inexorably being crushed to death. Three hours after dusk fell, at just after 7 p.m., a vet on the barge pronounced her dead. Northern bottlenose whales are a deep ocean species, and at that time of year – the middle of winter – she should have been hundreds of miles to the north, round the coasts of Caithness, Orkney or Shetland in northern Scotland, off Northern Ireland, or further north still, in Arctic waters.

A Royal Prerogative enacted in 1324 states that all whales, dolphins and porpoises found in English waters belong to the monarch and were to be known as 'Fishes Royal'. In 1913 the Natural History Museum was given the responsibility for investigating all UK strandings and, since 1990, has been a contributing partner of the government-funded UK Cetacean Strandings Investigation Programme. There have been more than 11,000 strandings so far. Following a post-mortem, scientists decided that the most likely explanation for the northern bottlenose whale's appearance in the Thames was simply that she got lost: following a navigational error, she took a wrong turn, and instead of swimming around the north of Scotland towards her Atlantic feeding areas, headed into the North Sea and upstream into the Thames Estuary to her inevitable death. Today her preserved skeleton forms part of the Natural History Museum's research collection.

Despite its tidal river, London seems an unlikely centre for whale sightings, but it was once one of the world's great whaling ports and the surgeon and naturalist John Hunter wrote the first scientific treatise on whales from specimens that had mistakenly penetrated the city's waterway. In 1783 a 6.4-metre-long female bottlenose whale was captured close to London Bridge. A surprising number of whales ventured into the Thames throughout Hunter's working life, as though auditioning for his collection (now the Hunterian Museum in Lincoln's Inn Fields). (And these were before the river was dredged and deepened, when it was an even less hospitable environment for cetacean visitors.) In 1759 a 7-metre grampus (also known as the killer whale, or orca) was caught at the mouth of the river and brought to Westminster Bridge on a barge. In 1772 another grampus, 5.5 metres long, was caught; in 1788 seventeen sperm whales were stranded on the Thames's lower reaches. And in 1791 a 9-metre orca was chased up the river as far as Deptford, and slain. As Philip Hoare describes in his wonderful book *Leviathan*:

When a whale was harpooned to death at Deptford in 1658, it was seen as an augury of the death of the dictator Oliver Cromwell. It happened to perish on the shore close to the estate owned by the diarist John Evelyn. Having inspected the carcass and its vast curtain of baleen with which it had once strained a ton of zooplankton a day, Evelyn marvelled that 'an Animal of so greate a bulk, should be nourished onely by slime'.

Its jawbones stood as a roadside arch in Dagenham for years, and are still remembered today in the name of Whalebone Lane.

An even more impressive whale skeleton hangs in the Natural History Museum, reminding all viewers that there is a creature alive today that is bigger even than the dinosaurs. The 25-metre-long blue whale skeleton was acquired for the museum shortly after it opened in 1881. The animal had beached at Wexford on the south-east coast of Ireland. The curators paid £250 for it in 1891. Every single bone is present.

'It's a fantastically complete specimen,' says Richard Sabin. 'It's also one of the largest of its kind on display anywhere in the world; and we know its history, we know how it was killed and processed, and that's quite rare.'

This skeleton is being moved into the entrance hall in 2017 so that it is the first object that visitors to the museum will see. Sir Michael Dixon, Director of the Museum, commented: 'As guardians of one of the world's greatest scientific resources, our purpose is to challenge the way people think about the natural world, and that goal has never been more urgent. The blue whale serves as a poignant reminder that while abundance is no guarantee of survival, through our choices, we can make a real difference.' As we stand and marvel at this vast creature, we are part of a rich tradition that goes back thousands of years. Our responsibility is now to make sure that it is safeguarded into the future.

ACKNOWLEDGEMENTS

This book would never have seen the light of day without the team at John Murray: Caroline Westmore expertly guided us through the proof stages and Sara Marafini came up with our beautiful cover and the weird and wonderful illustrations that head up each chapter. Huge thanks also to communications director Rosie Gailer and Yassine Belkacemi, Morag Lyall and Hilary Hammond, ace picture editor Juliet Brightmore, master indexer Douglas Matthews, Amanda Jones in production, Aimee Oliver and Vickie Boff in marketing, Ben Gutcher and Lucy Hale in sales, and Managing Director Nick Davies. It has been an immense pleasure working with such a dedicated and professional team – and especially with our wonderful editor Georgina Laycock, whose combination of constructive criticism, clear thinking and fine editorial brain have proved enormously helpful throughout.

At the Natural History Museum, we are very grateful to Chloe Kembery, Colin Ziegler and Helen Smith for all their help with the book, and to the following experts for their brilliant contributions: Professor Paul Barrett, Dr George Beccaloni, Dr Joanne Cooper, Paul Cooper, Oliver Crimmen, Theresa Howard, Dr Blanca Huertas, Dr Ronald Jenner, Dr Ken Johnson, Dr Sandra Knapp, Professor Adrian Lister, Miranda Lowe, James Maclaine, Professor Andrew Parker, Fred Rumsey, Douglas Russell, Richard Sabin, Dr Caroline Smith, Dr Mark Spencer and Dr Lorna Steel.

Other people who kindly commented on the text, and made

helpful suggestions and corrections include Miles Barton, Mike Benton, Lizzie Bewick, Phil Chapman, Mathias Clasen, Brother Guy Consolmagno, Jill Cook, Wendy Darke, Ed Drewitt, Ian Fergusson, Joyce Froome, Diane Johnson, Richard Kerridge, John Ó Maoilearca, Peter Marren, Ted Oakes, Matthew Oates, Ralph Pite, Ian Redmond and Lynn Rogers. In addition, Jonathan Elphick read through the whole text, for which many thanks. Any errors that remain are, of course, our own.

At BBC Radio 4 we would like to thank Commissioning Editor Mohit Bakaya and Controller Gwyneth Williams for greenlighting the series; and the BBC radio legal team Emma Trevelyan and Lesley Eaton for greenlighting the book. Thanks to Julian Hector, editor of Natural History Radio, for his continued encouragement and support, and to all the people at NHU Radio whose hard work and commitment got *Natural Histories* off the ground: you know who you are but we are eternally grateful to Andrew Dawes, Sarah Pitt, Jamie Merritt, Tom Bonnett and Ellie Sans.

But the one person we really couldn't have written this book without is the wonderful Mary Colwell, who steered the series with aplomb, somehow managing to juggle being series producer and the major scriptwriter on *Natural Histories*, with all kinds of other demands on her time. Her highly original take on the natural world has strengthened the series and this book beyond measure. Thank you one and all.

———•———

ILLUSTRATION CREDITS

Black-and-white chapter openers: © Dr George Beccaloni: 366–7. © Ryan M Bolton/Shutterstock: 18–19. © The British Library Board: vi. © Florilegius/The Trustees of the Natural History Museum, London: 100–1, 196–7, 212–13, 308–9, 320–1. © Kathy Gold/Shutterstock: 260–1. © Steven J. Kazlowski/Alamy: 244–5. © Henrik Larsson/Shutterstock: 352–3. © The Trustees of the Natural History Museum, London: xx, 38–9, 76–7, 112–13, 130–1,

TEXT PERMISSIONS

The authors and publishers would like to thank the following for permission to reproduce copyright material. 'The Frozen Mammoth' from *More Beasts for Worse Children* by Hilaire Belloc reprinted by permission of Peters Fraser & Dunlop (www.petersfraserdunlop.com) on behalf of the Estate of Hilaire Belloc. Extracts from 'Blue-Butterfly Day' and 'The Road Not Taken' from *The Poetry of Robert Frost* by Robert Frost published by Jonathan Cape, reprinted by permission of The Random House Group Limited and Henry Holt and Company, LLC. Excerpt from 'The Meteorite' by C.S. Lewis copyright C.S. Lewis Pte. Ltd. 1946. Reprinted by permission of The C.S. Lewis Company Ltd and Houghton Mifflin Harcourt Publishing Company. All rights reserved. Extract from 'The Daffodil Fields' by John Masefield reproduced courtesy of The Society of Authors as the Literary Representative of the Estate of John Masefield. Extract from 'Theory on Brontosauruses, by Anne Elk', from *Monty Python's Flying Circus, Just the Words*, vol. 2, reprinted by permission of Methuen.

Every reasonable effort has been made to trace copyright holders, but if there are any errors or omissions, John Murray will be pleased to insert the appropriate acknowledgement in any subsequent printings or editions.

FURTHER READING

Each chapter only gave us the space to write very briefly about every creature or phenomenon. If you want to find out more, here are books (both general and specific) that we have found valuable.

SERIES

Animal: over seventy individual volumes, each dedicated to a species or group. Species featured in *Natural Histories* appear in the following volumes: *Ape, Bear, Beetle, Cockroach, Crocodile, Gorilla, Lion, Monkey, Parrot, Shark, Snake, Whale* (Reaktion Books)

Handbook of the Birds of the World, ed. Josep Del Hoyo, Andrew Elliott, Jordi Sargatal and Andrew D. Christie (seventeen volumes, Lynx Edicions, 1992–2013)

Handbook of the Mammals of the World, ed. Don E. Wilson and Russell A. Mittermeier (eight volumes, five published to date, Lynx Edicions, 2009–)

GENERAL

Adcock, Fleur, and Simms, Jacqueline, ed., *The Oxford Book of Creatures* (Oxford University Press, 1995)

Allen, David Elliston, *The Naturalist in Britain* (Pelican, 1978)

Baker, Steve, *Picturing the Beast: Animals, Identity and Representation* (University of Illinois Press, 1993)

Berger, John, *Why Look at Animals?* (Penguin Great Ideas, 2009)

Birkhead, Tim, *The Wisdom of Birds* (Bloomsbury, 2008)

Cleene, Marcel de, and Lejeune, Marie Claire, *Compendium of Symbolic and Ritual Plants in Europe* (Mens & Cultuur Uitgevers, 2003)

Clifford, Sue, and King, Angela, *England in Particular* (Hodder & Stoughton, 2006)

Cocker, Mark, *Birds and People* (Jonathan Cape, 2013)

Demello, Margo, *Animals and Society: An Introduction to Human–Animal Studies* (Columbia University Press, 2012)

Fudge, Erica, *Animal* (Reaktion Books, 2002)

Grigson, Geoffrey, *The Englishman's Flora* (Phoenix House, 1955)

——, *The Shell Country Alphabet* (Michael Joseph, 1966)

Hurn, Samantha, *Humans and Other Animals: Cross-Cultural Perspectives on Human–Animal Interactions* (Pluto Press, 2012)

Kalof, Linda, *Looking at Animals in Human History* (Reaktion Books, 2007)

Mabey, Richard, *Flora Britannica* (Chatto & Windus, 1996)

——, and Cocker, Mark, *Birds Britannica* (Chatto & Windus, 2005)

Marren, Peter, *Bugs Britannica* (Chatto & Windus, 2010)

Ovid, and Innes, Mary M., *Metamorphoses* (Penguin, 1955)

Pliny the Elder, and Healey, John, *Natural History* (Penguin, 1991)

Thomas, Keith, *Man and the Natural World: Changing Attitudes in England 1500–1800* (Allen Lane, 1983)

Turner, David, *Was Beethoven a Birdwatcher?* (Summersdale, 2011)

GROUPS AND SPECIES

Chapter 1: Monkeys and Apes

Fossey, Dian, *Gorillas in the Mist: A Remarkable Story of Thirteen Years Spent Living with the Greatest of the Great Apes* (Weidenfeld & Nicolson, 2001)

Jenkins, Martin, and White, Vicky, *Ape* (Walker Books, 2008)

Morris, Desmond, *The Naked Ape: A Zoologist's Study of the Human Animal* (Vintage, 2005)

Chapter 2: Sharks

Ebert, David A., Fowler, Sarah, Compagno, Leonard, and Dando, Marc, *Sharks of the World: A Fully Illustrated Guide* (Wild Nature Press, 2013)

Kent, Sarah, *Shark Infested Waters: The Saatchi Collection of British Art in the 90s* (Philip Wilson, 2003)

Chapter 3: Butterflies

Barkham, Patrick, *The Butterfly Isles* (Granta, 2010)

Marren, Peter, *Rainbow Dust: Three Centuries of Delight in British Butterflies* (Square Peg, 2015)

Oates, Matthew, *In Pursuit of Butterflies* (Bloomsbury, 2015)

Chapter 4: Giant Squid

Cerullo, Mary M., and Roper, Clyde F.E., *Giant Squid: Searching for a Sea Monster* (Capstone Press, 2012)

Williams, Wendy, *Kraken: The Curious, Exciting, and Slightly Disturbing Science of Squid* (Abrams, 2011)

Chapter 5: Lions

Scott, Jonathan and Angela, *Big Cat Diary: Lion* (Collins, 2006)

Chapter 6: Burbot

Everard, Mark, *Britain's Freshwater Fishes* (Princeton University Press, 2013)

Chapter 7: Nightshades

Newton, John, *The Roots of Civilisation: Plants That Changed the World* (Murdoch Books, 2009)

Reader, John, *The Untold History of the Potato* (Vintage, 2009)

Stocks, Christopher, *Forgotten Fruits: The Stories Behind Britain's Traditional Fruit and Vegetables* (Windmill Books, 2009)

Chapter 8: Dinosaurs

Alvarez, Walter, *T. Rex and the Crater of Doom* (Penguin, 1998)

Fastovsky, David E., Weishampel, David B., and Sibbick, John, *Dinosaurs: A Concise Natural History* (Cambridge University Press, 2009)

Long, John, and Schouten, Peter, *Feathered Dinosaurs: The Origin of Birds* (Oxford University Press, 2009)

Chapter 9: Meteorites

Smith, Caroline, Russell, Sara, and Benedix, Gretchen, *Meteorites* (Natural History Museum, 2009)

Chapter 10: Corals

Sheppard, Anne, *Coral Reefs: Secret Cities of the Sea* (Natural History Museum, 2015)

Sheppard, Charles, *Coral Reefs: A Very Short Introduction* (Oxford University Press, 2014)

Chapter 11: Mammoths

Lister, Adrian, *Mammoths: Ice Age Giants* (Natural History Museum, 2014)

Shapiro, Beth, *How to Clone a Mammoth: The Science of De-Extinction* (Princeton University Press, 2015)

Chapter 12: Snakes

Inns, Howard, *Britain's Reptiles and Amphibians* (Princeton University Press, 2011)

Kerridge, Richard, *Cold Blood: Adventures with Reptiles and Amphibians* (Vintage, 2015)

Chapter 13: Daffodils

Kingsbury, Noel, *Daffodil: The Remarkable Story of the World's Most Popular Spring Flower* (Timber Press, 2013)

Chapter 14: Birds' Eggs

Cherry-Garrard, Apsley, *The Worst Journey in the World* (Vintage Classics, 2010)

Hauber, Mark E., and Bates, John, *The Book of Eggs: A Lifesize Guide to the Eggs of Six Hundred of the World's Bird Species* (Ivy Press, 2014)

Chapter 15: Bears

Brunner, Bernd, *Bears: A Brief History* (Yale University Press, 2009)

Pastoureau, Michel, and Holoch, George, *The Bear: History of a Fallen King* (Harvard University Press, 2011)

Chapter 16: Brambles

Mabey, Richard, *Weeds* (Profile, 2010)

Chapter 17: Parrots

Forshaw, Joseph M., *Parrots of the World: A Helm Field Guide* (Bloomsbury, 2010)

Juniper, Tony, *Spix's Macaw: The Race to Save the World's Rarest Bird* (Fourth Estate, 2003)

Pepperberg, Irene, *Alex and Me* (Scribe, 2013)

Chapter 18: Crocodiles

Trutnau, Ludwig, and Sommerlad, Ralf, *Crocodilians: Their Natural History and Captive Husbandry* (Edition Chimaira, 2006)

Chapter 19: Sea Anemones

Wood, Chris, *Sea Anemones and Corals of Britain and Ireland* (Wild Nature Press, 2013)

Chapter 20: Hornbills

Kemp, A.C., and Woodcock, Martin, *The Hornbills: Bucerotiformes* (*Bird Families of the World*) (Oxford University Press, 1995)

Kinnaird, Margaret F., and O'Brien, Timothy G., *The Ecology and Conservation of Hornbills: Farmers of the Forest* (University of Chicago Press, 2008)

Chapter 21: Oaks

Miles, Archie, *The British Oak* (Constable, 2013)

Young, Peter, *Oak* (Reaktion Books, 2013)

Chapter 22: Beetles

Bouchard, Patrice, Bousquet, Yves, and Pond, Sandra, *The Book of Beetles: A Life-Size Guide to Six Hundred of Nature's Gems* (Ivy Press, 2014)

Evans, Arthur V., *An Inordinate Fondness for Beetles* (University of California Press, 2000)

Chapter 23: Cockroaches

Bell, William J., Roth, Louis M., and Nalepa, Christine A., *Cockroaches: Ecology, Behavior, and Natural History* (Johns Hopkins University Press, 2007)

Chapter 24: Fleas

Rosen, William, *Justinian's Flea: Plague, Empire and the Birth of Europe* (Jonathan Cape, 2007)

Chapter 25: Whales

Hoare, Philip, *Leviathan* (Fourth Estate, 2008)

INDEX

The item should be returned or renewed by the last date stamped below.

Dylid dychwelyd neu adnewyddu'r eitem erbyn y dyddiad olaf sydd wedi'i stampio isod.

BETTWS

To renew visit / Adnewyddwch ar
www.newport.gov.uk/libraries

Swim into more

PuRRMaiDS

adventures!

The Scaredy Cat
The Catfish Club
Seasick Sea Horse
Search for the Mermicorn